The New York Times

Quick & Easy
Crossword
Puzzles

Puzzle 1 by Gregory E. Paul

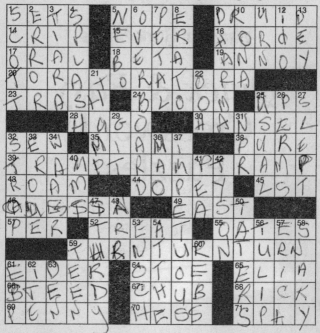

ACROSS

1 6-3, 5-7 and 6-4, e.g.
5 Yep's opposite
9 Ancient Celt
14 Los Angeles gang member
15 At any time
16 Raging group
17 Face-to-face exam
18 _____ carotene
19 Harass
20 1970 Pearl Harbor film

23 Landfill fill
24 Rose's beauty
25 Raises
28 Justice Black
30 Gretel's brother
32 Make dresses and things
35 Destination for many Cuban refugees
38 Containing no admixtures
39 Civil War song
43 Travel around

44 Disney dwarf who "never had anything to say"
45 W.W. II craft: Abbr.
46 Texas oil city
49 Atlantic states, with "the" ___
51 The "p" in r.p.m.
52 Pick up the tab for
55 Writer Joyce Carol ___
59 1965 #1 hit by the Byrds
61 Comforter stuffing
64 Western Indian
65 Charles Lamb, pseudonymously
66 War horse
67 Great Lakes fish
68 "Casablanca" cafe owner
69 Piggy bank deposit
70 Dame Myra
71 Neuter

DOWN
1 "Ivanhoe" novelist
2 Miscue
3 Princess topper
4 Swimming pool sound
5 Mount from which Moses viewed the Promised Land
6 "Man ___!"
7 Flower feature
8 Poet's muse
9 TV's "___ and Greg"

10 Barrett known for her dish
11 Still-life subject
12 Bachelor's last words
13 Susan of "L.A. Law"
21 Soundly defeat
22 "What a view!"
25 Customary
26 Salon works
27 Caught some Z's
29 "Shoo!"
31 "All Things Considered" network
32 Razor sharpener
33 Undermine
34 Vacillate
36 Long March leader
37 Trigger-happy, say
40 Month, in México
41 Potpie tidbit
42 80s–90s champ Mike
47 Well-built
48 Airport info next to "Dep."
50 Idahos, e.g.
53 Tennyson's Arden
54 ___ drop of a hat
56 Garden bulb
57 Kane of "All My Children"
58 Twisting
59 Adult-to-be
60 Graycoats
61 Second sight, for short
62 Suffix with Israel
63 Cub Scout unit

ACROSS

1 Etcher's need
5 Cut and paste
9 Liniment user
14 "Bet you can't . . .," e.g.
15 Fisher's plug
16 New, to Neruda
17 Bartender?
19 Food writer Claiborne
20 California giants
21 Fritter (away)
22 Petitions
23 "Bravo, torero!"
24 It's observed in Jan. in the Rockies
25 Modern surgical tool
28 Dian Fossey's home
30 Wood for a 61-Down
31 Trigonometry ratio
34 Employs
37 Put in the hold
39 Painter of water lilies
40 R. & B. singer James
41 Location
42 North, perhaps
44 Immeasurable period
45 Lustrous
47 Makes
49 Sigma's follower
51 Fleur-de-___
52 Kind of tide
54 From A to Z
56 Upright, in football
60 Saltpetre

61 Bartender?
62 Exonerate
63 Pot builder
64 What you might buy a Gucci bag in?
65 Sea swallows
66 Freshman, probably
67 Onion's cousin

DOWN

1 Throws in
2 Kind of package
3 Land of the Tigris and Euphrates
4 Render harmless
5 Beast of Borden
6 Alexandre, père ou fils
7 Nest eggs, for short
8 Lacrosse team
9 Old, in France
10 Bean ___ (tofu)
11 Bartender?
12 Pandora released them
13 Standard word reference
18 Guided trips
21 Missouri River tributary
23 Possessed
25 Lad's love
26 Piedmont wine center
27 Bartender?
28 Libidinous
29 Payable
32 It's in development
33 Spring features

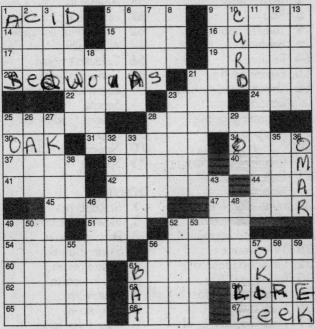

35 Prince's school
36 ___ serif
38 Like Burns's tim'rous beastie
43 Domain
46 Changes
48 Horrify
49 Coloring
50 Old womanish
52 Actor Nick of "Affliction"
53 "Have you ___?"
55 Algerian seaport

56 Trait carrier
57 30s migrant
58 Withered
59 Arduous journey
61 Louisville Slugger

ACROSS

1 Take it easy
5 Bag
9 They're kept in cabinets
14 Region
15 Distinctive flair
16 University town near Bangor
17 A small goodbye?
19 Happen again
20 "Open ___" (magical command)
21 Exile island for Napoleon
23 Mine diggings
24 "To ___ is human . . ."
26 Peas and beans
28 TV advertiser
32 Gambling mecca
33 Incinerate
34 Workshop gripper
36 Pack away
39 Andy's cohort, in old radio
40 Electronic clock feature
41 Turner who sang "What's Love Got to Do With It"
42 Pueblo dwellers
43 Employed
44 Bakery fixture
45 Score after deuce, in tennis
47 Cooks' "secrets"
50 University officers
53 Director Howard
54 Braun or Perón
55 Animal that gives milk
57 Pieces for piano class
62 "Three wishes" giver
64 A city elf?
66 Calcutta's home
67 Conservatives or liberals, say, in the Senate
68 Russian parliament
69 Step
70 Nautical direction
71 Spoken

DOWN

1 St. Louis gridders
2 New York canal
3 Parts of a min.
4 Skater Lipinski
5 Seamstresses
6 ___ française
7 Mammoth ___
8 Ring slowly
9 Search for food
10 Hot temper
11 A crazy cause?
12 Accustom
13 Tender spots
18 Sign for the superstitious
22 Military cap
25 Wanders
27 Clear, as a drain
28 Wrestling style
29 A socially correct goose in Boston?
30 Like a certain football kick

Puzzle 3 by Carol R. Blumenstein

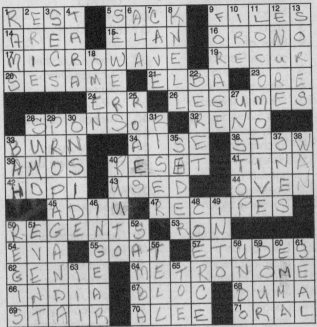

31 Step part
33 Scrooge's reply
35 Passover feast
37 Singles
38 Unnaturally pale
40 Eagerly approach
46 Engaged, as an auto engine
48 Force
49 Keen on
50 Kathie Lee's co-host
51 Happening
52 Brazilian dance

56 "Can you ___?" ("Is it obvious?")
58 Reverse
59 Forbidding
60 Austen heroine
61 Bewhiskered circus animal
63 Three on a sundial
65 Stocking's end

ACROSS

1 Slender-waisted insect
5 Pilot's spot
9 River of central Germany
13 ". . . baked in ___"
14 Plane measure
15 Soprano Tetrazzini
16 Rub the wrong way
17 Party pooper
18 Torcher's misdeed
19 Natural antidepressant
22 Compass doodle
23 Driveway blotch
24 Hold title to
25 Atmospheric prefix
27 Lawman Earp
29 Diplomat Deane
31 Before, to bards
32 Sleazy paper
34 Douglas ___
35 Smooth-talking
36 Tony Kushner play of 1993
41 "Listen!"
42 Popular card game
43 ___-Cat
44 Gift-wrapping time, for some
45 Ancient Britons
47 "Whistle While You Work" singer
51 Time div.
52 ___ glance
53 Big bird
55 "That's incredible!"
56 Raymond Massey film of 1945
60 Sword
61 Biblical birthright seller
62 Wholly absorbed
63 Oversized library volume
64 Actor Auberjonois
65 Baseball's Hershiser
66 Rind
67 Liberal pursuits
68 Hawaii's state bird

DOWN

1 1955 pact city
2 Beehive
3 Quartz material
4 Hammer part
5 Pilgrim to Mecca
6 Flynn and others
7 Jacob's first wife
8 Plantation bloom
9 Prefix with centric
10 P.M. before Gladstone
11 Abstruse
12 Campaigned
15 Landscapers' concerns
20 General Mills brand
21 Groups of bees
26 Singer McEntire
28 Boer migration
30 "Otherwise . . ."
33 NASA outfits
35 Cultivate
36 "Excuse me"

Puzzle 4 by Brendan Emmett Quigley

37 Handle the maps
38 1968 Winter Olympics site
39 Privately
40 Eventually become
45 Skating event
46 Trigonometry ratio
48 Staring fiercely
49 Go back into business
50 In fine ___ (fit)
54 Pouts
57 "Agreed!"

58 River of Flanders
59 Much of the earth's core
60 Easy dupe

ACROSS

1 Love, Spanish-style
5 Santa ___ race track
10 Tom Jones's "___ a Lady"
14 Merry-go-round or roller coaster
15 Fountain drinks
16 Item in a garage
17 Kind of joke
19 Ski lift
20 Peaceful
21 Easily defended
23 Wooden pin
26 Lady of La Mancha
27 Father
30 Race unit
32 Ring (in)
35 Son of Seth
36 Headmistress
38 Half of dos
39 Hoopla
40 Triangular sails
41 Air conditioner measure, for short
42 Like roses
43 Reluctant
44 Help a hoodlum
45 Clothesline alternative
47 "Can't Help Lovin' ___ Man"
48 It's catching
49 The "G" in EKG
51 Game with a jackpot
53 Nighttime view
56 Somewhat
60 Skin cream ingredient
61 Words of consolation
64 Kennedy and Koppel
65 Spooky
66 Toledo's lake
67 Singer/songwriter Axton
68 Ginger cookies
69 Split

DOWN

1 Places where Torah scrolls are kept
2 Coal site
3 Fragrance
4 Falls back
5 Cockeyed
6 Oui's opposite
7 Wedding vow
8 Delicate use of words
9 Proposed
10 "___ Cheerleaders" (1977 film)
11 Old-fashioned whoop
12 And others: Abbr.
13 Painful
18 Shoelace woe
22 Verb preceders
24 In seventh heaven
25 Sidelong pass
27 Benjamin Harrison was the last President to have one
28 Terminator
29 "I can't wait!"
31 Magician's word
33 Computer command

Puzzle 5 by Gregory E. Paul

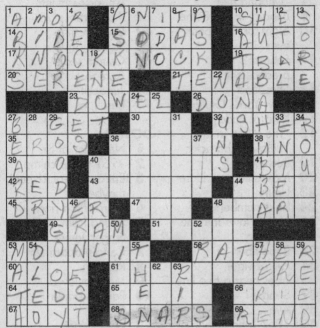

34 Way to go
36 Dallas cager, for short
37 38-Across, to us
40 "___ Theme" ("Doctor Zhivago" tune)
44 One more
46 Writer Hemingway
48 Goals or assists
50 Distributes, with "out"
52 Arbor Day honorees
53 Geometry, e.g.
54 Grocery list item
55 Following that

57 Roll call reply
58 Ireland
59 Hollow-stemmed plant
62 Memorable time
63 Kind of cord

ACROSS

1 "Unhand me!"
6 Behold, in old Rome
10 Sight for very poor eyes
14 Febrero's predecessor
15 Shredded
16 New York's Giuliani
17 Kind of buddy
18 "The Wind in the Willows" character
19 Bushelfuls
20 Makeshift procedure
23 Uglify
24 Links numbers
25 N.Y. follows it in the summer
28 Rope fiber
31 Full of vigor
35 Trees near a tree line
37 Shadow
39 Ave ___
40 1957 John Osborne play
43 Psychoanalyst Alfred
44 Medal recipient
45 Fender problem
46 Bank employee
48 Speakeasy owner's fear
50 "___ Rheingold"
51 December 24 and 31
53 Hindu title
55 "Be sensible!"
62 Choir member
63 It may be spun at sea
64 Museum embarrassments
66 Appearance
67 Uninteresting
68 Actress Shire
69 Church seats
70 Composer Janácek
71 Resell, as tickets

DOWN

1 Neighbor of Isr.
2 1961 space chimp
3 Entrance requirement, maybe
4 Man with a ring
5 Sound from 10-Down
6 Singer James
7 Certain apartment
8 Restrain
9 Make beloved
10 Parade staple
11 Oner
12 Lysol target
13 Information unit
21 Screen siren Garbo
22 Fragrance
25 Key of Haydn's Sonata No. 52
26 Semiconductor, e.g.
27 Fairy tale character
29 Speed-of-sound number
30 Stingy person
32 Exhorted
33 Tuscan city
34 Fruit desserts
36 Some are in closets

Puzzle 6 by Joy L. Wouk

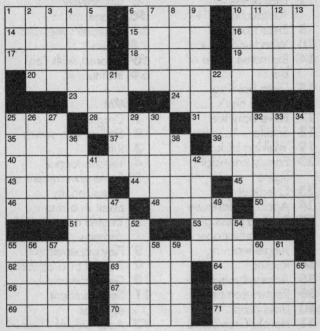

38 100 centesimi
41 Alla ___ (2/2 time)
42 Clamor
47 Summer cottage, often
49 Bartenders' servings
52 Ill-mannered look
54 Newton or Stern
55 Street fixture
56 Netman Nastase
57 Fret
58 Medley
59 Cold war foes

60 Bartlesville's home: Abbr.
61 Singer Young
65 Muttonhead

ACROSS

1. Eliot of the "Untouchables"
5. Error's partner
10. Woodworker's tool
14. Big name in the oil biz
15. Lawn bowling
16. Stick in one's ___
17. Have itchy feet
18. Schiller's "___ Joy"
19. Walking stick
20. Family financial figure
23. Overhaul
24. Apr. 15 addressee
25. Printing press gizmos
28. Some newspapers
33. Jungle warning
34. Ruckus
35. Actress Lupino
36. Reuters competitor
40. Links prop
41. Harold Gray's little orphan
42. Son of Zeus
43. Alberta's capital
45. Frightful
47. Walter Raleigh, for one
48. Bar mitzvah boy, barely
49. Company with two U's in its logo
56. Copycat
57. One of Columbus's ships
58. Roof edge
59. Medallion site
60. Collectively
61. Bridge
62. Baseball's Mel and others
63. Adored, with "on"
64. Incline

DOWN

1. Drug cop
2. Ending with switch
3. Ripoff
4. Tijuana topper
5. Some government issues, briefly
6. Event in a ring
7. Treated a sprain, perhaps
8. Play's opening
9. Treated as a celebrity
10. Greet obtrusively
11. Small amount of liquor
12. Actor Billy of "Titanic"
13. The clone Dolly, e.g.
21. Suffix with hotel
22. Hardly Mr. Right
25. Madder than mad
26. Pried (into)
27. Radio countdown host Casey
28. Enter, as a car
29. On the safe side?
30. Levels
31. 50s Ford flop
32. Insolent
34. Hand, to Hernando
37. "Shut up!"

Puzzle 7 by M. Francis Vuolo

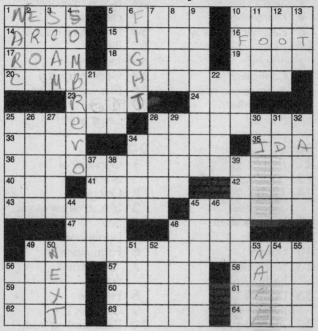

38 Very brave
39 Having the most precipitation
44 Figure in an Egyptian tomb
45 Jimmy's predecessor as President
46 Catholicism, e.g.: Abbr.
48 Lord or earl, e.g.
49 ___ the crack of dawn
50 Barber's cry
51 Flintstones pet
52 Biol. subject
53 Back of the neck
54 Indiana Sen. ___ Bayh
55 E-mail command
56 From ___ Z

ACROSS

1 Siesta
4 Pedro's home
8 Deceive, in a way
14 It's found in the ground
15 Canticles
16 Microscopic critter
17 Sweet melon
19 Fringed carriage
20 Gulf war ally
21 That is
23 "Don't give up!"
24 1968 third-party candidate
26 Very, to Verdi
28 Starlike
30 Uptight
33 St. Francis's birthplace
36 Doctor's interruption
38 Almighty
39 Kind of room
40 Late
42 Liked, hippie-style
43 Years ___
44 San ___, Italy
45 Botanical interstice
47 Leg up
49 Hereditary
51 Pesto ingredient
53 Moderate's opposite
57 One of the Chaplins
58 Pine product
60 Zilch
61 Nixon impeachment chairman
63 Himalayan capital
65 Picked
66 Tempers
67 Gone gray, say
68 Like some smiles
69 Rugmakers' supplies
70 Once called

DOWN

1 Opposite of "in any way"
2 Cologne
3 Like some servitude
4 Shy
5 Habit-forming
6 Farm machine
7 "___ forgive those . . ."
8 Endures
9 Ostrich's kin
10 Lines leading from pumping stations?
11 Hero's forte
12 Mind
13 Voiced turndown
18 China's Zhou ___
22 Soup follower
25 Catalogues
27 Took the wheel
29 Place to wipe the hands
31 Motown music category
32 Rim
33 Show horse

Puzzle 8 by Alfio Micci

34 Kind of lily
35 Cartoon dog
37 Underwrite
41 Author Zola
46 Minneapolis suburb
48 Crossword constructor, seemingly
50 Like many a rabbit's warren
52 Slice of wry?
54 Officially accepted works
55 Confuse

56 Summa cum ___
57 Area of the Big Apple
59 Start of a car accident
61 Sales slip: Abbr.
62 Book before Esth.
64 Post-B.A. degrees

ACROSS

1 City where "Phantom of the Opera" is set
6 Langley, for one: Abbr.
9 Where to put a pin on a jacket
14 By oneself
15 Ripken of the Orioles
16 Furious
17 "Come on, ducks, it's time to start!"
20 Clothes lines
21 A or B, on a record
22 ___-tse
23 Court dividers
25 Royal heirs
27 "Down with the glue factory proposal!"
31 1999 combatants
35 A Gershwin
36 Head, to Henri
37 Ancient city north of Jerusalem
38 Take the show on the road
40 Reagan Attorney General Edwin
42 Kind of bean
43 Historical records
45 Close
47 Tues. preceder
48 Make-a-million game
49 "Phooey! It's shearing time again!"
51 Up to speed
53 Late-night host Jay
54 Nabokov novel
57 Lady's man
59 Highway exits
62 "I need instructions on catching mice!"
66 Flood protector
67 Earl Grey, e.g.
68 Alternative to "window"
69 Step
70 1492 and 2001: Abbr.
71 Tibetan legends

DOWN

1 Chum
2 Pub brews
3 Uncreative education
4 Crazy
5 Part
6 Play a role
7 Queries on the Internet
8 Somewhat sky-colored
9 Permit
10 Biblical vessel
11 Kid's beach toy
12 Sicilian volcano
13 Toy building block
18 Holds in high regard
19 Hubbub
24 Place
26 Studio stages
27 Critically important
28 Maine university town
29 Ridicule
30 Actress Davis
32 Skewed square

Puzzle 9 by Stephanie Spadaccini

33 "It Had to ___"
34 Breezy talk
37 Do something courageous
39 Pro ___
41 Circus performer
44 Washington arm-bender
46 Escape
49 Pageant winner
50 Hollywood bio "___ Dearest"
52 Durocher or DiCaprio

54 Pointed tools
55 Eating regimen
56 Thomas ___ Edison
58 Addict
60 Nuisance
61 Songs for one
63 Flower garland
64 Possesses
65 "A Nightmare on Elm Street" creator Craven

ACROSS

1 Plotting group
6 "Get away!"
10 Propped open, perhaps
14 Radarange maker
15 Pal of Piglet
16 "But wait, there's ___!"
17 Person who looks exactly like another
19 Verne captain
20 District
21 Union Pacific et al.: Abbr.
22 1978 Burt Reynolds film
24 Constantly find fault with
25 Storage box
26 Make drinks
27 Vice President from Tennessee
29 School for martial arts
30 "Sprechen ___ Deutsch?"
31 Cater basely
33 Mark for life
34 Person who looks exactly like another
38 Got 100% on
39 High points
40 VCR button
41 German-built car
43 "Melt in your mouth" candy
47 "The Screwtape Letters" writer
49 Son of, in Arabic names
50 "Oh" de Cologne?
51 Closely trimmed
52 It precedes "Blastoff!"
53 Aptly named fruit
54 "Able was ___ . . ."
55 Person who looks exactly like another
58 At no time, in poetry
59 Yearn (for)
60 Porterhouse, e.g.
61 Airport info: Abbr.
62 Sauce thickener
63 Some people lock them

DOWN

1 Bathhouse
2 Unprincipled
3 No-goodnik
4 Novelist Seton
5 Young boy
6 Turn away
7 Corn leftovers
8 Prodigy alternative, for short
9 Leon Uris novel
10 Response to "Are too!"
11 "My Cousin Vinny" star
12 Azerbaijani's neighbor
13 Stock up on again
18 Prepare, as incoming students
23 ___ y plata (Montana's motto)

Puzzle 10 by Dave Tuller

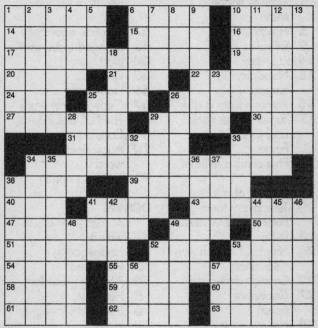

25 Ingredient in many cereals
26 Common cleanser
28 Kind of page
29 Bike stick-on
32 March of ___
33 Kind of dive
34 Winter driving hazard
35 Bid, in bridge
36 Flexible
37 Eliot Ness, e.g.
38 Inverse math function

41 Be in debt to
42 Greek odist
44 Stiletto or dirk
45 "American Pie" singer Don
46 Evades, as work
48 Tinker to ___ to Chance
49 Dow Jones Average, e.g.
52 Waikiki's island
53 Golden rule word
56 Author Umberto
57 Kind of: Suffix

ACROSS

1 They're honored in May
5 Hokey stuff
9 Great reviews
14 ___ vera
15 Nondairy spread
16 Remove from a disk
17 Turner in the Rock and Roll Hall of Fame
18 Five cents a minute, say
19 Partner of effect
20 Temporary town during the Depression
23 Put on
24 "Für ___" (Beethoven dedication)
25 Errand runner
27 Capital of Spain
30 Hollow pastry
33 Ostrich's kin
34 Bubbly drinks
37 French delicacy
38 Miniature ___
40 Get-well program
42 Bubbly drinks
43 City on the Rhône
45 Hand-dyed fabric
47 Attorney F. ___ Bailey
48 Home makers
50 Readiest for picking
52 Start of Caesar's boast
53 Greek sorceress

55 "Star Wars: The Phantom Menace" boy
57 Divorce, informally
62 Stringed instrument
64 Hurt
65 Coral ___
66 Floor layer
67 Genealogical work
68 The "U" of CPU
69 Coasters
70 Auctioneer's closing word
71 Gridiron option

DOWN

1 A calculator assists with it
2 Hodgepodge
3 Pre-stereo
4 Pitching great Tom
5 Hallway
6 Several Norwegian kings
7 Knot again
8 Sophisticated Coward
9 Proof of purchase
10 Coach Parseghian
11 Old-style entertainment
12 Old U.S. gas brand
13 Spotted
21 Yalies
22 China's ___-tse
26 "Dumb" girl of old comics
27 1990s actress Ward
28 "That's ___!"

Puzzle 11 by Elizabeth C. Gorski

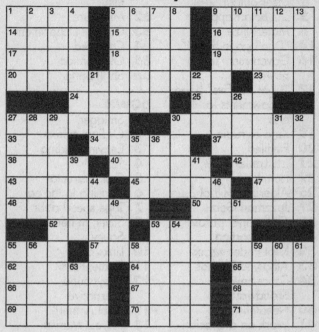

29 It's boring, daddy-o
30 H.S. junior's challenge
31 Fencing swords
32 VCR button
35 Young socialites
36 "There you are!"
39 Big party
41 Preflight snack?
44 Burglar alarm features
46 Chicken ___
49 Tear
51 Join in twos

53 Prefix with management
54 Lucy's neighbor
55 "Macbeth" has five
56 Singer Diamond
58 Back muscles, for short
59 Singer Horne
60 Hawaiian gifts
61 Newts
63 Conducted

ACROSS
1 Laser output
5 ___ Beta Kappa
8 Materialize
14 "Don't go in there!"
16 Government in power
17 "Light My Fire" band
18 Endowments for the arts
19 Kind of radio
20 Fulfilled
21 ___ Lanka
22 Humiliate
25 Algeria's Gulf of ___
27 Jazzman Getz
28 Cliffhanger phrase
31 Butter portion
32 Kept under wraps
33 Athos, to Porthos
34 Saucer-eyed Broadway star
40 Needlefish
41 Work on a Grecian urn
42 One of the Cyclades
44 "Zip-A-Dee-Doo-Dah" movie
49 Windshield feature
50 Obeyed a court order?
51 Makeup maker
52 Thrilla in Manila participant
53 Duty
54 Philandering fellow
56 "The Clemency of Titus" composer

58 1988 Burt Reynolds film
62 Miniature
63 Cabinet Department
64 Confused
65 Old Pontiac
66 Shrill barks

DOWN
1 Smidgen
2 Ordinal suffix
3 Enzyme ending
4 "___ X"
5 Coll. instructor
6 Pleasing to the ear
7 Tape speed abbr.
8 Silver, in heraldry
9 Saucy
10 Links org.
11 Element #99
12 Greyhound alternative
13 Plant runner?
15 Actress Marisa
20 Nth degree
22 "The Racer's Edge"
23 1950s Congressional grp.
24 Made an enemy of
26 Cinnamon candies
27 Formal introduction?
29 Rink grp.
30 Pale
35 Carry on
36 Web site address ending
37 Follower

Puzzle 12 by Brendan Emmett Quigley

38 Formerly, in newspaper announcements
39 "___ match?"
43 Diffident
44 Like grain that's out of the rain
45 Addressed a crowd
46 "The X-Files" network
47 Fry, in a way
48 Mrs. who owned a famous cow
49 The Bucs stop here

53 Ebony or mahogany
55 Aware of
57 Its point is to make holes
58 18-wheeler
59 K.G.B. rival
60 Alley ___
61 Couples: Abbr.

ACROSS

1. Passing mention?
5. Bucks and bulls, e.g.
10. Toddler's bed
14. Snack (on)
15. Humiliate
16. Seine feeder
17. Rod for a hot rod
18. Word before mail or vote
19. Some TVs
20. It's old
23. "It __ Necessarily So"
24. Walk back and forth
25. Holler
28. Reagan military program, for short
30. Tears into
34. Common aquarium fishes
36. Emergency PC key
38. Omega's preceder
39. It's very old
43. Regret
44. Three, in Napoli
45. Frank acknowledgment
46. Nursery rhyme Jack
49. Cold call?
51. __ Banks, "Mr. Cub"
52. Hour not found on a grandfather clock
54. Bern's river
56. It's very, very old
62. Angel's prop
63. Praises
64. On the qui __
66. King's land in a Broadway musical
67. Comic DeGeneres
68. French summers
69. 98, in the car world
70. Old Russian despots
71. Grate

DOWN

1. Out __ limb
2. Squared at the edges
3. Wight, for one
4. Synonym books
5. Expert
6. Calls off, as a mission
7. Dismissed, with "off"
8. Daydreamer
9. "Later!"
10. Eye tissue
11. Wedding shower?
12. "__ Mommy Kissing Santa Claus"
13. Porgy's love
21. Behemoth
22. Student's place: Abbr.
25. Twinklers
26. In a lather
27. In __ words
29. Postpone, as enrollment
31. Give birth to
32. Very, in music
33. It may change with a promotion

Puzzle 13 by M. Francis Vuolo

35 One who gives orders: Abbr.
37 Half a Latin dance
40 Electrons, in wave functions
41 Turn inside out
42 Study carefully
47 They're universally accepted
48 1–1 score, e.g.
50 Oakland gridder
53 Coastal feature
55 Orgs.

56 Mock words of understanding
57 Do perfectly
58 Attired
59 Oahu dance
60 Beatles' meter maid
61 The "Y" of Y.S.L.
65 Sixth sense

ACROSS

1 Plays a part
5 Purple color
9 American symbol
14 Boutique
15 Left the couch
16 Implore
17 Snit?
20 Dodges
21 Wall upright
22 Noted Downing Street address
23 Maiden name indicator
24 Give the gas
26 Garden store purchase
28 Not the glad-handing sort
30 Slanders
34 Hope/Crosby "Road" destination
37 Gunk
39 Permeate
40 Autobiography?
43 Late singer Mel
44 Carve
45 Comic Bill et al.
46 Detective
48 Harbor sights
50 Use a mop
52 Downed
53 High ___ kite
56 Trash bag accessory
59 Designer Cassini
61 Like a baguette

63 Ambivalent?
66 Lively
67 Geometry calculation
68 Hawaiian bird
69 Oozes
70 Airy home
71 Baseball's ___ Slaughter

DOWN

1 Western ski area
2 2,880-mile-long country
3 Close-fitting hat
4 Tater
5 Charisma
6 Bagel topper
7 Mail org.
8 Track-and-field contests
9 Not localized
10 Brewery product
11 Polite fellow
12 Alençon product
13 Paradise
18 A Saarinen
19 Paris gridwork
25 Chapter's partner
27 They harass the insane
28 Kind of paper or test
29 Oxidizes
31 "What ___!" ("Don't pass up this offer!")
32 Part of an ancient inscription

Puzzle 14 by Stephanie Spadaccini

33 Arranges, as music
34 Morsels
35 Missing at roll call, maybe
36 Marco's money
38 Russian country house
41 ABC, CBS, etc.
42 Small talk
47 "Stop!"
49 François's father
51 Dramatist Brendan
53 Grayish
54 Office worker

55 Actor Lew
56 Big basins
57 Regarding
58 Singer Brickell
60 Actor Richard
62 The ___ Reader (magazine)
64 One means of knowing
65 Horror film director Craven

ACROSS

1. ___ Major
5. Dayan of Israel
10. Velvet drape
14. Je ne ___ quoi
15. Consumed
16. Vocal solo
17. Roe
18. Not level
19. News bit
20. Mediocre
23. Ripken of the Orioles
24. Dehydrated
25. Actress Dawber
28. Congressional meeting place
32. Steeped beverage
33. ___ Maria
34. Kind of rug
35. Common auto option
37. More refined
39. Thunder preceder
43. Troubadours' instruments
44. Female rabbit
45. Western brush
46. WNW's reverse
47. Circulars, basically
50. Blowhard's talk
52. Koppel of "Nightline"
53. Sudden jolt
55. ___ Jima
56. It may be called for in a recipe
61. Katharina, to Petruchio
64. Kentucky college, or its town
65. Bishop of Rome
66. Object of devotion
67. Change
68. Canal with a mule, in song
69. Kind of stand
70. Curls up with a book
71. Shuffleboard locale, maybe

DOWN

1. Computer operator
2. Pasta sauce brand
3. Omen
4. Person who's not yet a full partner
5. Common potluck dish
6. Solemn promise
7. Pigpens
8. Biker's protection
9. Whole
10. Jack and Jill's vessel
11. Carney of "The Honeymooners"
12. Prevaricate
13. On the ___ (fleeing)
21. Dieter's concern
22. Vaulted
25. Persona non grata
26. Pay back
27. Big Wall Street news
28. Nautical rope
29. Stir up
30. Struck repeatedly

31 "___ Abner"
36 Clear (of)
38 Like a drain after a drain cleaner
40 City of southern Honshu
41 Old salt
42 Chopper landing spots
48 Expel from law practice
49 Connive
51 It can be inspired
54 1950s war site
56 Place to pick up a sandwich
57 Ward (off)
58 Minute opening
59 Like some proportions
60 Stink to high heaven
61 Cleverness
62 Boise's state: Abbr.
63 Sly one

ACROSS

1 Southwestern art center
5 English exam finale, often
10 Lime drinks
14 Exile isle
15 "Touched by an Angel" co-star
16 Phone bug, e.g.
17 School on the Thames
18 Birth-related
19 Don Juan's mother
20 Funny
23 Cocks and bulls
24 "___ Howdy Doody time . . ."
25 Grounded birds
28 Bother terribly
30 Many N.Y.C. dwellings
33 Galley slave's tool
34 Payback time for Wimpy
37 Stats, e.g.
38 Delectable
40 Harness racer's gait
42 Walks feebly
43 Altar assent
44 Concert hall section
45 John Lennon hit
49 Syrup source
51 AT&T rival
53 More than impress
54 Scary
59 Uprising at Attica
61 Face-to-face exams
62 Inter ___
63 Human rights org.
64 Fergie, formally
65 Air outlet
66 Like one end of many pools
67 Manicurist's aid
68 Advantage

DOWN

1 Something tots do
2 Tennis great Gibson
3 Double-reed player
4 Belted one out
5 Dadaist Max
6 Elite divers
7 ___ time limit
8 Rush job notation
9 Hand-in-the-car-door reaction
10 Kind of acid
11 Call from the front door
12 Barely make, with "out"
13 "___ who?"
21 Ask, as for money
22 Picks out of a lineup, for short
26 Klutz
27 Sellout sign
29 Working hard
30 "___ which will live in . . ."
31 War ender
32 Bambino

Puzzle 16 by Elizabeth C. Gorski

35 This, to Jorge
36 Los Angeles woe
37 ___ many words
38 Object of a tax lawyer's search
39 Professor Corey
40 Comic Conway
41 Vitamin bottle info
44 Grazing ground
46 Sent in
47 Cafe sunshade
48 Cancel
50 Abate

51 Bicuspid neighbor
52 Undemanding, as a job
55 Wine choice
56 Way around London, once
57 Scale down
58 Jay's competition
59 "Awesome!"
60 Diamonds, to hoods

ACROSS

1 Side of a gem
6 "Planet of the ___"
10 Family pillar
14 Overflowing
15 Symbol of goodness
16 Manipulative sort
17 "Lighten up!"
19 Michelin product
20 Ophthalmologist's study
21 Around
22 Beer parties
24 Richly decorate
25 Gummed flap
26 Edit, as film
29 Nuances
33 Give up
34 Common street name
35 "Dumb" girl of old comics
36 Designer Klein
37 Y chromosome carriers
38 Dentist's request
39 Noon, in France
40 Is bedridden
41 Work, as dough
42 Nervously excited
44 Bank robberies
45 Suit to ___
46 Café au ___
47 Walk a beat
50 Lancelot and others
51 "This ___ fine how-do-you-do!"
54 New York canal
55 "Lighten up!"
58 Gets on in years
59 Norse war god
60 Patronize, as a restaurant
61 Wrongful act
62 Dalmatian docs
63 "___ Daughter" (1970 film)

DOWN

1 There's no changing it
2 "Shoo!"
3 Order for a party caterer
4 Reverse of WNW
5 Dangerous place for skating
6 Leading
7 Old TV host Jack
8 Chicago trains
9 Tofu makings
10 "Lighten up!"
11 Sale words
12 Lively
13 Greek war god
18 Prefix with conferencing
23 Boy
24 "Lighten up!"
25 Balks, as a horse
26 Turbaned sage
27 Start a closeup shot
28 Singer/photographer McCartney
29 TV's ___ Jessy Raphael

Puzzle 17 by Margaret Watson

30 Slangy denials
31 Super
32 Former Vegas hotel
34 Pale yellow
37 "Congratulations!"
41 Target of a good, swift kick
43 "Who am ___ say?"
44 Spy Mata ___
46 Property claims
47 Kind of moss
48 Jason's ship
49 Ballpark level

50 Pique
51 Least bit
52 Beautiful swimmer
53 Picnic spoilers
56 Poem of praise
57 Word repeated before "in" and "out"

ACROSS

1 Dobbin's tow, perhaps
5 Action film highlight
10 Paul Bunyan's ox
14 King of the road
15 Pass-the-baton race
16 Bolshevik Trotsky
17 River delta, e.g.
20 Easter egg need
21 Sole
22 Almost ready for the tooth fairy
23 Archeological sites
24 Go hurriedly
26 Easter event
29 Bed supports
30 [see other side]
31 Visually teasing images
32 Circle ratios
35 Tour bus stop
39 Pull the plug on
40 "Move ___!"
41 Carpet store calculation
42 ". . . only with ___ eyes"
43 Walk with a cane, say
45 Part of A.T.M.
48 John Paul II, e.g.
49 Little hooter
50 Franklin D.'s mother
51 Wino
54 Summer time

58 Meat-stamp letters
59 Hostel visitor
60 Caffeine-yielding nut
61 Sullivan had a really big one
62 King with a golden touch
63 Widemouthed pitcher

DOWN

1 Herring kin
2 Smoke or order preceder
3 Up to the task
4 "___ rang?"
5 Shrink in fear
6 Makes well
7 Friend in need
8 Bummed out
9 Storm center
10 Garden display
11 "The Fox and the Grapes" storyteller
12 Gem State capital
13 "C'mon in!"
18 Word on a sample check
19 Nebraska river
23 Mend
24 Colorful talk
25 Golfer's transport
26 John Paul II, e.g.
27 Mary Kay competitor
28 Tim of "WKRP in Cincinnati"
29 Coward's lack
31 "Six ___ and half a dozen . . ."

Puzzle 18 by Arthur S. Verdesca

32 Fresh-mouthed
33 "That's clear"
34 Lower-left phone button
36 One of the Society Islands
37 Ken or Lena of Hollywood
38 Judge
42 It's often laid down
43 Sacred scrolls
44 Norwegian saint
45 ___ operandi

46 Inundated
47 Bonnie's partner
48 Ziti or spaghetti
50 Dress shirt ornament
51 Pre-cable problem
52 Lecher's look
53 Old autocrat
55 Workout spot
56 ___ polloi
57 Yegg's haul

ACROSS

1 Support, with "up"
5 Naturally curly hairdo
9 Swindle
13 "___ Man" (Estevez film)
14 Foreigner
15 Sharpen
16 Arena shouts
17 Boxing start
19 Destination of one who walks?
21 Spine-tingling
22 Walk stiffly
23 Workers on duty
25 Drink in a cup
26 City southwest of Tehran
28 Name in many a hospital name
30 "Mamma ___!"
33 Word for a king
35 Licorice sources
38 Concludes
40 Inferior
42 Opportunity for a football squad
44 ___ instant (quickly)
45 Showy flower
46 ___-do-well
48 Criterion: Abbr.
49 Lightly sprayed
51 The "L" of L.A.
53 Republicans, for short
55 Circus sites
57 Copycats
61 English topic
63 Subway danger
65 Bronze medal
67 "___ small world . . ."
68 Western lily
69 Correo ___ (Spanish airmail)
70 Fed. agents
71 Yin's opposite
72 Marries
73 Piquancy

DOWN

1 Univ. teachers
2 Ignited again
3 "Lohengrin," e.g.
4 Unmarried partner, in modern lingo
5 Rose by any other name?
6 Finishing order
7 Return to office
8 Toronto's prov.
9 High heel, e.g.
10 Paramours
11 Comics orphan
12 Jiltee of myth
14 Mil. jet locale
18 Money back
20 Bout enders, in brief
24 Pajama material
27 Assign a wrong year to
29 Singer ___ Te Kanawa
30 Western plateau
31 Don Juan's mother
32 Big planning on Madison Avenue
34 Checkers color
36 "L'___, c'est moi"

Puzzle 19 by Manny Nosowsky

37 Transmit
39 Songs for one
41 Be indebted to
43 Made a home in a tree
47 Freeway, e.g.
50 Main order in a restaurant
52 Little squirt
53 Full of nerve
54 Actor Milo

56 Large and petite
58 Wonderland cake words
59 Small hills
60 Bias
62 Old-fashioned sailors' drink
64 Bygone car
66 Manhandle

ACROSS

1 On the loose, after "at"
6 Orange throwaway
10 Bad day for Caesar
14 Orally
15 La Scala highlight
16 Richard of "Runaway Bride"
17 Pondered
18 Place for a phone number, often
20 John Glenn or Davy Crockett, e.g.
22 Bring up
23 Copier additive
27 Extreme cruelty
30 Spy's writing, perhaps
33 N.Y.'s Fifth, e.g.
34 Leap for Lipinski
35 Floods on purpose
37 Beatles hit sung by Ringo
40 Kindred feelings
41 Price tag
42 "Go, team!"
43 Parasite's home
44 Cultural group
46 Sarcastic
48 Icicle's locale
49 Man with a monkey, stereotypically
56 Torus-shaped candy
59 Spread salt on, perhaps

60 At any time
61 Webmaster's creation
62 D-Day beach
63 Turner and Williams
64 Attention-getter
65 Disinfectant brand

DOWN

1 Dalai ___
2 Homecoming figure
3 Crimson Glory, for one
4 Castro, prior to 1959
5 Whirling currents
6 "M*A*S*H" role
7 Anemic's need
8 Close at hand
9 Carp's kin
10 Hemispherical home
11 N.J. neighbor
12 Notable time
13 Sun. delivery
19 Daniel of Nicaragua
21 Pushrod pusher
24 Republic
25 "Despite all that . . ."
26 Puts back to zero
27 Grid great Gale
28 Hewer
29 Oracle site
30 Salad oil holder
31 Spheres
32 Not too brainy

Puzzle 20 by David Ainslie Macleod

1	2	3	4	5		6	7	8	9		10	11	12	13
14						15					16			
17						18				19				
20					21									
			22							23		24	25	26
27	28	29					30	31	32			33		
34						35					36			
37				38	39									
40									41					
42				43				44	45					
46			47				48							
			49		50	51	52					53	54	55
56	57	58							59					
60					61					62				
63					64					65				

35 Fertility goddess
36 Lex Luthor, to Superman
38 Catchall category
39 One of the five W's
44 Musician's asset
45 Small-screen heartthrob
47 Idlers' opposites
48 Everglades wader
50 ["Good heavens!"]
51 Budget rival
52 Trawlers' gear

53 "Buenos ___"
54 Canyon sound
55 Heartfelt
56 Voided tennis shot
57 "___ Got a Secret"
58 Spooned in

ACROSS

1 Leader opposed by the Bolsheviks
5 Stockholm native
10 Prefix with distant
14 Gymnast Korbut
15 Like some kitchens, in real estate ads
16 Moscow's land: Abbr.
17 Rosy, as a complexion
20 Dwindles, with "out"
21 Surgeon's assistant
22 "Tinker to __ to Chance"
23 Manicurist's board
25 To the __ degree
28 __ Moines, Iowa
29 Rude look
30 Peek-__
31 Entree fowl
33 Alaskan islander
34 Speckled, as hair
38 Nun's wear
39 Fussy relatives, stereotypically
40 Take apart
41 Montana metropolis
43 Egyptian cobra
46 Architect I. M. __
47 Someone __ (not mine)
48 Trattoria sauce
50 Madame with a Nobel
52 Detects
53 Fundamental, as issues
57 Baby-faced
58 Spanish mistress
59 Writer __ Stanley Gardner
60 Hot tempers
61 Jack who would eat no fat
62 Numbered rds.

DOWN

1 Surpassed
2 Record holder
3 Glass marbles
4 Soapbox derby entrant
5 Visits
6 Lived
7 Fraternity letter
8 Sit-down affair
9 Hang on
10 Bumbles
11 She has lots of workers
12 It's between Can. and Mex.
13 Theory suffix
18 "48 __"
19 Boo-hoo
23 School with historic playing fields
24 Authorization
26 Take the show on the road
27 Sizzling
29 Health resort
30 Hannibal's challenge

Puzzle 21 by Fran and Lou Sabin

31 Muse of history
32 Long distance inits.
33 Suitable
34 Not loco
35 Step down
36 Implants
37 WSW's reverse
38 Drill sergeant's call
41 They're often pulled at night
42 Exhausted
43 Categorize

44 British essayist Sir Richard
45 Sheriffs' aids
47 Time to remember
48 Shooter ammo
49 "Step right in!"
51 Western tribe
52 Rebounds, e.g.
53 Long distance inits.
54 Where Switz. is
55 The "p" of m.p.h.
56 "Put ___ Happy Face"

ACROSS

1 Contralto's counterpart
6 Richard of "Pretty Woman"
10 Arm or leg
14 Consumer
15 Part of I.C.U.
16 Racetrack
17 Castle feature
19 Shuttle scheduler
20 50 minutes with a psychiatrist, e.g.
21 Yeses
23 Ready for overtime
25 Clear, as a disk
26 "Joe"
30 Honors
33 Home to 9,000 Maine collegians
35 "Oh, for Pete's ___"
36 Elsie's greeting
39 Absolutely best part
43 Old spy org.
44 Result of melting
45 Gown fabric
46 Troop formation
49 Hardy heroine
50 Bewildered
53 PBS Emmy winner
55 Plotzed
58 African member of OPEC
63 Time to make a move
64 Fruit or mincemeat, e.g.

66 Duel tool
67 "I had no ___!"
68 Any song by the Supremes
69 Slash
70 Filly's brother
71 Adam and Mae

DOWN

1 Resting places
2 Swiss stream
3 Stops on the I.R.T.
4 Wraps (up)
5 Once around the world
6 Kind of pig
7 Butt
8 Latvia's capital
9 Summers in France
10 Antisocial types
11 Former Mrs. Trump
12 Flag places
13 Not at all excited
18 Disturb
22 High-quality
24 Part of sweeping efforts?
26 Skater Starbuck
27 God of war
28 Promises
29 Chemical ending
31 When repeated, enthusiastic
32 Squeeze (out)
34 Passé
36 Underground type
37 Predators on mice
38 End drawer in a till

Puzzle 22 by Elizabeth C. Gorski

40 Roth ___ (investment choice)
41 Zip
42 Grind, so to speak
46 Wrote
47 Like some yogurt
48 The Louis whose mother was Marie Antoinette
50 Second photo in a testimonial ad
51 Hose shade
52 Signal to pull over

54 Radiant
56 "Ulysses," for one
57 Queen of Carthage
59 Big fashion magazine
60 Clears (of)
61 "What's ___ for me?"
62 Ripens
65 Sushi order

ACROSS

1 False god
5 Buddy
9 Atlanta-based airline
14 Pasture portion
15 Tip-top
16 Turn inside out
17 Flushing field
18 Barbershop request
19 Rope fiber
20 "Yikes!"
23 Nobelist Wiesel
24 Prohibition ___ (1920–33)
25 1900
28 Society crasher
31 Menlo Park monogram
34 Out in front
36 Be sick
37 The "A" in B.A.
38 "Yikes!"
42 Malt kiln
43 Iowa's state tree
44 City near Dayton
45 Rd. for a mail carrier
46 Prince Philip, to Queen Elizabeth
49 Calendar square
50 Gobble up
51 Like the driven snow
53 "Yikes!"
60 Kindergarten adhesive
61 Without: Fr.
62 Brainstorm
63 Four duos
64 Out of the wind
65 Little tykes
66 Eye drops
67 Flippant
68 "If all ___ fails . . ."

DOWN

1 Quite a party
2 Result of overexercise
3 Neck of the woods
4 Shove off
5 Tabby's tempter
6 Derby participants
7 Platoon or squadron, e.g.
8 Bulletin board notice
9 Gila monster's home
10 "Don't Cry for Me, Argentina" musical
11 More or ___
12 Carhop's aid
13 Part of NATO: Abbr.
21 Give the slip
22 Funnyman Milton
25 Business Administration or English Lit., e.g.
26 Use crib notes
27 Former Attorney General Edwin
29 Carpet fasteners
30 Lungful
31 What's happening
32 Parts of hearts
33 Piece in "Harper's"

Puzzle 23 by Gregory E. Paul

35 Fitting
37 Copycat
39 Genealogy
40 ___ Bernardino
41 Old paperboy's cry
46 Midshipmen's rivals
47 First of two baseball games
48 Autumn apple
50 Go in
52 Upper echelon
53 Shoestring
54 "The Thin Man" dog
55 "Immediately!"
56 Cabbage
57 1-Across, e.g.
58 Nov. 11 honorees
59 Convenience
60 Flower's place

ACROSS

1 Italian autos
6 Jack's companion, in rhyme
10 Country bumpkin
14 Model Everhart
15 Conception
16 Addict
17 Run after a comic?
19 Litigant
20 Long, long time
21 Small amount
22 Natural gas ingredient
24 Impaled
26 In a stall, as a horse
27 Wide shoe specification
28 Kama ___
29 Maniacs
32 Chemical suffix
33 Byway
37 Sophisticated military plane
38 Big expense for newspapers
39 Pre-PC counters
40 The two of them
41 N.Y.C. line
42 Stir
43 "Thriller" singer's nickname
45 "This means ___!"
46 Fixes, as a shoe
49 Driveway endings
53 Tennis star Gibson
54 Saharalike
55 Sight from Lucerne
56 Take a dogleg, e.g.
57 Hurt a politician's wife?
60 Paradise
61 ___ Stanley Gardner
62 Nonnuclear family member
63 Wet, as morning grass
64 Any day now
65 "Beau ___"

DOWN

1 Confronts
2 ___ water (up the creek)
3 Guam's capital, old-style
4 "___ the season to be jolly"
5 Hothouse features
6 Islamic crusade
7 Alter ___ (exact duplicate)
8 "My Name Is Asher ___"
9 Newborn's paraphernalia
10 Hurry an actress along?
11 Ordinary
12 Designer Geoffrey
13 Blew it
18 Canadian Indians
23 Blacken
25 Make a baseball player sit out the game?

Puzzle 24 by Stephanie Spadaccini

26 Submerged
28 ___ Domingo
29 Just great
30 ___ Jima
31 "Dig in!"
34 "Red" or "white" tree
35 Bandage brand
36 Cacophony
38 Ticks off
39 Presenter's task
41 Deep freezes, so to speak
42 Hang around for

44 Pub brew
46 Scored
47 Get away from
48 Throw here and there
49 Verdant
50 Stares
51 Vote in
52 Bender
54 Folk singer Guthrie
58 Tijuana gold
59 Crusty one?

ACROSS

1 In ___ straits
5 Impassive
10 Arrangement of the hair
14 Drug addict
15 Antidrug cop
16 BMW competitor
17 Shoppers' mecca #1
20 Sen. Kennedy
21 Work units
22 "The Wizard of Oz" locale
23 Dairy case item
24 Grant of "An Affair to Remember"
25 French city on the Strait of Dover
28 Plague carriers
29 Contend (for)
32 Scents
33 Change the furnishings
34 ___ Lee Corporation
35 Shoppers' mecca #2
38 "Holy smokes!"
39 Catcher's need
40 A ship to remember
41 Place for a home office, maybe
42 Ballpoints, e.g.
43 School paper holder
44 Guys' partners
45 Dressed
46 Charlotte ___, Virgin Islands
49 Nutcase
50 Uncle who "wants you!"
53 Shoppers' mecca #3
56 Home of Iowa State
57 Gin's partner
58 Miles away
59 Playwright Hart
60 Notable period
61 Newborn

DOWN

1 Airpipe, e.g.
2 ___ of Man
3 Marsh growth
4 Notable period
5 Traps
6 Ballroom dance
7 Horrid giants
8 Polar formation
9 Parakeet's cousin
10 Shrewd
11 The double of a double play
12 Inkling
13 Pines
18 Enjoy with gusto
19 Big donkey features
23 Propelled a canoe
24 West Pointer
25 Intimidated
26 Saying
27 Navigational system
28 Takes five
29 In effect
30 Goodnight girl of song
31 Diner

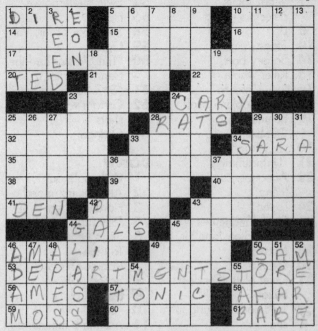

33 Sights at Angkor Wat
34 Valiant fight
36 Brunch staple
37 Eskimo boats
42 Unexciting poker holding
43 Irregular spot
44 Tumbler
45 Like orange traffic markers
46 Funnyman Sandler
47 Office note
48 Simians

49 Numbers game
50 Divan
51 Basra native
52 A ___ pittance
54 Finish, with "up"
55 Coca-Cola Co. brand

ACROSS

1 What some detectors detect
6 Lip
10 Stage item
14 Battery part
15 Killer whale
16 "___ Camera"
17 Good-lookin' fellah
19 Summers in Québec
20 ___ Majesty
21 "Unfortunately . . ."
22 Adequate, as a living
24 Layer
25 Skillful maneuver
26 1992 Elton John hit
29 Mass part
30 Less
31 Chief of staff under Nixon
32 Traditional hazing site
36 Sleep like ___
37 Brief role
38 Robin Cook thriller
39 Snack
40 Nile reptiles
41 Betray
42 Popular mints
44 Fireplace supplies
45 One who's experienced release
48 Low-cal
49 Principles
50 "Little Women" woman

51 Tree juice
54 Swim's alternative
55 Hon
58 Sushi bar order: Var.
59 Ogled
60 "The Cloister and the Hearth" writer
61 "So what ___ is new?"
62 Certain volleyball shots
63 Change

DOWN

1 Unthought-out
2 At times it's upped
3 Hardly upbeat
4 Tally (up)
5 Stays behind
6 To date
7 Canine sounds
8 School subj.
9 Padre's place
10 "Easy!"
11 A dime a minute, and others
12 Signs
13 Wallop
18 Oscar-nominated Peter Fonda role
23 Loaf part
24 Not the easiest person to deal with
25 Common side order
26 Investigator, of sorts
27 Hawaiian city
28 Deputy sheriff of TV's Hazzard County
29 Bivouacs

Puzzle 26 by Elizabeth C. Gorski

31	Speed
33	Kind of learning
34	Love, to Luis
35	Catches some rays
37	Strokes
41	90s-style nest egg
43	Spreading tree
44	Sex symbol Brad
45	Old hat
46	Variety of symmetry
47	Skating sites
48	English university city
50	Borscht need

51	To-do
52	Helper
53	Equal
56	___ peace accord (1998 agreement)
57	Wriggler

ACROSS

1 Pre-entree course
6 ___ Canaveral
10 Cheetah feature
14 Palate appendage
15 Mozart's "Il mio tesoro," e.g.
16 Soothing succulent
17 Spillane detective
19 Completely demolish
20 Cover
21 Quills
23 Worked the field
26 Enzyme suffix
27 "Don't get any funny ___!"
29 Abominable Snowman
31 Number after due
34 Telephone attachment
35 Hercules type
36 Popular dog's name
37 "Gimme ___!" (start of an Iowa State cheer)
38 Deduces
40 ___ de France
41 Nada
42 Ohio tire city
43 Watering holes
44 Actor Mineo
45 Tavern offering
46 Like craft shows
48 Darjeeling or oolong
50 One who's been initiated
52 Turns away
55 Like pottery
59 ___ of Arc
60 Grade school marching orders
63 After-hours money sources, for short
64 Shade provider
65 Scrawny chicken parts
66 Musical symbol
67 Swami
68 Sugary snack, say

DOWN

1 Kind of wrestling
2 Tel ___
3 Book before John
4 Warned
5 Showy bloom
6 Oasis animal
7 Take up weapons
8 Epitome of easiness
9 Obstacles for barbers
10 Madras dresses
11 Flights
12 Seep
13 Golfer's bagful
18 Is under the weather
22 Nuisances
24 Rundown shack, e.g.
25 Evil one
27 Ancient Aegean land

Puzzle 27 by Joey Crumley

28 Precision squads
30 Turn into leather
32 Race with a baton
33 Men in Liz's past
34 Trash holders
35 Sheik's bevy
38 Morocco's capital
39 Barely make, with "out"
43 Aerial assailant
46 Genesis brother
47 Sublet
49 Dadaist Max

51 Former NBC newsman Frank
52 Not fully closed
53 November exhortation
54 J.F.K. arrivals
56 Cheese lovers?
57 Actress Chase
58 "___ la vie"
61 Golden-ager's nest egg, for short
62 A photog saves it

ACROSS

1 Special home installations
5 After dusk
9 Boot out
14 Aquarium
15 Black
16 With 32-Across, Best Picture nominee of 1979
17 Young Ron Howard role
18 ___ Strauss & Co.
19 Negative sort of person
20 Broadway show about a gang war at Macy's?
23 Standing
24 Puppeteer Lewis
25 Angel's topper
28 Western timber tree
32 See 16-Across
35 Actress Taylor of "The Nanny"
38 German "a"
39 Broadway show about a "chewsy" cowgirl?
43 Bowl over
44 Aroma
45 Look in (on)
46 "Nonsense!"
49 Mix up
51 1996 Leonardo DiCaprio role
54 Social class
58 Broadway show about an old Chinese gent?
61 "The Wreck of the Mary ___"
63 Peru's capital
64 Singer Vikki
65 The Little Mermaid
66 ___ plaisir
67 Sandwich cookie
68 Fine's partner
69 Teller's stack
70 5-Down loaves

DOWN

1 Vermont ski resort
2 Mill output
3 Licoricelike flavor
4 Drawing
5 Supermarket section
6 Under the covers
7 Gads about
8 Jewish turnover
9 "One more time!"
10 One who "borrows" a car
11 Marine eagle
12 Roman 901
13 Tic-___-toe
21 Gaze
22 Street material
26 Journey part
27 Teller's stack
29 Pudding ingredients
30 ___ to one's ears
31 Big name in fine wines
32 Grate
33 Voting "no"

Puzzle 28 by Stephanie Spadaccini

34 Plenty, informally
36 Yadda-yadda-yadda . . .
37 Peepers
40 Like some night vision
41 Can. province
42 New York city
47 Godforsaken
48 Comic Philips
50 Resentment
52 Key of Beethoven's "Sonata No. 26"

53 Martini staple
55 À la King
56 DEF, on a phone
57 New money on the Continent
58 Central
59 "You said it!"
60 PC alternatives
61 Pop
62 Pitcher's stat.

ACROSS

1 Feelings, informally
6 Young miss
10 Garden with the tree of life
14 Wipe, as a blackboard
15 Get ___ (board)
16 Lymph bump
17 Mechanical man
18 Skyscraper support
19 Swenson of "Benson"
20 Unspecified number
21 Frugal lunch-eater
24 Boyfriends
26 What a swish shot doesn't touch
27 Immediately
29 In working condition
34 No-good sort
35 Planetarium display
36 President after Jimmy
37 Accompanies musically sans words
38 The first "M" in M-G-M
39 Catcall
40 Suffix with computer
41 Artist's cap
42 Use a divining rod
43 Kitchen gadget
45 North African tribesman
46 Scale units: Abbr.
47 Caterpillar hairs
48 Torturous task
53 Prone
56 Tick off
57 Sea World attraction
58 Movie with a saloon fight, maybe
60 Tennis score after deuce
61 Skip
62 Actress Worth
63 Be in awe
64 Custom-___
65 To the point

DOWN

1 Aloe ___
2 It's pumped in gyms
3 Fortysomething, say
4 "___ Beso" (1962 song)
5 Relapse
6 University of New Mexico's nickname
7 From the top
8 Saxophonist Getz
9 Hat dance hat
10 Mystery
11 Doorbell sound
12 Upper hand
13 At hand
22 Regret
23 Pretense
25 Son in Genesis
27 Partner of pains
28 Kind of fund
29 Playful animal

30 Divide with a comb
31 Bully
32 Baggy
33 Register
35 Dried up
38 Public facility
39 Bar mitzvah dance
41 Kind of lettuce
42 Where General Motors is headquartered
44 Certain hydrocarbon
45 The ___ Gees

47 It has wheels on its heel
48 Talk big
49 Opera set in Egypt
50 Football foul
51 Witty Bombeck
52 Ascorbic ___
54 Highlighters, e.g.
55 Branch headquarters?
59 "___ you kidding?"

ACROSS

1 Idaho, e.g.
6 Calcutta dress
10 Alain's girlfriend
14 Accustom
15 Caddie's offering
16 Bad luck cause
17 Single year's record
18 Cuts, as branches
19 Lotion ingredient
20 Be mildly surprising, to an egotist?
23 Trip up a mountain
24 Wine city near Turin
25 ___ Mahal
27 Still in the womb
32 Office transmittal
36 Iran's ___ Shah Pahlavi
39 Lively French dance
40 Long-lost friend, to an egotist?
43 Carpet fiber
44 Altimeter units
45 Job for a body shop
46 More than dislike
48 . . . . . _ _ . . .
50 Ocean prowlers
53 Pursued
58 With surprising speed, to an egotist?
63 ___ Clinic
64 Kismet
65 Longest river in Europe
66 Fuse units
67 "Trinity" author
68 Prolific writer on calculus
69 Swim contest
70 Word with contact or zoom
71 With subterfuge

DOWN

1 Princess' headgear
2 Magnani and Christie
3 Part of a military uniform
4 Make blank
5 Give in
6 Round building
7 It may be picked up in a tobacco shop
8 Items in bell towers
9 Undisturbed
10 Open a bit
11 Actor O'Shea
12 "___ pronounce . . ."
13 Divorcées
21 Skittish move
22 Evening fare at some churches
26 Newsman Greenfield
28 Wren or hen
29 Double curve
30 Havoc
31 Habitat for 28-Down
32 Motel employee
33 Start of North Carolina's motto
34 Hand holder
35 Eye up and down
37 Playwright Akins

Puzzle 30 by Ed Early

38 God of war
41 1946 Literature Nobelist
42 Nasdaq offering
47 Bath water quantity
49 Elbows
51 Trumpet emanation
52 1960s protest
54 Run ___ of
55 Rand of fan dancing fame
56 Broadway conductor Lehman ___

57 "Dear" book
58 Shi'ite leader
59 Be specific about
60 Key in
61 Virus's target
62 Loch of Scotland

ACROSS

1 Play parts
5 Atty. Gen. Janet
9 Greek column style
14 ___ & Chandon (champagne)
15 With, en français
16 Onetime Trump
17 Prince Charles's top
19 Exploding stars
20 Bowler's 7-10, e.g.
21 Sends to a certain fate
23 Likely
24 Actor's minimum wage
26 Architect I. M. ___
27 Hurry
28 Chinese Chairman
30 Steffi Graf's footwear
33 Out-of-doors, as dining
35 Absorbed, as a loss
36 She said "I do"
37 New Year's ___
39 Tear down
43 Old gray mare, say
46 Ushered
49 Cal Ripkin's lid
53 Gridders' scores
54 McClanahan of "The Golden Girls"
55 Place to recuperate
56 Combat zone
58 Height: Abbr.
59 Name on a children's book
61 "Casablanca" cafe
64 Birth-related
66 Picabo Street's outerwear
68 Muralist Rivera
69 Roughly
70 It's rounded up in a roundup
71 Sen. Thurmond
72 "___ here" ("Ditto")
73 Goofs up

DOWN

1 Stereo parts
2 City dwelling
3 Chews out
4 Impassive
5 Cheerleader's cry
6 Prosecutor's presentation
7 Roman "fiddler"
8 Squids' relatives
9 "Really! It's MY treat!"
10 Ab ___ (from the beginning)
11 Arizona Indian
12 Where to find baked blackbirds
13 Social classes
18 Senator's constituency
22 Phoenix neighbor
25 ___ États-Unis
28 Paw's mate
29 MacGraw of "Love Story"
31 Steinbeck work
32 Frau's counterpart
34 Philosopher Descartes

38 Avoidance of reality
40 Assailant
41 A's opposite, in England
42 Begley and Bradley
44 King David's wayward son
45 Stare with lax jaw
47 Mustang or Lynx
48 "Carmen," e.g.
49 Ranches and corporations have them
50 Café ____
51 Irish canine
52 Rodeo ropes
57 Specialty
60 Gumbo staple
62 Brynner's co-star in "The King and I"
63 Norms: Abbr.
65 Back from now
67 Coffee, slangily

ACROSS

1 Poet Khayyám
5 "Naughty you!"
10 Went for the cuspidor
14 F.B.I. info
15 Place for croutons
16 Mafia bigwig
17 Halloween wear
19 Geraint's lady
20 ___ Tafari (Haile Selassie)
21 Trash bag accessory
22 City on the Arno
23 Burglar's advance man, maybe
26 Tending to grab
28 Smokers' needs
32 "The Purple People Eater" singer Wooley
33 "O Sole ___"
34 Triangular road sign
36 Not a stylish dresser
39 A throw
41 "Eating ___" (1982 black comedy)
43 Milky Way unit
44 Neither sharp nor flat
46 Trainees learn these
48 Singing syllable
49 Pack down
51 Study of prison management
53 Crimson
56 Good gymnastic scores
57 "The Time Machine" people

58 Brit. lexicon
60 Move it
61 Balm ingredient
62 Feature of some radios
67 Laces (into)
68 Sal of "Exodus"
69 Aunt Bee's boy
70 Audition
71 Preserves, as pork
72 Withdraw gradually

DOWN

1 Wide of the mark
2 Aging orbiter
3 "Aladdin" prince
4 "That I have but one life to lose for my country," to Hale
5 Air France fleet members
6 End of a bray
7 Came to rest
8 Hoodoo
9 Detroit duds
10 Regalia items
11 Pusher's target?
12 Imitative
13 NBC debut of 1/14/52
18 He followed Franklin
23 Small role for a big star
24 Kind of flu
25 Infantry assault group
27 14 and up, for short
29 Gas station offering
30 Wine taster's concern

31 Single-master
35 Trick
37 Blue-haired Simpson
38 Earnestly hopes
40 Most likely to break a scale
42 Football Hall-of-Famer Dawson
45 Singer Sumac
47 Like some booms
50 Some golf tourneys
52 Stay out of sight
53 Coward's lack

54 Kate's TV partner
55 Daniel's "Sonnets to ___"
59 Frontiersman Boone, for short
60 Med. care grps.
63 Not active: Abbr.
64 Unlock, in verse
65 Cloak-and-dagger org.
66 Barbie's doll

ACROSS

1 Weeps uncontrollably
5 [Nothing but net]
10 Midbody muscles
13 Stage device
14 Electrical pioneer Nikola
15 Cabal's plans
16 "Like, no way!"
17 "The Breakfast Club" actress
19 Pro's opposite
20 "Gomer ___, U.S.M.C."
21 Thrill-seeker's cord
22 Duelist's warning
24 Actor Lugosi
25 Star of TV's "Veronica's Closet"
30 Image that may be burned
33 Brinker with silver skates
34 Fury
35 Break off from a mother's milk
36 "___ Misérables"
37 Roman wrap
38 Like some stocks, for short
39 Vaudeville bit
41 Key of Chopin's "Piano Concerto No. 2"
43 1980's sitcom
46 Spy Aldrich
47 It doesn't look good

51 Little piggy that went to market?
54 Muscat's land
55 Phone transmission
56 "Love Story" actress
58 Wind instrument
59 Severe sentence
60 Boxing site
61 Marty Feldman role in "Young Frankenstein"
62 Came across
63 Dull, as text
64 Shut (up)

DOWN

1 Extraterrestrial realm
2 With 6-Down, Citizen Kane portrayer
3 Sound of a spring
4 Coppertone no.
5 Keep out of the rain
6 See 2-Down
7 ___ of Wight
8 Foxy
9 Faded star
10 "Shake ___!"
11 Foreshadow
12 47-Across, literally
15 Prison-related
18 Luau dances
20 Bluenose
23 Like, with "to"
24 Slant
26 Iota preceder
27 Its pride is its pride
28 Thus
29 Two semesters

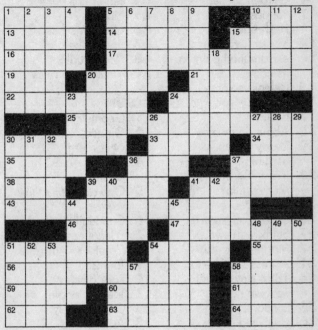

30 Friendly "Star Wars" creature
31 Cheese from sheep's milk
32 It's true
36 Box tops
37 20-20 and 7-up
39 Pago Pago site
40 Patella
41 Abandon the nest
42 Bearing
44 Words on a Wonderland cake
45 Noted French auto race
48 Mature
49 Kept going and going and . . .
50 Exercise
51 Pain soother
52 Tennis's Nastase
53 Present
54 Nabisco cookie
57 Dog's warning
58 Bigwig

ACROSS

1 Garden shelter
7 Put past?
11 Hush-hush org.
14 Musical with an exclamation point in its name
15 Defensive spray
16 "So . . .?"
17 Nullify
18 About, in memos
19 Ready for an asylum
20 Hip 1984 Bill Murray film
23 ___ la Douce
26 Sailor's affirmative
27 Suffix with switch
28 Marine food fish
31 Actress ___ Chong
34 1884 Helen Hunt Jackson novel
35 Londoner, e.g.
36 Uninvited guests
41 Grandson of Adam
42 Mouth puckerers
44 Encouraged
48 Mark the boundaries of
49 Inside view?
50 "There but for the grace of God ___"
52 Solidifies
53 Women who go after other women's men
58 Mad. ___
59 Furnace output

60 "Stop bugging me!"
64 Tennis call
65 Not busy
66 German subs
67 Bard's "before"
68 "Hey, bud!"
69 Violates the rules

DOWN

1 Geometry suffix
2 Ginger ___
3 Quick turn
4 "Green Acres" co-star
5 One of Alcott's "little women"
6 Creme-filled snack
7 Friendliness
8 Capital of Australia
9 Tannish
10 Poor grades
11 Tourist's staple
12 Consecutively
13 Appends
21 Carrier to Stockholm
22 English poet laureate Hughes
23 Jerusalem's home: Abbr.
24 Gather
25 "Red hot" person
29 Paid to hold hands?
30 Refuse
32 Many an airline seat request
33 One of the Barrymores

Puzzle 34 by Kevin McCann

35 Apt. features
37 Solidifies
38 Discharge
39 Palatine Hill site
40 Angry state
43 Patrick and Paul: Abbr.
44 Blow out
45 Sesame Street character
46 Egg, for one
47 Optometrist's interest
48 Cartoonist Browne

51 String ensemble, maybe
54 Party manager, in Congress
55 Lipstick shades
56 Prefix with lateral
57 Massages
61 Tit for ___
62 Judge in 1996 news
63 "'Tis a pity"

ACROSS

1 Plane reservation
5 Brief fight
10 Person whose name starts with Mac-, maybe
14 Burn balm
15 Scout group
16 ___ Alto, Calif.
17 Horne who sang "Stormy Weather"
18 Tending (to)
19 The Emerald Isle
20 1967 Robert Knight hit
23 Not "dis," in Brooklyn
24 More complete
25 Group of bees
28 Country estates
31 Louisville's river
32 South Pacific islander
33 It once billed itself "The most trusted name in television"
36 Inventor's impossible goal
39 "Take your hands off me!"
40 Rigid bracelet
41 Supply-and-demand subj.
42 Rich pastries
43 Fire sign
44 Word on express mail
47 Republicans, for short
48 1995 Deepak Chopra book

55 Belonging to us
56 Steamed
57 San ___, Italy
58 Fit of fever
59 Sneakers with swooshes
60 Popular online auction company
61 "___ of the D'Urbervilles"
62 Beau ___
63 Soap actress Linda

DOWN

1 Dollar days event
2 Abbr. on a contour map
3 Top-notch
4 Sign of unhappiness
5 March 17 honoree, briefly
6 Goes astray
7 Horn sound
8 Novelist Morrison
9 Danger near an aerosol spray
10 Incantations
11 "God Rest Ye Merry, Gentlemen," e.g.
12 Fruit on a toothpick
13 Printer need
21 On the ___ (fleeing)
22 Rich fertilizer
25 Frosh, next year
26 Cry on a roller coaster
27 Subject to a draft
28 Speak boastfully of
29 Mirror ___

Puzzle 35 by Robert Frank

30 Takes it easy
32 Amazing
33 Puerto ___
34 Person in an apron
35 Writer Rice
37 U.S. investment instrument
38 Moderated
42 Past, present, and future
43 Henry V, to Henry IV
44 Sub that sank Allied ships

45 Cheek coloring
46 Mentors
47 Farmyard honkers
49 Lake near Niagara Falls
50 Fifth Avenue retailer
51 "Let it stand"
52 Singer McEntire
53 Crime buster
54 It has its ups and downs

ACROSS

1 The Crimson Tide
5 "Cool!"
10 Collecting Pokémon cards, and others
14 One-spots
15 Flower of the primrose family
16 Zeno's birthplace
17 HAIR
20 Caviar, for one
21 Hawaii's Sen. Daniel
22 Dash units
23 Mideast chief: Var.
24 Steps over a fence
27 Troublemaker
31 Smut
32 Parts of Polynésie
33 The Buckeyes, for short
34 HERR
38 Little troublemaker
39 Sleeveless garment
40 Kind of energy
41 City income tax classification
44 Part of a dying fire
45 Blue eyes producer, maybe
46 Vijay Singh org.
47 Surfing locale
50 Dish seasoned with sake
55 HARE
57 Next-door
58 Russian range
59 Secret sign
60 Stickum
61 Almost worthless Italian coins
62 Vientiane is its capital

DOWN

1 Madam
2 Reason to see a dentist
3 Airline serving
4 ___ spumante
5 Anonymous
6 Business bigwigs
7 Confederate
8 Make fast
9 Great expectations
10 Hat with a curled brim
11 Ballplayer Moises
12 Like some morning grass
13 All there
18 Leopardlike cat
19 Hissy fit
23 Ten-percenter
24 English Channel feeder
25 Dancers' gaffes
26 Those holding office
27 Tilting
28 Printed French cotton
29 Award for Judi Dench
30 German industrial valley

Puzzle 36 by Bernice Gordon

31 Twosome
32 Goddess of peace
35 Memorable, as a trip
36 Daily delivery
37 San Francisco's ___ Hill
42 Give the cold shoulder
43 Kind of breath
44 Means of escape
46 Capital of ancient Macedonia
47 Punch
48 Low-down louse

49 Biblical twin
50 Ski lift
51 Protest long and loud
52 Where 62-Across is
53 Gambling game
54 Ticks off
56 Christina's dad

ACROSS

1 Not white, as meat
5 Free, as a ticket
9 Choir voice
13 Skin softener
14 Before surgery
16 Spare
17 Wine container
19 Checker, perhaps
20 "Crackers"
21 Hot sauce
23 Egg container
27 Part of the Corn Belt
31 Carted
32 Olive container
34 Civilian clothes
39 Bob of the Bob and Ray comedy team
40 Sermon
42 Mongol invader
43 Moonshine container
44 Field
47 Father
48 Soda pop container
53 Partitions
54 River spanned by the Bagnell Dam
59 Relatives of ostriches
60 Garbage container
64 Gondola propeller
65 Muddle
66 ___ mater
67 Victim of a 1917 revolution
68 Hardly demanding
69 Requisite

DOWN

1 Time to crow
2 Baseball brothers' name
3 Edible part of a parsnip
4 Popular sneakers
5 Book balancer, for short
6 Bobby of hockey
7 Mal de ___
8 Emily Dickinson's field
9 Hitching post
10 Minimum
11 Mexican silverwork center
12 Tear bringer
15 Rank
18 Conk
22 Villain
24 Mil. staff officer
25 Rear end, site of many falls
26 Prominent dachshund feature
27 The Beach Boys' "___ Around"
28 Stewpot
29 Animator Disney
30 It's east of the Urals
33 Dishonorable
35 Colorado Indians
36 Pacific island getaway
37 Sightseeing trip
38 "Come Back, Little Sheba" playwright
40 Suffix with psych-

41 Barrett known for dishing

43 Uncle ___

45 When lunch ends, maybe

46 Islam adherent

48 Highly skilled

49 Prom transports

50 Part of the back of the mouth

51 Scrooge

52 "___ don't!" (words of denial)

55 Put into the computer without typing

56 Competent

57 Willing

58 "Holy cow!"

61 Tree feller

62 Let a judge hear the case

63 Tollway: Abbr.

ACROSS

1 Funny Fannie
6 Mordant Mort
10 Taj Mahal city
14 Ancient land near Lydia
15 Gus Kahn song "The ___ Love"
16 Ooze
17 "Knots Landing" co-star
19 "Livin' La Vida ___" (Ricky Martin hit)
20 Rate affected by the Fed: Abbr.
21 Schnozz ending
22 Exits
24 High lights
26 Not go according to plan?
27 Premieres
30 It will knock you out
32 Concur
33 Shift, e.g.
34 Scoundrel
37 Deposits
38 "A Journey to the Center of the Earth" writer
39 Rum-soaked cake
40 Gilbert and Sullivan princess
41 Speed ___
42 Monteverdi opera
43 Straight's partner
45 Fife player
46 Waterloo
48 Bar orders
50 Warned
52 "Wonderful!"
53 Johnny ___
56 "Look!" in La Mancha
57 Theme of this puzzle
60 Good thing to have in a storm
61 Some TVs
62 Greedy person's demand
63 Eye problem
64 Grayish
65 Pitcher Gregg ___

DOWN

1 So-called "crossroads of the South Pacific"
2 Nutcase
3 Med school subj.
4 Tonic's go-with
5 Old French dance
6 Source of waves at sea
7 Santa ___, Calif.
8 Stampeding group
9 Ditto
10 Obliquely
11 "Bolero" star, 1934
12 Prefix with linear
13 Woman with ___
18 "Poor me!"
23 Zadora and Lindstrom
24 Takes to court
25 Woes
27 Picasso contemporary
28 "Omigosh!"
29 Roxy Music lead singer

Puzzle 38 by Elizabeth C. Gorski

31 The Big Apple's ___ Station
33 Music sampler
35 Help in crime
36 Southwestern resort
38 Bone in a column
39 Warner ___
41 "Shoot!"
42 Busy
44 Freshen
45 Surgeon General with a beard
46 Moistens

47 "The Mill on the Floss" author
49 ___-totsy
51 Shrinks, e.g.
53 Record speeds, for short
54 "Tickle me" doll
55 "___ there, done that"
58 "Wonderful!"
59 Furnace fuel

ACROSS

1 Support, with "up"
5 Conveyance for Huckleberry Finn
9 Dinner fowl
14 Arizona Indian
15 Singer Guthrie
16 Popular pain reliever
17 No couch potato, him
18 500 sheets
19 Fathered
20 French germ fighter in Missouri?
23 ___ the task
24 Now's opposite
25 Visited
28 Adversaries
29 Female G.I.
32 Italian baritone Pasquale ___
33 Land of shamrocks
34 Hence
35 "M*A*S*H" star in Indiana?
38 Buffalo's lake
39 Exploit
40 "La Gare Saint-Lazare" artist
41 "Get it?"
42 Dolt
43 Accumulations
44 "One Life to Live," e.g.
45 Writer Jaffe
46 Mexican muralist in California?
52 Handed down a decision

53 Nothin'
54 Revered object
55 Coke vis-à-vis Pepsi
56 Disney's "___ and the Detectives"
57 Africa's longest river
58 Tent-pitching need
59 Actress Russo
60 Hardens

DOWN

1 High degrees?
2 Cheer (for)
3 German auto
4 Ballet whirl
5 Hen's tooth, e.g.
6 Response to "Am not!"
7 Hoo-ha
8 Crimson shade
9 Social strata
10 Not from Earth
11 Llama country
12 ___ easy (eggs order)
13 Celebrated outlaw ___ Kelly
21 Violin stroke
22 Transparent
25 Casual eateries
26 Love, in Roma
27 Osmond or Curie
28 Punished in addition to giving jail time
29 Small songbirds
30 Come to terms
31 Expenses
33 Morning coffee, for one

34 Helping to avoid humiliation
36 1952 and 1956 candidate Stevenson
37 Muscat resident
42 Treat tenderly
43 It should be raised on a ship
44 Move furtively
45 "The Thinker" sculptor
46 Three-piece apparel
47 Thomas ___ Edison
48 Willing to take part

49 Singer Adams
50 Restaurant freebie
51 Pub brews
52 They have Xings

ACROSS

1 James of "Brian's Song"
5 "Hurry!"
9 It's west of Togo
14 Regarding
15 Berg opera
16 "You've got nothing to worry about!"
17 What a tough puzzle can give you
18 Sonny and Cher's "___ You Babe"
19 Film projection
20 Emmy-winning newswoman of the 80s–90s
23 Ink, in France
24 Kind of artery
25 Prince of Broadway
28 Obi-Wan player
30 Refuse to follow suit
32 Onetime network of 20-Across
35 Not a nice feeling
38 Sting operation
39 Never say die
43 The Mideast's Gulf of ___
44 Prefix with -hedron
45 Fresh
46 Infrequently
49 Reagan Sr. and Jr.
51 Werner Erhard teaching
52 Hot sauce
55 Brewer's need

59 1966 musical starring Gwen Verdon
61 Count with a keyboard
64 Prefix with physics
65 Winged youth of myth
66 Honor ___ thieves
67 Finito
68 His dying words were "What an artist the world is losing in me!"
69 Ballroom staple
70 Wasp's home
71 First place

DOWN

1 Cappuccino, e.g.
2 One of 3.5 billion
3 Cobweb site
4 Cosa ___
5 "Put ___ on it!"
6 Make easier to swallow
7 Without equal
8 Enter a harbor
9 Prominent Edsel feature
10 Fashion lines
11 In the style of
12 Carp, carp, carp
13 Can
21 Andrew Wyeth subject
22 Canal site
25 Marsh wader
26 Wide open
27 Cartoon skunk

Puzzle 40 by Arthur S. Verdesca

29 Unit of work
31 High degree
32 Event for foxhounds
33 Portends
34 Took part in a bee
36 Cobbler, e.g.
37 Intermissions
40 Finis
41 Like hit shows
42 Singer Tucker
47 New York city, county, or river
48 West of films

50 Unclouded
53 Problematic car
54 Allen or Martin
56 Televised
57 Put away
58 Boxer with a nasty bite
59 Carol
60 Male deer
61 Vampire ___
62 Docs' org.
63 Last word in many company names

ACROSS

1 Wolf's tooth
5 Ice hazard
9 ___ a clue (is out of it)
14 S-shaped molding
15 Queen of the Heavens
16 Baseball great Banks
17 Nostalgic song by 64-Across
20 Toadies
21 Catch in the act
22 Played chef to
23 Priest's robe
24 Indulgent song by 64-Across
27 Kind of women's shoe
31 Where China is
32 Chum
33 1930s Depression org.
35 Hold back a year in school
39 Drowsy song by 64-Across
44 Make cutting remarks
45 Moray, e.g.
46 Links peg
47 Dr. Seuss's "Horton Hears ___"
50 Babe in a maternity ward
53 Prom finale by 64-Across
57 Motorists' org.
58 Computer screen, for short
59 4-Down exclamation
60 Polynesian wrap

64 Composer born Nov. 22, 1899
68 Very, in music
69 Bridle strap
70 Not-so-lazy river
71 At the minimum setting
72 Booty, in slang
73 An orange, minus the juice

DOWN

1 Old ___ (not the modern type)
2 Pulitzer writer James
3 Revivalists
4 Munich citizen
5 Often-bumped part of the leg
6 Meadow
7 Shackles
8 Canal site
9 "Watch it, buster!"
10 Elbow's site
11 Haughty response
12 Frisco footballer
13 Classic doll
18 Moolah
19 Budding entrepreneurs, for short
25 Biography
26 "Le Roi d'Ys" composer
27 Chooses
28 Frequent chess sacrifice
29 "The Time Machine" people

Puzzle 41 by Frances Hansen

30 Before
34 Mimic
36 ___ snuff
37 N.Y. Met, e.g.
38 Eager
40 Practice in the ring
41 Off-color
42 Hankering
43 Harmonious
48 1950s Red-hunting grp.
49 Hollywood treasures
51 W.W. II female

52 Go from pub to pub
53 Stupid jerk
54 Scottish resort town
55 To any degree
56 Hurled
61 Honolulu's location
62 Moon walker Armstrong
63 Food served with a ladle
65 Sports car
66 "That hurts!"
67 "Mamma ___!"

ACROSS

1 Best ___ (most excellent)
6 Entreaty
10 One of the Three B's
14 Boom box
15 Deli breads
16 Canyon comeback
17 Rookie pianists' duet
19 Get a move on
20 Infomercials, e.g.
21 Fork feature
22 N.F.L. no-nos
23 Fruity, flaky dessert
26 Breakfast nook
29 Allies' foe in W.W. II
30 Bright thought
31 Leprechaun's land
32 Krazy critter of the comics
35 Theme of this puzzle
40 Singer-songwriter Barrett
41 Study of the body: Abbr.
42 Stunning triumph
43 Like a bug in a rug
44 Adds on
47 Jerry Garcia's band, with "the"
51 Wranglers alternative
52 Respond to a bore
53 Toothed tool
56 Current with
57 Seam finisher

60 Estrada of "CHiPs"
61 Poverty
62 Sworn ___
63 Pinhead
64 Dome covers?
65 Fills

DOWN

1 Killer whale
2 Saudi Arabian king
3 Tempests in teapots
4 Bit of insolence
5 Went ballistic
6 One who hopes to succeed?
7 French school
8 "A rat!"
9 Dummkopf
10 Intoxicates
11 Malfunction
12 Some like it hot
13 Gymnastics apparatus
18 Hair colorer
22 Barely visible
23 Nasty
24 Foal's mother
25 Lighted sign over a door
26 Claim-staker's claim
27 One way to stand by
28 Poverty
31 N.Y. winter hours
32 Fort ___ (gold site)
33 Fluish feeling
34 Sugar servings: Abbr.
36 Copenhageners

Puzzle 42 by Nancy Salomon

37 Adequate, informally
38 Prego rival
39 Topped a torte
43 Well lit?
44 Changes with the times
45 Part of CNN
46 1598 edict city
47 Stuck (on)
48 Copy, briefly
49 Steer clear of
50 Telling tales
53 Leave in

54 High point
55 Kids' questions
57 Internet letters
58 "Bali ___"
59 One ___ million

ACROSS

1 Nuisance
5 Play segments
9 First name of six U.S. presidents
14 Lotion ingredient
15 Campbell's product
16 "Don Giovanni," for example
17 One of Columbus's fleet
18 Mannheim Mr.
19 Lawn sprinkler output
20 Breakfast course #1
23 Scatter
24 4%, say, on a bank acct.
25 At a distance
29 Breakfast course #2
33 Fellow
37 Order at the Pig & Whistle
38 Ornament
39 ___ stone (hieroglyphics key)
41 Empress to Napoleon III
43 Also known as
44 Frequently, in poetry
45 Florida's Miami-___ County
46 Breakfast course #3
50 "Auld Lang ___"
51 Terrier's cry
52 Siesta taker
57 Breakfast course #4
61 Authenticated

64 Occasions to serve crumpets
65 Elevator pioneer
66 F.B.I. datum
67 Corn units
68 Observe
69 Less green
70 "Phooey!"
71 Fencing sword

DOWN

1 One-third of a three-piece suit
2 Poet T. S. ___
3 Antisub device
4 Make fun of
5 '75 Wimbledon champ
6 Like most colleges today
7 Power station equipment
8 Leaped
9 "No way, ___!"
10 Acclaimed
11 French sea
12 Old NOW cause
13 Recite
21 Lowest VHF channel
22 Communications conglomerate
26 '90s singer Apple
27 Sharp-tasting
28 Actress Zellweger of "Jerry Maguire"
30 Squealer
31 Fla. neighbor
32 English sports car, for short

Puzzle 43 by Richard Chisholm

33 Curmudgeons
34 Christmas greenery
35 ___ flu
36 Postwar period
40 "For shame!"
41 Gee preceder
42 Southwest Indian
44 Bad season, perhaps
47 Bounder
48 Speechified
49 Web site address ending

53 Composition of an endangered layer
54 "Legs" rock trio
55 Choice
56 Watch again
58 Frankfurt's river
59 Poet Teasdale
60 "Hey, there!"
61 Home film player
62 Jackie's second
63 A boxer might have a fat one

ACROSS

1 Waldorf ___
6 Per
10 Home paper
14 Sorbonne, e.g.
15 Number of Heinz flavors in old Rome?
16 Columnist Bombeck
17 Uninvolved
18 How some kids ride
20 A book one shouldn't miss
22 Good drink for the flu
23 Opposite of a ques.
24 Tempe sch.
25 "Star-Spangled Banner" preposition
26 Diagonal (to)
31 Some Surrealist works
32 LAX posting
33 It goes with the flow
37 Part of the German/Polish border
38 The privileged
40 Singer Redding
41 Barbershop call
42 Source of iron
43 Voting groups
44 Where to pontificate
47 Union foe: Abbr.
50 Show presenter on base, briefly
51 Part of E.U.: Abbr.
52 Veep who went to a Graduate School of Religion
54 They're between D's and E's on guitars
59 Diners' requests
61 Key material
62 Shake up
63 "Garfield" dog
64 Grand ___
65 Guarded rapier
66 Desires
67 Largest tributary of the Missouri

DOWN

1 It's in stitches
2 It may take a case pro bono
3 British "rest stations"
4 Gobs
5 Helps pay for
6 Rio Grande city
7 Enthusiastic
8 Smoke, informally
9 They can rock the boat
10 National ___
11 Muse of poetry
12 One who rules the roast
13 Senegal's capital
19 "What's ___ pleasure?"
21 S.A.S.E., e.g.
24 Pay to play
26 "Let's go!"
27 West Wing worker

Puzzle 44 by Elizabeth C. Gorski

28 Frightening dinosaur
29 Reason to sue
30 Celebrate
33 Take it easy
34 Sitting on
35 "Veni, vidi, ___"
36 Secy.
38 Part of an estate's staff
39 Folk's Guthrie
43 It's full of beans
44 Hide well
45 Affirmatives
46 "___ a lid on it!"

47 Training group
48 Sailing vessel
49 Texas A&M athlete
53 Look up and down
54 Opposed, in Dogpatch
55 Currier's partner
56 ___ care in the world
57 Tavern order
58 End of a New Year's Eve song
60 Soft drink

ACROSS

1 Family head
5 Taken ___ (surprised)
10 50s–60s singer ___ Domino
14 Whiff
15 Winner of 1968 and 1972
16 Help in a holdup
17 Drill instructor's 41-Across
19 Folk stories
20 TV's Kovacs
21 A portion
22 Sugar unit
23 Item on a high school jacket
25 Princeton's Tiger, e.g.
27 Ireland, poetically
29 More than bad
32 Blacken
35 Fuddy-duddy
39 Bibliographical suffix
40 Derby, for one
41 See 17- and 64-Across, and 11- and 34-Down
42 Op. ___
43 "Wherefore ___ thou Romeo?"
44 Circa
45 Wine and dine
46 Freshmen, usually
48 New money on the Continent
50 "___, My God, to Thee"

54 Like bad bruises
58 Cracker spread
60 Lapsed
62 Base runner's achievement
63 Ardent
64 Drill instructor's 41-Across
66 It may be reflecting
67 Bring out
68 What's more
69 Diarist Frank
70 Extend, as a subscription
71 Vegas sign

DOWN

1 Architect's construction
2 Like a lot
3 ___ Rushmore
4 Judge
5 Actress Sue ___ Langdon
6 Bridle parts
7 It's a given
8 Pause sign
9 Croucher's sore spots
10 Unused, as a field
11 Drill instructor's 41-Across
12 School session
13 Dance lesson
18 Satyr's stare
24 Hardship
26 Jack or 10
28 Nautilus captain

Puzzle 45 by Gregory E. Paul

30 The "U" in I.C.U.
31 Like the White Rabbit
32 Tête-à-tête
33 Aesop's also-ran
34 Drill instructor's 41-Across
36 Down Under bird
37 Western writer Grey
38 Become, at last
41 José's house
45 Computer language
47 Knitting tool
49 Trick

51 Rodeo performer
52 Avoid, as capture
53 What many incumbents do
55 "The Old Wives' Tale" playwright
56 Cow catcher
57 Rock's ___ John
58 Mate of 1-Across
59 Stratford's stream
61 Derby, e.g.
65 Morning moisture

ACROSS

1 Give and take
5 There are three in a tbs.
9 Record player
14 Rhine feeder
15 ___ monde (high society)
16 News bit from a supermarket tabloid
17 Boar
19 Boredom
20 Impassive
21 Ham comedian's ploy
23 Painter of the Barbizon School
25 Sigma follower
26 Boor
32 English county
33 Spot for a sweat bead
34 Puzzle doer, apparently
35 Mah-jongg piece
36 Completely off drugs
38 Pillow filler
39 It might help wash down a banger
40 Miscellanies
41 ___ a fiddle
42 Bore
46 Dead-on
47 Belief
48 Requests for quiet
52 Ordinarily
56 Main stream
57 Boer
59 Cream cheese base
60 Velvet spread
61 "So long!"
62 Make, as an effort
63 Eyelid swelling
64 Reproaches

DOWN

1 They go back and forth in the woods
2 "Hold on!"
3 Guthrie with a guitar
4 Treat for the feet
5 Foil
6 Jack-tar
7 Wit's end?
8 Florist's unit
9 Like some sports programs
10 Put down the phone
11 Prefix with present
12 Sentence starter
13 Not a copy: Abbr.
18 Teatime treat
22 180, so to speak
24 Like the text on proof sheets
26 Kind of sauce
27 Ship from Valdez
28 Jungle danger
29 Former capital of Japan
30 Hawkeye
31 Women with vows
32 Photo finish?
36 $100 bill

Puzzle 46 by Norman S. Wizer

37	Hasty escape
38	Preoccupy
40	Garage surface
41	Sideshow attraction
43	Egg rolling time
44	Lustrously white
45	Provide storage for forage
48	Kemo ___
49	Put-on
50	Itch
51	Easy dupes
53	Les États-___
54	Reporter's news source
55	Love child
58	Blubber

ACROSS

1 Actress Turner
5 One of baby's first words
9 Coke bottle size
14 Get the wrinkles out
15 Composer Stravinsky
16 Home base for humans
17 Takes risks
20 Casual top
21 Unnecessary accessory with 20-Across
22 Unit of conductance
23 Average grades
25 "Waiting for the Robert ___"
28 Takes risks
34 Follower of Mar.
35 Beaver's project
36 Shorthand takers
38 Infectious bacteria, briefly
41 Chop
43 Spar (with)
44 Feels sorry for
46 Afternoon break
48 Mexican Mrs.
49 Takes risks
53 Ooze
54 Instrument on a Greek vase
55 Austrian peak
58 Afire
60 Hidden
64 Takes risks
68 Cybernotes
69 New York's ___ Canal
70 Explorer called "the Red"
71 Hunky-dory
72 Cell-phone button
73 Bulletin board item

DOWN

1 Santa checks it twice
2 Boats like 3-Down's
3 Biblical captain
4 Monkeyshines
5 Bloat
6 Many years ___
7 Cautionary advice
8 More affected
9 Gift in Honolulu
10 Fleming of 007 novels
11 In good physical condition
12 Draw on copper, say
13 Prefix with -stat
18 ". . . ___ saw Elba"
19 Sen. Jesse from North Carolina
24 Overthrown Iranian leader
26 "Cómo ___ usted?"
27 Pitcher
28 Fight for breath
29 Kind of nerve
30 Poetry Muse
31 Modify
32 Psychiatrists treat it

Puzzle 47 by Dave and Diane Epperson

33 "Tag, ___ it!"
37 Mark with a branding iron
39 One of 12 popes
40 "Take this!"
42 Sirens do it
45 Inscribed pillar
47 Eager to proceed, slangily
50 Gets back at
51 "I smell ___"
52 Hush-hush
55 Stunned

56 Tibetan monk
57 Blueprint
59 BF Goodrich item
61 Jewish dance
62 Many a DeMille film
63 Where to play shipboard shuffleboard
65 Tyke
66 Foxy
67 Tonic's partner

ACROSS

1 Georgia ___
5 Seven-time A.L. batting champ Rod
10 Architect of St. Paul's Cathedral
14 Monster
15 Plus end
16 Mortgage consideration
17 Christo, notably
19 Concerning
20 ___ Percé (Western tribe)
21 Postal workers have them: Abbr.
22 Very uneven
24 Shipboard functionary
26 Part of beauty pageant attire
27 Stat for 5-Across
28 Certain sneakers
32 Interstate hauler
35 It sometimes thickens
37 Impede legally
38 Factory
40 "What Kind of Fool ___" (1962 hit)
41 Part of a subway entrance
42 Friend in a sombrero
43 Kind of room
45 Pre-owned
46 I.R.A. renewal
48 Little toymaker
50 New Haven collegians
51 Cold symptom
55 Result of ironing
58 Couple
59 ___ Alamos
60 It's rounded up in a roundup
61 Take train stations by force?
64 "Picnic" playwright
65 Giving goosebumps
66 Carpet layer's calculation
67 "D"
68 Hans Christian Andersen and others
69 Slothful

DOWN

1 Villages
2 Protected bird
3 Beanie Babies, e.g.
4 With it, in the 50s
5 Travel on a road
6 Chipped in
7 18 Louises
8 CBS's Bradley and others
9 Symbol of limpness
10 Airplane wings, propellers, etc.
11 Phoned
12 To be, in Toulouse
13 Penury
18 ___-Israeli relations
23 "Angela's ___"
25 Laundry cycle supervisor?
26 Protester's ploy
28 Quite a hit
29 Inventor Elisha

Puzzle 48 by Richard Chisholm

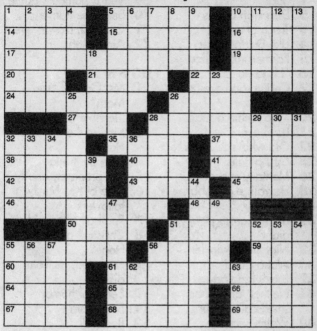

30 Tent support
31 Went 80, say
32 Box
33 Ticklish fellow
34 Armor of interlinked rings
36 Disables
39 Factory things
44 Deliberative bodies
47 Watched
49 Eye parts
51 "If You Knew ___" (Eddie Cantor favorite)

52 Fauna's partner
53 Golf pro Nancy
54 Emerson work
55 Golf shot
56 It's NE of Tahoe
57 Therefore
58 Hollywood's Bruce or Laura
62 Actor Stephen
63 Jazz guitarist ___ Farlow

ACROSS

1 Spat
5 Dish with beans
10 Trace of smoke
14 Like Darth Vader
15 Former intl. airline
16 "I had no ___!"
17 Cerium and erbium, e.g.
20 Map within a map
21 Bowl over
22 Old what's-___- name
23 Golf pitfalls
26 Mentally spaced out
28 Hawaii, e.g.: Abbr.
30 Statutes
32 Brit. recording giant
33 Nighttime twinkler
35 Aloha gifts
37 Lucy's landlady
41 Neither large- nor small-caliber guns
44 Watch secretly
45 Adult-to-be
46 Harvard rival
47 Rubber ducky's spot
49 Nutty
51 ___ Moines, Iowa
52 "Pow! Right in the ___!"
55 Green stuff
57 Newsman Koppel
58 Gave the once-over
60 Scottish inlets
63 Compliment from a Brit
67 ___ -Day vitamins

68 "Cool!"
69 Vegas numbers game
70 Belgrade native
71 Churchill Downs event
72 Aide: Abbr.

DOWN

1 Ms. Garr of "Mr. Mom"
2 "Terrible" czar
3 Mrs. in the White House
4 One on the lam
5 Tax preparer, briefly
6 One of two hardy followers
7 Football stats: Abbr.
8 Christine of "Chicago Hope"
9 Protected, as from disease
10 Sense of humor
11 Boise's state
12 Baseball commissioner Bud
13 Skip a turn
18 Catchall abbr.
19 Tooth protector
24 Date maker
25 "No ___!" ("Easy!")
27 In an apt way
28 Doctrines
29 Big first for a baby
31 Fathered
34 They're a laugh a minute
36 Cook, as clams
38 Major nuisances

Puzzle 49 by Nancy Salomon

39 Writer ___ Stanley Gardner
40 Cleaning cabinet supplies
42 Brand-new
43 The low-down
48 Out of reach of
50 Tattled
52 Nancy Drew's creator Carolyn
53 Time waster
54 Actress Taylor of "The Nanny"
56 Opa-___, Fla.
57 Terrible time?
59 Turtledove
61 ___ Christian Andersen
62 Predicament
64 Chemist's workplace
65 Wagering locale, for short
66 Myrna of "The Thin Man"

ACROSS
1 Laddie's love
5 Vehicles with bells
10 Nursery item
14 "Tell ___ the marines!"
15 French assembly
16 Operatic heroine
17 Big fat mouth
18 Delaware Indian whose name is French for "a friend"
19 Diving bird
20 Like some purchases
23 Hustle
24 Taking the booby prize
25 Two trios
29 Line of trousers
31 Soccer star Hamm
32 Dined
33 Time-tested
37 ___ facto
40 Really liked, man
41 Redding of R&B
42 Hardly gentlemanly
47 Koufax's was 2.76
48 Writer ___ Blount Jr.
49 Less trying
53 Reach
55 Bounders
57 Miracle-___ (lawn products brand)
58 Unharmed
61 Roentgen's discovery
64 "Smoke Gets in Your Eyes," e.g.
65 Sir's partner
66 Long ago
67 Heavy-plus
68 The "I" in "The King and I"
69 Gusto
70 Post office gizmo
71 Fall in April?

DOWN
1 Chinese fruit tree
2 Vehicle for Duke Ellington
3 Positions of equilibrium
4 Frosh follower
5 Wave of destruction
6 Tears
7 Put on ___ (pretend)
8 Doll's cry
9 Adds gradually
10 Flower part
11 Earth Summit host, 1992
12 Words preceding a kiss
13 Shut out
21 Apple growth retardant
22 Peruse
26 Pucker-producing
27 Needle holder
28 Caddie's bagful
30 School for British princes
31 Traveling trio

Puzzle 50 by Richard Hughes

34 Mini-whirlpool
35 Flop
36 Children's Christmas wish
37 Notion
38 Harbor city
39 Kind of team
43 Soprano's song, maybe
44 Like some items on a grocery store receipt
45 Cousin of a wapiti
46 Soviet news agency

50 Large lizard
51 Title bandit in a Verdi opera
52 Dennis of the N.B.A.
54 To this point
55 West Pointer
56 Drink flavoring
59 Isle of exile
60 Persian poet
61 The ___ Affair (1797 imbroglio)
62 Fish eggs
63 ___ longa, vita brevis

ACROSS

1 Deep sleep
5 Reminder of a swordfight
9 Customs
14 Milky gem
15 "Catch a Falling Star" singer, 1958
16 Plain as day
17 Telescope part
18 Famous ___
19 Word before hop or top
20 Shakespearean play with the clown Touchstone
23 Do tailoring
24 Computer giant
25 U.C.L.A. quarterback, perhaps
27 Gave a hoot
31 Hardly a neatnik
33 Café additive
37 Break in the action
39 Have bills
40 Four-star
41 Soap opera set in Oakdale
44 Hipbones
45 Mount Rushmore pres.
46 Sonnet section
47 Advertising sign
48 Heal
50 Arctic explorer Robert
51 City west of Tulsa
53 Reuters competitor
55 Met display
58 Faulkner novel
64 Injures with a horn
66 British blue blood
67 Rev. Roberts
68 Woodstock or the Super Bowl
69 TV's Nick at ___
70 Zero, on a court
71 Down at the heels
72 "___ bien!"
73 Pants part

DOWN

1 Pepsi, for one
2 Unlocks, in poetry
3 Umpteen
4 The first "a" in aka
5 Richter ___
6 Funnies
7 In a frenzy
8 Annual Pasadena doings
9 "All for one and one for all," e.g.
10 Eggs
11 Civil War soldiers
12 Author ___ Stanley Gardner
13 Cook, as tomatoes
21 Needless
22 Plants securely
26 Contract provision
27 Item of neckwear
28 Space between pews
29 2:1, e.g.
30 Flammable fuel

Puzzle 51 by Gregory E. Paul

32 Sophia of "Two Women"
34 Main line from the heart
35 Kind of tube
36 Cantankerous
38 Beturbaned wise men
42 Not insubordinate
43 Lukewarm
49 Eva Perón's maiden name
52 Spiteful
54 Gomer and others

55 Census data
56 Gad about
57 Shoe stiffener
59 Retreat
60 The sun, in sunnyside up
61 Vitamin tablet supplement
62 Where the congregation sits
63 Tickled-pink feeling
65 Tackle's teammate

ACROSS
1 Charlie Parker's music
5 High-five sound
9 "Gunga Din" setting
14 Fortuneteller's beginning
15 Adorable
16 Has to have
17 It has a broad side
18 Cupid
19 Lowlands, to poets
20 Black eye
23 Do something
24 ___ Master's Voice
25 It goes from C to C
29 Analogous
31 "___ Rosenkavalier"
34 Detergent target
35 Rose's Broadway beau
36 Lavish attention (on)
37 Red-eye
40 "Mrs. Bridge" author Connell
41 Abbr. in many company names
42 Lancelot's attire
43 Room to relax in
44 Peter or Paul
45 On pins and needles
46 Prior to, to Prior
47 Genetic inits.
48 Pinkeye
56 Burn soothers
57 Carry on
58 Opposed

60 Color faintly
61 Jai ___
62 Lute shape
63 Like a sweep's uniform
64 End-of-class signal
65 Pound of poetry

DOWN
1 Triangular sail
2 Job order notation
3 Definitely a flunking score
4 Founder of Stoicism
5 Like cabs on a rainy day
6 "Serpico" director Sidney
7 Resting on
8 Where the Amazon rises
9 To no avail
10 ___ -foot oil
11 Pickle purveyor
12 Logical start?
13 Org.
21 Poe called it "grim, ungainly, ghastly, gaunt, and ominous"
22 Chop shop supplier
25 Gawked at
26 Hunger for
27 Moon of Saturn
28 "Right on!"
29 Dislike, and then some
30 Do-it-yourselfers' needs

Puzzle 52 by Randall J. Hartman

31 Doctrine
32 Cultural values
33 Take another shot
35 Taj Mahal site
36 Awful
38 "Ghosts" playwright
39 Island west of Maui
44 Reliable
45 Show for the first time
46 Tape deck button
47 Letterman, to Leno
48 "Memory" musical

49 Mixed bag
50 Eating peas with a knife, e.g.
51 Grouch
52 Whopper
53 End of a dash
54 Don Juan's mother
55 Top banana
59 Author Levin

ACROSS

1 Spring event
5 Central American Indian
9 Land with half of Mount Everest
14 Massive
15 "Deutschland ___ Alles"
16 Like Bo-Peep's herd
17 And others: Abbr.
18 Cushy fabric
19 Subjects of many New Year's resolutions
20 "Shh . . ."
23 Singer-actor Kristofferson
24 Chapeau
25 Goddess of the hunt
28 Badly claw
30 Staff of Life, for short
33 "Little Women" author
35 I.R.S. employee: Abbr.
36 Get ___ the ground floor
37 "Shhh . . ."
40 Mideast's Gulf of ___
41 Notebook projection
42 Bug
43 Danson of "Cheers"
44 Judge's apparel
45 Perch
46 Fellows
47 Homeless child
49 Reply to 20- or 37-Across
57 Comment to the audience
58 Actions at Sotheby's
59 This doesn't need to be fixed, but it can be
60 Writer Ira
61 Rim
62 Stratford-upon-___
63 Rendezvous
64 Wine dregs
65 Mailed

DOWN

1 The Huxtable boy, on "The Cosby Show"
2 Certain Rwandan
3 Actor John of "Sands of Iwo Jima"
4 Famous
5 Civilian clothes
6 Aids in crime
7 "Gimme an A! . . .," e.g.
8 Commedia dell'___
9 Words of refusal
10 Throw out in the street
11 Where a ship comes in
12 Poker starter
13 "___ we forget . . ."
21 Steamed
22 "Stop talking!"
25 Sponge gently
26 ___-France
27 Did stage work
28 Alternative to yes or no
29 Long, long ___

30 Put an ___ (stop)
31 Some stadium features
32 Hägar the Horrible's dog
34 Wyoming range
36 To the degree that
38 Catch red-handed
39 Eagle's nest
44 Show remorse
46 Calf-length skirts
47 Pie slice
48 Dolts

49 Brewery grain
50 Belgian river, a W.W. I battle line
51 Roman historian
52 Cain's brother
53 Go by horse
54 Wash
55 Kind of jacket
56 Bad impression?

ACROSS

1 A crow's-nest tops it
5 Person with a puffy white hat
9 Stew server
14 Toe stubber's cry
15 Partner of now
16 In progress
17 Grimm beast
18 Turner who was called "The Sweater Girl"
19 ___ Domingo (Caribbean capital)
20 Salty septet
21 Demand too much of
23 Hence
24 ___ publica
25 Opposite WNW
26 Connecticut town near New London
29 Tin foil, e.g.
33 Auto manufacturer's woe
36 Recently stolen
37 "At ___, soldier!"
38 Bikini, e.g.
39 Longing
40 Instrument with fingerholes
41 Some J.P. Morgan hldgs.
42 Beaver's work
43 Ironing challenge
44 Mother of Apollo
45 Hurled word
47 Caviar
49 New Deal inits.
50 Hops kiln
54 Football squad warm-ups
58 Acknowledge frankly
59 Cropped up
60 Barley beards
61 Poor, as excuses go
62 Turn red, perhaps
63 Give stars to
64 Marcel Marceau, e.g.
65 Bottomless pit
66 Took a gander at
67 Inuit's transport

DOWN

1 Archie's dimwitted pal
2 Boring tool
3 Scrawny one
4 George W. Bush story?
5 ___ hydrate (knockout drops)
6 Angels' place
7 1954 Literature Nobelist
8 North Carolina's Cape ___
9 Wears well
10 No more begging?
11 Lady of Lisbon
12 "An Iceland Fisherman" author Pierre
13 School on the Thames
22 Faction
27 Under the weather
28 Charged particle
30 Actor Julia

31 "The Thin Man" pooch
32 Social equal
33 Scold harshly, with "at"
34 Basic French verb
35 Chesterfield or ulster
39 Jabber
40 Hostile force
42 Regard as
43 Performed a ballet step
46 Thirty, in Montréal

48 Broken mirrors and others
51 Be of use to
52 English Channel feeder
53 Coarse wool fabric
54 ___ Lee Corporation
55 Baby's bed
56 Cordlike
57 Bern's river

ACROSS

1 Seldom seen
5 China's Chairman ___
8 Gomorrah's sister city
13 Profess
14 Ripsnorter
15 Words to live by
16 Foremost
17 ___ were (seemingly)
18 Cosmopolitan's ___ Gurley Brown
19 Classic Disney character
21 Debt acknowledgment
22 ___ Baba
23 "Listen up!"
24 Archeologists' finds
28 Varieties
30 Close loudly
31 Was on a jury
32 Mystery writer's prize
33 Close
34 Like Playboy models
35 Hard-to-eat-just-one item
38 Rickshaw
41 Legislative excess
42 December 25 visitor
46 Colorado Indian
47 Bees' home
48 Time capsule activity
49 Say another way
51 "Oh yeah? ___ who?"

52 Docs, for short
53 Decorative vessel
54 Shakespeare's shrew tamer
57 ___ Island (immigrants' site)
59 Dr. Frankenstein's assistant
60 Suffix with origin
61 "Live free or die," to New Hampshire
62 Snaillike
63 Typesetting unit
64 Merlin of football and TV
65 WNW's opposite
66 Connery of 007 fame

DOWN

1 Rioting
2 Was of use
3 Slowing a horse, with "in"
4 Brain-teasing Rubik
5 Like corn flakes sitting in milk
6 Et ___ (and others)
7 Unfortunate
8 Sharp divide
9 Black-and-white cookies
10 Actor Dom
11 Old poem
12 Tue. preceder
14 Shoestrings
20 French dear
25 "Holy smoke!," e.g.

Puzzle 55 by John Greenman

26 Lenient
27 Mudhole
29 Riveted with attention
30 Stock unit
33 Lincoln's hat
34 Skyrocket
36 Roasting rod
37 Mazda competitor
38 Snarly dog
39 Grazed
40 Outcomes
43 Lingerie item

44 Traditional pudding ingredient
45 Election loser
47 Pop group with the 1997 hit "MMMBop"
48 Fruit on a bush
50 Old hat
51 Feed, as a fire
55 Clashing figures?
56 Beanies
57 Funnyman Philips
58 Response to an online joke

ACROSS

1 Boston team, informally
6 Plant with a frond
10 Popular pens
14 Unique
15 ". . . baked in ___"
16 Kind of testimony
17 1966 sci-fi classic
20 H.S. requirement
21 Baker's dozen?
22 Having crow's-feet
23 Christie's "Death on the ___"
24 Some go for 6 or 12 mos.
25 1970s–80s TV hero, with "the"
32 Red Cross supply
33 Sea sound
34 Dundee denial
35 Haughtiness
36 One with a smiley face?
38 Motivate
39 Dodger, Brooklyn-style
40 "In a minute"
41 Wee one
42 Lurid pulp magazine founded in 1926
46 Lodge member
47 List wrap-up
48 Persian Gulf port
51 Hawk's gripper
53 "No ___" (menu phrase)

56 "Man of La Mancha" tune, with "The"
59 Simone de Beauvoir, to Sartre
60 Just lying around
61 "Butterfield 8" author
62 Princes, e.g.
63 Look
64 Away

DOWN

1 Joe, in France
2 Zip
3 Overshot
4 Rubble-maker
5 Albatross, e.g.
6 Like cows before slaughter
7 Sweeping story
8 Like chocolate-chocolate cake
9 Ariz. neighbor
10 Winningly youthful
11 Mujahedin base
12 Zoo feature
13 Winter toy
18 Garage activity
19 ___ but wiser
23 Base figures, for short
24 "Braveheart" group
25 Another name for ancient Troy
26 Bellini opera
27 Dungeon restraints
28 Gift beautifier
29 Remove, as a 28-Down

Puzzle 56 by Fran and Lou Sabin

30 Retreats
31 Composer Jerome
32 Rum cake
36 Go kaput, with "out"
37 Cabin element
38 Go yachting
40 "___ Marner"
41 "Beverly Hills 90210" fellow
43 Six in a million?
44 Person with lots of bills
45 Native Oklahoman

48 Civil rights concern
49 Bullets, e.g.
50 It may be on a tennis ball
51 Almanac topic
52 Skilled
53 Lamb, e.g.
54 Draped dress
55 Gangster chaser
57 Wine tasting?
58 Pi's follower

ACROSS

1 Smokes
5 Sandbar
10 Con game
14 Aboard a ship
15 Primary blood carrier
16 Quiz option
17 Atlanta landmark #1
20 August meteor shower
21 Strong fishing nets
22 "You ___ here"
23 Tiny scissors cut
24 Bill Clinton's number two
28 Pillow covering
29 Ooh and ___
32 French revolutionary Jean Paul
33 Unwanted e-mail
34 Gumbo pods
35 Atlanta landmark #2
38 Front-page stuff
39 Walk nervously
40 J.R.'s mother, on "Dallas"
41 Hosp. workers
42 Similar to
43 They hold 27-Down
44 Jaywalker's punishment
45 Dernier ___ (last word)
46 Large African expanse
49 Area including Turkey and Israel
54 Atlanta landmark #3

56 "This ___ my day!"
57 Not glossy
58 Peace proponent
59 Flagmaker Betsy
60 Hardly the macho type
61 Captain Hook's helper

DOWN

1 "Li'l Abner" cartoonist
2 Psychiatrist's response
3 Neutral or first
4 Small pouches
5 Lampoon
6 Throng of people
7 Smeltery materials
8 Chowed down
9 Washington or Irving
10 Subway handhold
11 Stage workers
12 "The Clan of the Cave Bear" author
13 "Amazin'" team
18 Vigorous
19 Barber's job
23 Barber's job
24 Modify
25 Less plausible, as an excuse
26 Gets bigger
27 Galley propellers
28 Ginger or cinnamon
29 James Bond's "A View to ___"

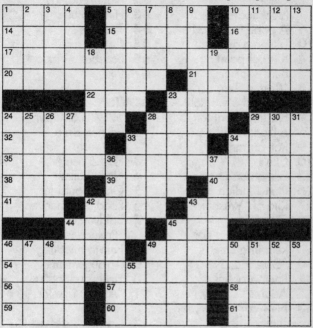

30 Bandleader Shaw
31 Grant's successor
33 Venom carrier
34 Norway's capital
36 Ready to fight
37 Bring back on staff
42 Milan money
43 Comedian Ullman
44 Lowdown
45 Popular mints
46 Move a muscle
47 Mock words of
understanding

48 Coop group
49 Butterfly snarers
50 Extremities
51 Molecule part
52 Golfer
Ballesteros
53 Branch site
55 Mai ___

ACROSS
1 Clear the blackboard
6 A pope may lead it
10 Ultimate diet
14 Kind of paint
15 Burn soother
16 "Coffee, Tea, ___?"
17 Result of a workout
18 Starting point for a flight test?
19 Roll-on target
20 CPA's
23 Edmonton's home
26 Plains Indian
27 Rita of "West Side Story"
28 Jewelry that's not kept in a safe
30 "Give it ___!"
31 Photographer Adams
33 New-car feature, for short
36 Potluck dinner dish
41 Tackle a slope
42 "Merrily we roll ___"
43 Certain turn
44 "___ Hope" (former soap)
47 Tea type
49 Fund-raising effort
52 Colony members
53 Features of many signs
56 Cartoonist Thomas
57 Furrow former

58 Europe's "boot"
62 Novel ending?
63 Hindu music
64 Tea type
65 Cattail, e.g.
66 Baseball's Vizquel
67 Pix

DOWN
1 1997 U.S. Open winner Ernie
2 Like sushi
3 Had a beef?
4 Navy builder
5 On the outside
6 Food from heaven
7 Baldwin of "Prelude to a Kiss"
8 Fair-to-middling
9 Arrangements
10 Heels and loafers
11 "As You Like It" forest
12 Camper's dessert item
13 To the point
21 When many people have lunch
22 Cole who was "King"
23 "___ for All Seasons"
24 NBC's peacock and CBS's eye
25 Babbler
28 Laugh waves
29 As well
32 Read a bar code
34 Stupid louts

Puzzle 58 by Nancy Salomon

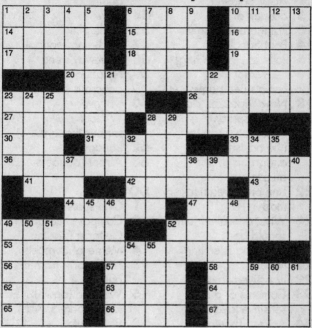

35 Writer's angle
37 Ran
38 Sleep sound
39 Vain voyages?
40 Poached edibles
45 Shoot the breeze
46 Football star's title
48 Lend an ear
49 Li'l one
50 Diner serving
51 Mail, in Marseille
52 Battling
54 Jack of "Rio Lobo"

55 Robe
59 Wanted-poster letters
60 Chop (off)
61 "Absolutely!"

ACROSS

1 Actor Baldwin
5 Scarlett of Tara
10 Paint amateurishly
14 Poet Sandburg
15 Jolly ___ (pirate flag)
16 ___ Major
17 Lamb's pen name
18 New York's ___ Place
19 It's transparent
20 Noted philosopher (the basis for three anagrams in this puzzle)
22 Line on a weather map
24 What a swollen joint should be
25 Its calling is calling
26 Mists
29 Bar giveaways
33 Contents of a sensitive layer
34 Actress Thomas
35 Napkin's place
36 "How sweet ___!"
37 Puts into piles
38 Pelt
39 Spy novelist Deighton
40 Writer Loos
41 Luxurious material
42 Shows peevishness
44 Virgil epic
45 Become bushed
46 Hollywood heartthrob Pitt
47 Office chair problem

50 Factor in college admissions
54 Glow
55 Tickle pink
57 ___ Bator, Mongolia
58 Driveway's end
59 Neighbor of the pancreas
60 Discovery
61 Without serious thought
62 Rundown
63 Airport dangers

DOWN

1 One-spots
2 Composer Schifrin
3 Guitarist Clapton
4 Medieval trumpets
5 Holds forth from the pulpit
6 Watered (down)
7 F.B.I. workers: Abbr.
8 Early auto
9 Airport area
10 Company that makes Teflon
11 Dashing horse
12 Annapolis inits.
13 Boxer Max
21 Farm unit
23 Middlin'
25 It comes from the heart
26 "And there you are!"
27 Ancient Mexican
28 North, south, east, or west

Puzzle 59 by Randall J. Hartman

29 À la ___ (one way to order)
30 Upper crust
31 Forearm bones
32 Opposite of 50-Down
34 Wavelike design
37 Divers' gear
38 Manacle
40 Where India is
41 Word with high or seven
43 High school sweetheart
44 25-Down, e.g.
46 Kind of breath
47 Madras dress
48 Part of Q.E.D.
49 Russia's ___ Mountains
50 What pack rats do
51 Mishmash
52 "You ___?"
53 Pass receivers
56 More than stretch the truth

ACROSS

1 B-school entrance exam
5 Tablelands
10 Porgy's woman
14 Junction point
15 Just ___ of the tongue
16 Condo division
17 Zoning measure
18 A Judd
19 Longish skirt
20 Dad says "no"
23 Cousin of the bossa nova
24 Crossword worker?
25 ___ salts
29 More lofty
33 Nick and Nora's pooch
36 Backseat driver, e.g.
38 First daughter Carter
39 Dad says "yes"
42 Pay stub?
43 Render immobile, rodeo-style
44 Bauxite and others
45 Bodega's place
47 Journalist Joseph or Stewart
49 Silver State sch.
51 Part of TNT
55 Dad says "maybe"
61 Rolling in dough
62 Dazed and confused
63 Ocean predator
64 Price of a hand
65 Change the price of
66 April 1 victim
67 Lose traction
68 Vial measurements
69 Peaty areas

DOWN

1 Chews like a chipmunk
2 Starbucks order
3 To the point, to lawyers
4 Publication with features on boy bands
5 "Look ___ hands!"
6 Jacob's twin
7 Trudge through the mire
8 Actress Anouk
9 Polishes, army-style
10 Cause of a limp, maybe
11 Oklahoma city
12 Bar or car starter
13 To-do
21 Big mouth
22 In the cooler
26 Jungle gym's place
27 Not a dup.
28 Man in the 'hood
30 Salon's concern

31 Name in plus-size modeling
32 Whiskey choices
33 ". . . ___ for Superman!"
34 Toni Morrison novel
35 Pre-1917 ruler
37 Slave away
40 Use one's bean
41 Request to a gas pumper
46 Applied to Sigma Chi, say

48 Yoko ___
50 November lever puller
52 Pang
53 Scout's job, for short
54 Face-to-face exams
55 Mardi ___
56 Sty cry
57 Curtain-raising time
58 Org. for Borg
59 Enlarge, as a hole
60 "Cosmo" and "GQ," e.g.

ACROSS

1 Four-poster, e.g.
4 Carpeting calculation
8 Old name for the phone company
14 Regret
15 Laze about
16 Charlotte ___, Virgin Islands
17 Perform in plays
18 Border on
19 Like some salads
20 Breakfast treat
23 Goofs
24 Summer TV offering
25 Comic Costello
28 Usher to a different part of the theater
30 Floor's opposite
33 Jump rope variation
36 Homeric epic
40 Lobster eggs
41 Writer James and ballplayer Tommie
42 Twists and turns in a bowling alley
45 Three-time Wimbledon winner
46 Newlyweds get them
51 Distress call
52 Look of scorn
55 Tackle box item
56 Vodka, cream, and Kahlúa cocktail
59 Night flight
62 Went by train

63 King in a Steve Martin song
64 In disagreement
65 Notion
66 Australian bird
67 Command before "Go!"
68 Snaky fishes
69 Tree juice

DOWN

1 Stimulating drink
2 Trick-taking card game
3 Dissuades
4 [Sigh]
5 Oscar-winner Benigni
6 Escape from
7 Place to exchange rings
8 Afternoon show
9 Singer Tori
10 Big party
11 Chicago trains
12 "The dog ate my homework" is a classic one
13 Was in front
21 From Neb. to Ky.
22 Cell parts
25 Lo-cal
26 Fairy tale start
27 Exclamations of disgust
29 Viper
31 The Gem State
32 ___ nut (wheel fastener)

Puzzle 61 by Peter Gordon

34 High-priority
35 Manute ___ of basketball
36 Some PC's
37 Nutso
38 Midmonth date
39 Writer Rand
43 Most prying
44 German pastry
47 Capp and Capone
48 Multiroom hotel offerings
49 Psychological injury
50 Parodied
53 Spooky
54 Wear away
56 Marries
57 Jekyll's alter ego
58 Caribbean and others
59 Aid for a maid
60 French summer
61 Web site address part

ACROSS

1 On ___ with (equal to)
5 Provide, as with a quality
10 Take one's cuts
13 Odense citizen
14 Play the flute
16 Original sinner
17 Person not to be messed with, in song
19 Boggy area
20 "Here ___, there . . ."
21 1950s Wally Cox sitcom
23 Tooth doctors' org.
24 Fare for Miss Muffet
26 What's more
27 Like rock 'n' roll's Richard
29 Regatta rower
32 Inventor Sikorsky
33 Stay put
36 50s TV detective couple
41 Parlor piece
42 In ___ (stuck)
44 Encroachments
48 Curie's title
50 One may be proper
51 To ___ (unanimously)
53 By way of
54 Chicagoan in 1871 news
58 Headed for overtime
60 It may be framed
61 Anne Bancroft role of 1967

64 Up to, in ads
65 Opposite of all
66 Other, in Oaxaca
67 Japan finish?
68 Spread seed
69 NASDAQ rival

DOWN

1 U.S.N. bigwig
2 Exemplar
3 Disney artist
4 Clinton Cabinet member
5 Somme time
6 "I didn't do it!"
7 Bride's worldly possessions
8 Lone Star State sch.
9 Gen. Robert ___
10 Happened to
11 Unwilling (to)
12 Stretching muscle
15 Ethyl finish
18 New Year's Day game
22 Buddy
23 Rope-a-dope boxer
25 Did a sheepdog's job
28 ___ -la-la
29 Enclosure to an ed.
30 Hollywood industry
31 A numero
34 C.P.R. givers
35 Mohawk-sporting actor
37 Code-cracking org.

Puzzle 62 by A. J. Santora

38 "Far out!"
39 Distorted imitation
40 Cigar holders
43 Tetley product
44 Con
45 Chuck of "Code of Silence"
46 Gather, with "up"
47 Lennon's lady
49 Nay sayer
51 "One way" symbol
52 Gershwin's "___ and Only"

55 K-O connection
56 Lustful god
57 Concerning
59 ___ a secret
62 One of the B's in B & B
63 Dundee denial

ACROSS

1 Thermonuclear blast maker
6 Trot or canter
10 "Listen!"
14 Golfer Palmer, informally
15 Killer whale
16 Place to put a thimble
17 Corporate recruiter
19 "Mama" speaker
20 Wheat or barley covering
21 Wild time
22 Sty
24 Sty animals
25 Identical
26 Quiet spot to sit
29 September birthstone
33 Market price
34 Treadmill unit
35 Keats pieces
36 Lemon and orange drinks
37 Like some renewable energy
38 ___ moss
39 Gin flavor
40 Thigh muscle, for short
41 Garden tool
42 Long workday, perhaps
44 ___ Pieces
45 Lena or Ken of film
46 Violinist Leopold
47 Philadelphia N.F.L.'ers
50 Book before Romans

51 Disputed skill, for short
54 Didn't have traction
55 Snob
58 Fishing need
59 Buffalo's county
60 Jonah's swallower
61 Not far
62 Cub Scout groups
63 Besmirch

DOWN

1 Response to a comic
2 Make beer, e.g.
3 ___ even keel
4 ___-Atlantic
5 Serve well
6 Deep bells
7 Pretentious
8 Freezer stuff
9 Roofing material
10 Crop-dusting plane
11 Surmounting
12 "First in, first out," e.g.
13 Pottery oven
18 Impulse
23 Mischievous sort
24 Census taker's target
25 Meal gotten from a garden
26 "Stop!," to Popeye
27 Soup scoop
28 60s–70s Mets star ___ Jones
29 Marner of fiction
30 Think tank products

Puzzle 63 by Gregory E. Paul

31 "The Cloister and the Hearth" author
32 ___ Park, Colo.
34 Grieve
37 Stepped on, as a bug
41 Goes up and down
43 ___ Miss
44 Buzzi of "Laugh-In"
46 Partner of pains
47 "SportsCenter" channel
48 Ingredient in facial tissues

49 ___ monster
50 Opposed to, hillbilly-style
51 And others: Abbr.
52 Unload, on Wall Street
53 Zebras, to lions
56 Ill temper
57 Wed. follower

ACROSS

1 Snacks in shells
6 Panty raid site
10 Quartet on a baseball field
14 First Hebrew letter
15 "Zip-___-Doo-Dah"
16 Mosaic piece
17 Bulldogger's event
18 "Oh, my aching head!," e.g.
19 Big chemical company
20 Movie with a hard-to-rhyme name
23 In a funk
24 Ages and ages
25 Midafternoon, on a sundial
26 Some E.R. cases
27 Black-eye soothers
32 Bump off
35 Demagnetize, as a tape
36 Shoebox letters
37 King with a hard-to-rhyme name
41 Suffix with hero
42 "Crazy" singer Patsy
43 "___ Wonderful Life"
44 Reaches the wrong party
46 Kind of dance or bride
48 Old biddy
49 1/24 case
50 Take steps

53 Pirate with a hard-to-rhyme name
58 Boor
59 It may get a licking after dinner
60 Wavelike design
61 Nave neighbor
62 Links carrier
63 "Stormy Weather" composer
64 Herbicide target
65 Proposer's prop
66 Most trifling

DOWN

1 Bite-size pies
2 Hello from Ho
3 Handed over
4 Crude cartel
5 Chased away
6 Runyon or Wayans
7 Bad whiff
8 Bring in
9 28-Down handout
10 Ideal spot
11 Pipe-smoking former Congresswoman Fenwick
12 Ballet bend
13 D.C. V.I.P.
21 ___ Altos, Calif.
22 Not so green
26 Olive of "Thimble Theatre"
27 Shackles
28 See 9-Down
29 Anka's "___ Beso"
30 Toga party needs

31 "Did you ever ___ lassie . . .?"
32 Triathlon leg
33 Actress Virna ___
34 Home to the down-and-out
35 Pianist Gilels
38 Cupcake topper
39 Part of a recipe title
40 Televise
45 In need of body work
46 Used to be

47 Kind of magnetism
49 100 smackers
50 St. Teresa's birthplace
51 First known asteroid
52 Lott of Mississippi
53 Run easily
54 Bookworm's counterpart
55 Algerian port
56 Roll call call
57 Tribal tales
58 Corpus juris

ACROSS

1 Grab
6 Wood strip used as a bed support
10 Talented
14 Indiana basketballer
15 Munich Mister
16 Vast emptiness
17 Sports facility
18 "___ bitten, twice shy"
19 Opposer
20 Finally understood
23 Cat with a bowl of milk, e.g.
27 Medicinal plants
28 Singer Guthrie
29 Revolutionary War firearm
34 Makes level
36 Sidewalk material
37 Owns
40 Ocean predator
43 Needle part
44 Put down forcibly
45 Kingdom in the South Seas
46 Imaginary
48 ___ canal
49 Open-mouthed
53 Set aflame
55 One who can have you going around in circles?
60 Created
61 Affirm positively
62 Artist's prop

67 Notion
68 What you might be in when you're out
69 Crème de la crème
70 Midterm, say
71 Pool exercise
72 "Saturday Night Fever" music

DOWN

1 Resort
2 A barber might nick it
3 Winter road hazard
4 Kind of Buddhism
5 Delete
6 Film or play
7 Loaned
8 Keystone place
9 Shade giver
10 Be of use
11 Drum played with the hands
12 Like a ballerina's body
13 Revises, as copy
21 Sleeve's contents
22 Most recent
23 Wood shop machine
24 Set out for display
25 Showy feather
26 Robert Frost writing
30 Wedding helper
31 Commemorative marker
32 Australian "bear"

Puzzle 65 by Nancy Kavanaugh

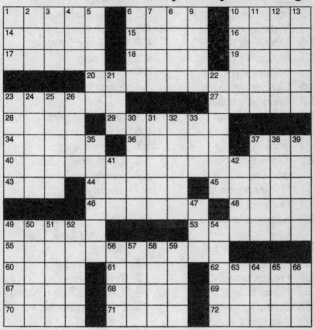

33 Finish
35 Part two
37 Vietnam's capital
38 Specialized vocabulary
39 Rollerblade, e.g.
41 What computer programs do
42 Taxi feature
47 Prevaricate
49 Allow in
50 A+ or C-
51 Helpers

52 Skirt fold
54 Monopolist's trait
56 British raincoats
57 State openly
58 Tractor-trailer
59 Cable car
63 Boxer Muhammad
64 Female sib
65 And so forth
66 Virgo's predecessor

ACROSS

1 G.I.'s lullaby?
5 Forty-niner's filing
10 Visually dull
14 Mate's shout
15 Barbera's partner in cartooning
16 Go backpacking
17 Worrier's habit
19 Hillside shelter
20 Oscar-winner Sophia
21 Kramden's pal on "The Honeymooners"
23 Hot and dry
26 Sending to one's fate
27 Language of the Koran
28 French novelist Honoré de ___
29 Salome's seven
30 Aladdin's enabler
31 Vladimir Putin's onetime org.
34 French 101 verb
35 Redhead's dye
36 Gin flavoring
37 ___ Bingle (Crosby moniker)
38 Toss back and forth
39 Begins to flutter the eyelids
40 Shuttle plane
42 Jolson's river of song

43 Noted Parthenon sculptor
45 In the middle of
46 Small wound
47 Drink for Dracula
48 Mélange
49 Amazing to behold
54 Small amount of milk
55 Rent out again
56 Met song
57 Gets soaked
58 Up to one's ears
59 TelePrompTer display

DOWN

1 "The Joy Luck Club" author
2 "Caught you!"
3 Taro dish
4 One of 17 in a haiku
5 French president Jacques
6 Head toward evening
7 Have ___ (be connected)
8 Quaint lodging
9 Mississippi's state tree
10 TV's "___ and Greg"
11 Highly amusing
12 Ohio tire center
13 Living thing
18 Mussorgsky's Godunov
22 Move like molasses

Puzzle 66 by Frances Hansen

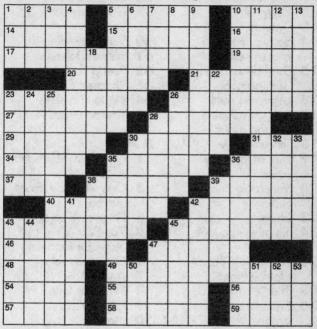

23 "___ by the bell!"
24 Mountain ridge
25 Like a horror movie
26 Actor DeVito
28 Diver's dread, with "the"
30 Ranking above species
32 Tennessee political family
33 Assailed on all sides
35 "Carmen" highlight
36 Hold one's ground

38 Vivacity
39 Attack like an eagle
41 Cementheads
42 Not chunky, as peanut butter
43 Raindrop sounds
44 Sun: Prefix
45 Suisse range
47 Horror icon Lugosi
50 Archery wood
51 High dudgeon
52 Put the kibosh on
53 Gangster's gun

ACROSS

1 Old Russian leader
5 Hogwash
10 Dressed
14 Early political caucus state
15 Land divided at the 38th parallel
16 Letterman rival
17 Al-___ (valuable support group)
18 Tehran native
19 Hint of things to come
20 Venerable public servant
23 Sharp
24 Timothy who took trips
25 Frankie of "Beach Blanket Bingo"
28 The "E" in Q.E.D.
30 Fish's breathing organ
31 Occurring involuntarily
36 Three ___ match
37 Children's card game
39 "___ Got a Secret"
40 "Burr" author
42 Search, as the horizon
43 Who, what, or where sentence: Abbr.
44 Presentable
46 Capital of South 15-Across
49 Stubborn as ___

51 Coleridge character
56 Lay ___ the line
57 Give a speech
58 Verve
60 Verne captain
61 Führer's followers
62 Puerto ___
63 "Jurassic Park" terror
64 Big tournaments
65 Tibetan beasts

DOWN

1 Grp. with informants
2 Area
3 One who's off base, maybe
4 Klugman's co-star in 70s TV
5 Slope for slaloming
6 Least desirable
7 Angry
8 Horne or Olin
9 Café au ___
10 Near
11 Auxiliary proposition, in math
12 Lend ___ (listen)
13 An Osmond
21 Prefix with system or sphere
22 Endangered antelope
25 Intensely interested
26 In ___ veritas
27 Banned orchard chemical
28 And others: Abbr.
29 Louis XIV, e.g.

Puzzle 67 by Randy Sowell

31 Does sums
32 Thurman of "The Avengers"
33 Cheese nibblers
34 A "terrible" 1-Across
35 Penny
37 Rudimentary seed
38 Tell whoppers
41 March 21 occurrence
42 Overlook's offering
44 Coercion
45 Yale student
46 Benevolent one

47 Go in
48 Entreaty to "all ye faithful"
49 Wow
50 Morning, in Montmartre
52 Unacceptable act
53 Links hazard
54 Charles Lamb's pseudonym
55 Torture device
59 Phone book listings: Abbr.

ACROSS

1 One of the worlds in "The War of the Worlds"
5 Baby's first word, maybe
9 Designer Donna
14 Touch on
15 PC pic
16 Alpha's opposite
17 Kennedy matriarch
18 The N.F.L.'s Aikman
19 Dentist's request
20 Start of a quip
22 Stuffed bear
23 Cache
24 Final approval
28 Quip, part 2
34 Paul Simon's "Slip ___ Away"
38 Form of evidence, these days
39 Frankfurt's river
40 Crescent shapes: Var.
41 Skill
43 Word for Yorick
44 Stars and Stripes land
47 Compassionate
48 End of the quip
51 Verso's opposite
52 Ancient Greek colony
57 Mrs. Gorbachev
61 Speaker of the quip
63 Cockeyed
64 Gyro meat
66 Prefix with second
67 Cubic meter
68 Devil's doing
69 Town on the Thames
70 Model at work
71 Like Marilyn Monroe
72 Learning the times table, e.g.

DOWN

1 Home-run champ until 1998
2 Up's partner
3 Rene of "Tin Cup"
4 Beef on the hoof
5 Catcher's need
6 Unlike this answer
7 Jersey greeting?
8 "___ luck?"
9 Bow and scrape
10 Grenoble girlfriend
11 Foxx of "Sanford and Son"
12 Like fine wine
13 Word before "a soul"
21 Ledger entry
25 "Then what?"
26 Hither's partner
27 Wrap in bandages
29 Make certain
30 1947 Oscar-winner Celeste
31 Light bulb, figuratively
32 Chattanooga's home: Abbr.
33 One-named designer
34 Meat loaf serving

Puzzle 68 by Dorothy E. Donaldson

35 Lollapalooza
36 ___ the finish
37 Half a 50s sitcom couple
42 Decorated Murphy
45 [not my error]
46 Toward the rear
49 Cash register part
50 Star of silent oaters
53 Title holder
54 "Rad!"
55 Comeback in a kids' argument
56 Make amends
57 Coarse file
58 Concerning
59 Alibi ___ (excuse makers)
60 Withered
62 With adroitness
64 "___ Miz"
65 Forum greeting

ACROSS

1 Itsy-bitsy
4 Jerks
9 Mob
14 Ewe's mate
15 Field of play
16 Easy-to-carry instruments
17 Part of an octopus
18 Not now
19 Harass
20 What Rick Blaine never said
23 Endings for hydrocarbons
24 Bambi's mother, e.g.
25 Ordered (around)
28 Leopold and ___ (big 1920s murder case)
30 Wharton degree
33 Semester's-end events
34 Robe for Caesar
35 Hardly a genius
36 One-man show about President Truman
39 Yemeni port
40 Simplify
41 Signs to beware of
42 Beatty or Rorem
43 ___ and sciences
44 High-priced furs
45 ___ Baba
46 Prefix with plane
47 Plaintive plea in the 1919 Black Sox scandal

54 It makes a clicking noise
55 Tony-winner ___ Lenya
56 Before, for a bard
57 Actor John of "The Addams Family"
58 Dutch painter Jan
59 ___ Aviv
60 Places for hinges
61 Where to find dates?
62 Message in a bottle?

DOWN

1 Coat or shawl
2 Rank below marquis
3 Austen heroine
4 Certain Indonesians
5 Speechified
6 Followers of epsilons
7 Force on Earth: Abbr.
8 "Nobody doesn't like ___ Lee"
9 Schmooze (with)
10 Overly overweight
11 Parks on a bus
12 Consider
13 N.Y.C. clock setting
21 Toadies
22 Rating a 10
25 Commenced
26 Rust, for one
27 Put in the bank
28 Fertile soil

29 Look like a wolf?
30 Mushroom
31 Carried
32 Yawning gulf
34 "___ does it!"
35 Shoots in the jungle?
37 Kind of badge for a scout
38 Makes husky, as a voice
43 Martians and such
44 Sofa
45 Sailor's "yes!"

46 Poker stakes
47 "Comme ci, comme ça"
48 Chrysler, e.g.
49 "The Sun ___ Rises"
50 Trivial bit
51 New York footballers
52 Black-and-white cookie
53 Congers
54 Plenty ticked

ACROSS

1 Menachem's 1978 co-Nobelist
6 "Get out!"
11 ___ de Triomphe
14 Hanging need
15 Card game authority Edmond
16 Dull card game
17 Actress who was married to Dudley Moore
19 Fuss
20 Puts on a computer hard drive
21 Jeweled headpieces
23 Set down
24 Old Hartford hockey team
25 Rouse
29 Singer Cara
30 Hoops player
31 Say confidently
32 "___ Boot"
35 California city by Joshua Tree National Park
39 Blue
40 Sport ___ (popular vehicles)
41 "The Waste Land" poet
42 Summits
44 Hand-dyes with wax
45 Pilgrims to Mecca
48 "Wait a ___!"
49 Acid neutralizer
50 Most sugary
55 Compete
56 Trusting act
58 Night before
59 Golden award
60 Arm bones
61 Court divider
62 Rudder's place
63 Suspicious

DOWN

1 Prefix with disestablishmentarianism
2 Adjective follower
3 Afflictions
4 Like some mgrs.
5 Warning on the Enterprise
6 In a demure manner
7 Cud chewers
8 Deli bread
9 Sane
10 Highway divider
11 Not spaced-out
12 What Fuzzbusters detect
13 Angry
18 Fed head Greenspan
22 McSorley's product
24 Songbirds
25 New Testament book
26 Trumpet sound
27 Getting on in years
28 Mattel doll
29 Harvard, Yale, Brown, etc.
31 Poker starters

Puzzle 70 by Peter Gordon

32 Half of MCIV
33 Run ___ (go crazy)
34 Fast jets, for short
36 Most tasty
37 Tranquil
38 Hgt.
42 In the style of
43 Parts of string quartets
44 Complaint
45 Whiz
46 Martini garnish
47 ___ shooting

48 Like court testimony
50 Practice in the ring
51 A fisherman may bring one home
52 "___ kleine Nachtmusik"
53 Restaurant review symbol
54 Those people
57 Good service?

ACROSS

1 "It's us against ___"
5 Backtalk
9 Data disk
14 What an optimist always has
15 This, south of the border
16 Bakery enticement
17 The "U" in I.C.U.
18 Larger ___ life
19 Circus star with a whip
20 1966 Johnny Rivers hit
23 Doozy
24 Suffix with pay or play
25 Capt.'s superior
28 Rock band ___ Mode
31 Cinder
34 Yale of Yale University
36 "Just ___ thought!"
37 Chorus member
38 Hospital ward alternative
42 Pentagon inventory
43 "Tip-Toe Thru the Tulips With Me" instrument
44 Make up (for)
45 Mudhole
46 Israeli parliament
49 Gave supper
50 ___ -Cat (winter vehicle)
51 Currier's companion
53 1997 Best Picture nominee

60 Attacks
61 Opposed to, in dialect
62 Annapolis inits.
63 Tour of duty
64 Oodles
65 ___ for oneself
66 Short-tempered
67 As a result
68 Lawyers' charges

DOWN

1 As a result
2 Sharpen, as on a whetstone
3 "Ben-Hur," e.g.
4 Geo model
5 Medium-sized sofa
6 Equivalent to B flat
7 Dateless
8 Levelheaded
9 Longhorns, e.g.
10 Pulitzer Prize category
11 Capital of Italia
12 Gathering clouds, for one
13 Ruin
21 Turn out to be
22 Like a rare baseball game
25 Monument Valley features
26 On the ball
27 Force open, as a lock
29 Place for icicles
30 Civil War side: Abbr.
31 Standoffish
32 Slingshot ammo
33 ___ in on (neared)

Puzzle 71 by Gregory E. Paul

35 Towel stitching
37 College major
39 Kind of sentence
40 Mamie's man
41 Moth-___
46 Hard to saw, as some pine
47 What a stucco house doesn't need
48 Be that as it may
50 Meager
52 Cram
53 After curfew

54 Sale caution
55 Doom
56 Composer Stravinsky
57 "Now it's clear"
58 Shakespeare's ___ Hathaway
59 Boys
60 Monogram of 40-Down's predecessor

ACROSS

1 Farmland unit
5 News source of old
10 Summer getaway
14 Parade spoiler, perhaps
15 Ready to come off
16 Coloratura's piece
17 Back to being friends again?
19 Seasoned sailor
20 Ran into
21 They're sometimes fine
22 Choctaw and Chickasaw
24 St. Francis' birthplace
26 Actor James
27 Humor that doesn't cause a blush?
33 Do watercolors
36 "___ la vista"
37 Suffix with project
38 Big concert equipment
39 Skin suffixes
40 Worked-up state
41 Kelly's "___ Girls"
42 Mildew and such
43 Fountain drinks
44 Mentally sound?
47 One with an "Esq." tag
48 Zoo showoffs
52 Certain fir
55 Peak in Thessaly
57 Author Rita ___ Brown
58 Hullabaloos
59 Relapsing?
62 ___ -majesté
63 Norman Vincent ___
64 More than suggest
65 Lascivious look
66 Mexicali mister
67 Batik artisan

DOWN

1 Sachet quality
2 Champs Élysées sights
3 Breaks in relations
4 Suffix with exist
5 Pastor
6 Dig like a pig
7 Written promises
8 Attendance fig., often
9 Goes back to the top
10 Pit boss's place
11 Riyadh native
12 Track event not in the Olympics
13 Praises for pups
18 Word before "a prayer" or "a clue"
23 Big Indian
25 Charged particles
26 "Far out, man!"
28 Writer with an award named after him
29 Florida's Key ___
30 Warm-hearted
31 Essayist's alias
32 6–2, 5–7, 6–3, etc.
33 ___ Alto

Puzzle 72 by John Greenman

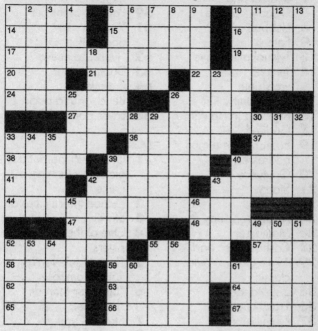

34 Hymn sign-off
35 ___ facto
39 They chase "bunnies"
40 Arrange logically
42 Greek cheese
43 Stiff hairs
45 Sadat's predecessor
46 Like much Jewish food
49 Manicurist's tool
50 Singer's span
51 Passover feast

52 Bouncer?
53 "Zip-___-Doo-Dah"
54 Get checkmated
55 In the blink ___ eye
56 Normandy battle site
60 License's cost
61 Nasty campaigning

ACROSS

1 Subject of a "People" profile
6 Hubbub
9 Father
13 Tylenol alternative
14 Temple worshiper
15 Single unit
16 Big crop in Hawaii
18 Goaded
19 End of some e-mail addresses
20 Opulence
21 Starry
22 Fix
24 Miami's ___ Bay
26 Mediocre
28 Cash register part
29 1941 Orson Welles classic
33 ___ Mahal
36 Fruity coolers
37 Note before la
38 Prefix with -nautics
39 Face off in the ring
40 Making a fuss
44 Pat Boone's "___ That a Shame"
45 Worry
46 Late prize-winning San Francisco columnist
50 Reef materials
54 Lucky charm
55 Diamond Head locale
57 Step to the plate
58 San Francisco footballer, briefly
59 Popular painkiller
61 Woman's lip application
62 "Feliz ___ nuevo"
63 Door swinger
64 E-mailed
65 Bench with a back
66 Law's partner

DOWN

1 One checking out a place in planning a crime
2 Escape the clutches of
3 Starting advantage
4 One of the Gabor sisters
5 "Symphonie fantastique" composer
6 "Stronger than dirt" sloganeer
7 Star in Cygnus
8 Have debts
9 Yahoo! or Lycos, e.g.
10 Furious
11 Song of triumph
12 Flummox
15 Biceps or triceps
17 Unlucky charm
21 "Q ___ queen"
23 Sale sign
25 Like slanted type
27 Kind of inspection
29 Taxi
30 Wedding vow
31 Cowboy's moniker

Puzzle 73 by David J. Kahn

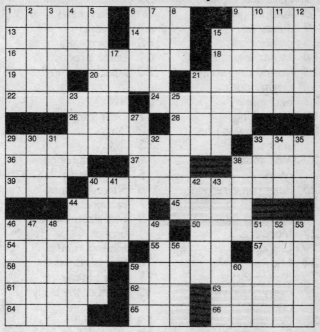

32 Some ring outcomes, for short
33 4:00 affair
34 Mr. Onassis
35 Music's ___ Bon Jovi
38 Tennis whiz
40 Kitchen gizmos
41 Med. school course
42 Cheesy snack
43 The mustachioed brother
44 Most skilled
46 Puts up, as a painting

47 Novelist Zola
48 Talk nonstop
49 Nary a soul
51 In ___ (trapped)
52 Oscar-winning Jessica
53 Navigate
56 Confess
59 Get a little shuteye
60 Tire filler

ACROSS

1 Hula skirt material
6 Arafat's grp.
9 It may be secondhand
14 Moses' mountain
15 Varnish ingredient
16 Downy duck
17 Befuddle
18 Not cutting
20 Woman who's not very sharp?
22 Mad magazine's genre
25 Paint can direction
26 Addis Ababa's land: Abbr.
27 Mad. ___
29 Clip out
34 Chowed down
35 Stately shader
37 Every 9-Down has one
38 Girl who's got her facts wrong?
43 "Star Trek" extra
44 Cobbler
45 Windup
46 More spiteful
49 Chem. pollutant
51 Canonized Mlle.
52 New Mexico art center
54 The "N" in "N × P"
56 Man who's annually in the doghouse?
60 Aspirin target, maybe
61 Propelled a boat
65 The Little Mermaid
66 Coffee vessel
67 Extremist
68 Lavatory sign
69 Lipton product
70 Attack ad, maybe

DOWN

1 Govt. property org.
2 Purge
3 &
4 Pheasant ragout
5 ___ Nevada
6 Surveyor's map
7 Plasterwork backers
8 Fair-sized musical groups
9 Managua miss
10 Longish dress
11 Thor's father
12 Clark of the Daily Planet
13 Work unit
19 Cast-of-thousands film
21 Early evening
22 Chantey singer
23 Number one Hun
24 Grad student's work
28 Polar worker
30 Watch the kids
31 Most artful
32 Tooth: Prefix
33 Give, as an apology
36 Unruly locks
39 Harden
40 Hanky embroidery

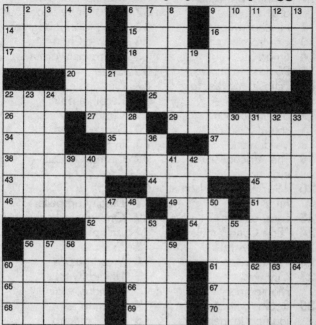

41 Saw along the grain
42 City non-Muslims may not enter
47 Man addressed as "My Lord"
48 Cheap liquor
50 Louisiana waterways
53 English place name suffix
55 Poem of King David
56 Insignificant
57 Totally botch

58 Baseball's Saberhagen
59 Comedian Carvey
60 Henpeck
62 Rd. or hwy.
63 Unit of geologic time
64 Patriotic org.

ACROSS

1 Worker protection org.
5 Nuclear weapon
10 Cry from a crib
14 Smart-___
15 Rome's river
16 Eclipse, maybe, to the ancients
17 Shuttle launch sound
18 Verdi work
19 The African Queen, e.g.
20 1967 Van Morrison hit
23 Lose, as skin
24 "Erie Canal" mule
25 "___ la vista!"
28 The U.S.A.'s "uncle"
31 City west of Montgomery
35 Rooms with stairs leading to them
37 "Skip to My ___"
39 China's Chou En-___
40 Flowers given to the Preakness Stakes winner
44 Place with microscopes
45 14, in old Rome
46 Nail polish
47 Liability's opposite
50 Unused
52 Swap
53 Jabber
55 Reagan's first Secretary of State
57 1970 hit by Sugarloaf
63 Bring to 212 degrees
64 Charlie Chan portrayer Warner ___
65 Ooze
67 "Just this ___ . . ."
68 Recoil in pain
69 Close tightly
70 Shade of red
71 In the buff
72 Grand Ole ___

DOWN

1 Dinghy propeller
2 One whose business isn't picking up?
3 Listen to
4 Word puzzle
5 United (with)
6 Humans, e.g.
7 Listen to
8 A ___ pittance
9 Slender nails
10 Ceiling-hung art
11 Love, Spanish-style
12 Lunch or dinner
13 Aardvark's tidbit
21 Hit with a bang
22 Car fill-up
25 "Usted ___ español?"
26 Map site
27 Knife wounds
29 Tylenol competitor
30 Up-to-date
32 Incan transport
33 Like a horse or lion

Puzzle 75 by Gregory E. Paul

34 Bridal path
36 Reason for an X rating
38 Put to work
41 Yang's counterpart
42 Before
43 ___ Sea, in the North Atlantic
48 Hole for a lace
49 Menlo Park monogram
51 From what place?
54 On the map

56 Threw in
57 Auctioneer's last word
58 Paddy crop
59 Director Kazan
60 U.S. soldier in W.W. II
61 Not shallow
62 Four seasons
63 Go up and down in the water
66 Thickness

ACROSS

1 Current units
5 Many comedy teams
9 Squirrel away
14 Some is junk
15 Archer of "Patriot Games"
16 Marseille menu
17 Collection in Old Icelandic
18 Carpe ___
19 "The ___ Incident" (1943 Fonda film)
20 Assume what's being asked
23 Parting word
24 Not happy
25 Flushed
27 Trinity member
28 Ginnie ___
30 Mystery writer Josephine
31 Mr. Potato Head part
32 Early Microsoft offering
33 "A mouse!"
34 Captures
35 Wake sleeping dogs, so to speak
39 ___ Jones's locker
40 NASDAQ listings: Abbr.
41 Speakers' pause fillers
42 Ending with methyl
43 Round Table title
44 Indy 500 logo
45 Place to take a cure
48 Cone bearer

49 Italian poet Torquato ___
51 Suffer a loss, slangily
53 Get closer to home, in a way
56 Not level
57 Like service station rags
58 Black-and-white hunter
59 ___ fatale
60 At liberty
61 Victory signs
62 Long lock
63 A.T.F. agents
64 To be, to Tiberius

DOWN

1 One-celled pond dwellers
2 Got by
3 Hardly the Queen's English
4 List of candidates
5 Miami-___ County
6 More than unusual
7 Get the better of
8 Academic term
9 Shipmate of Bones and Spock
10 Downtown cruiser
11 Like sloths and tree toads
12 Alley Oop's time
13 Chop down
21 Sitcom material
22 Search for
26 Welby and Kildare: Abbr.

Puzzle 76 by Nick Grivas

(grid)

29 Not gregarious
32 Like some martinis
33 Sci-fi visitors
34 Air rifle ammo
35 Item that may be slid down
36 Paycheck booster
37 Least fortunate
38 Called balls and strikes
39 Rock's ___ Leppard
43 The contiguous 48
44 Dirty

45 Oddballs may draw them
46 Zodiac fishes
47 "Ten-hut!" undoer
50 Talia of "Rocky"
52 Beyond's partner
54 "Desire Under the ___"
55 Cereal grasses
56 Toward the tiller

ACROSS

1. Linemen's protectors
5. Light-refracting crystal
10. Marries
14. Coward in "The Wizard of Oz"
15. Author Bret
16. Like slanted type: Abbr.
17. The New Yorker cartoonist Peter
18. ___ a time (individually)
19. Kind of wrestling
20. Buddhist discipline
21. Soul singer from California?
23. Slowly, to a conductor
25. Bullfight bull
26. California prison
29. Big airplane engine
33. Lustrous gems
35. Levi's material
37. Coronado's gold
38. Prayer opener
39. Kind of boom
40. Fake
41. Greyhound, e.g.
42. Heard, but not seen
43. Intelligence
44. Old-time Japanese governor
46. Tried and true
48. "What are the ___?"
50. St. Petersburg's Hermitage, e.g.
53. Pop singer from Texas?

58. Wizards and Magic org.
59. Grad
60. Mt. Everest locale
61. "___ calling"
62. Italian money
63. Jalopy
64. Darjeeling and oolong
65. Hit the runway
66. Snake shapes
67. Johnson of "Laugh-In"

DOWN

1. Public square
2. On TV
3. Country singer from North Dakota?
4. ___ -Cat (off-road vehicle)
5. Snaps
6. Indian princess
7. Infuriates
8. Get the ball rolling
9. Momentarily dazzling
10. Opposite of ignorance
11. Sewing case
12. Cousin of "Phooey!"
13. Wade (through)
21. Works at the Louvre
22. Short drink
24. Olympian's quest
27. Nose tickler
28. ___ Work (road repair sign)

Puzzle 77 by Dave and Diane Epperson

30 Folk-rock singer from Colorado?
31 Great times
32 Scholarly book
33 Cutlass or Eighty Eight
34 "Tush!"
36 Christie's "Death on the ___"
39 Big film festival name
40 Envisages
42 Autobahn car
43 Flabbergast

45 Became angry
47 Beams
49 Litigants
51 German sub
52 Parsonage
53 ___ Mall (London street)
54 Inter ___
55 Become a traitor
56 They'll get you in hot water
57 Noted gallery
61 ___ loss for words

ACROSS

1 Atty.-to-be's exam
5 Edith who sang "La Vie en Rose"
9 Key of Mozart's Symphony No. 39
14 Court records
15 Stewpot
16 Said à la the Raven
17 Feature of some shirts
19 "I give!"
20 "Seinfeld" miss
21 Bite, as the heels
23 Crisscross pattern
25 Catch in the act
26 Big goon
29 Decade divs.
30 "Minnie the Moocher" singer
33 See 13-Down
34 "Gil Blas" writer
35 Neuter
38 "Not ___ bet!"
40 Alkaline solutions
41 Help run, as a party
44 Part of WASP
47 Qatar, for one
49 Cone bearer
52 Fighter in gray
53 Biddy
54 Fish in a can
56 Part of a TV feed
58 "The Devil's Dictionary" author
59 In any respect

62 Baltimore chef's specialty
64 Kindled anew
65 Roof projection
66 Get out of bed
67 Intense media campaign
68 Amscrayed
69 Tolkien tree creatures

DOWN

1 In recent days
2 Like some variables
3 Times up
4 Unspoken
5 Malodorous animal
6 Needing hospital care
7 Astronaut Shepard
8 Hot breakfast dish
9 Steady
10 "Candid Camera" man
11 ___ cit. (footnote abbr.)
12 U.S./U.K. divider
13 With 33-Across, Montreal's subway
18 In a state of abeyance
22 Heavy sheet
24 River of Aragón
26 On vacation
27 Web designer's creation
28 Baby blues
31 Sir Arthur ___ Doyle
32 Capital on a fjord

33	"Butt out!," initially
35	Surgery result
36	Dermal opening
37	Ishmael's captain
39	Tiny colonists
42	Klink's aide in "Hogan's Heroes"
43	Two-___ sloth
45	Got one's mitts on
46	Ira Gershwin's contribution
48	Social welfare org.
49	Quarter-barrel
50	Theme of "Oedipus Rex"
51	___ Pieces
55	"The Wreck of the Mary ___"
56	Touched down
57	Like some vaccines
59	Wall St. whiz
60	Bus. card abbr.
61	___ Baba
63	Caesar's hello

ACROSS

1 Pinball message
5 Saloon orders
9 "A Lesson From ___"
14 Soprano's song, maybe
15 Nod off
16 One of the senses
17 Hiker's woe
18 Colorado skiing destination
19 Follow
20 Intermittently
23 A single time
24 "___ it or lose it"
25 Frequently, to Shakespeare
28 Exterminator's target
31 Nod off
34 Arc de Triomphe locale
36 Mexican gold
37 "Livin' la Vida ___" (Ricky Martin song)
38 Intermittently
42 Surf's sound
43 Shipment to a mill
44 Rephrases
45 Guggenheim display
46 Brand-new business
49 Nintendo product
50 Expire
51 Lennon's in-laws
53 Intermittently
61 Sailors are famous for them

62 Fur, say
63 Down-to-earth
64 Pal
65 Excited about
66 Food for Fido
67 Reveal
68 Like a billionaire's pockets
69 Wall Street inits.

DOWN

1 Word before shell or Bell
2 Remove the wrinkles from
3 Peseta : Spain :: ___ : Italy
4 Argentine dance
5 Reply from Ann Landers
6 Repair shop substitute
7 Basso Pinza
8 The first "S" in S.A.S.E.
9 "Relax, soldier!"
10 Jessica of "Tootsie"
11 Bones, to a doctor
12 Pins and needles holder
13 Spotted
21 On pins and needles
22 Fold-up mattress
25 Where to hear a 14-Across
26 Party handout
27 "Trick or ___"
29 Necessity at a golf club

30 George Gershwin's brother
31 Like a pitcher's perfect game
32 Vinegar: Prefix
33 Colorful violet
35 Abbr. on sale items
37 Inc., in Britain
39 Jottings
40 ". . . man ___ mouse?"
41 Train station
46 Squelches
47 Until now
48 Remove a clog from
50 Muralist Rivera
52 Kitchen wrap
53 Slanted type: Abbr.
54 Identify
55 Fly like a butterfly
56 Amino, for one
57 Second to ___
58 Bank (on)
59 Memorial Day solo
60 ___ gin fizz

ACROSS

1 Sixth sense
4 Sprightly dances
8 Egypt's Sadat
13 Designer Cassini
15 Taj Mahal site
16 Bellini opera
17 Caretaker for a baby
18 Sticky stuff
19 Gnawed
20 Austrian observance of April 30
23 Meadow
24 Like wind chimes
25 British observance of April 23
31 Onetime Argentine leader
32 ___ Perot
33 How to address a Fr. lady
36 The Emerald Isle
37 Airport abbr.
38 Ukraine's capital
39 Prevail
40 Fisher's rental
42 Stretched tight
43 Indian observance of April 13
45 Connecting strips of land
48 Trivial Pursuit need
49 United States observance of April 14
55 Perform penance
56 Evictee from paradise
57 ___ Bator
59 Deluxe sheet material
60 One-liner, e.g.
61 Aggregate
62 Golf great Sam
63 Stout relatives
64 Mack or Danson

DOWN

1 Ages and ages
2 Order at KFC
3 Pitcher Alejandro
4 Black-spotted cat
5 Composer Stravinsky
6 Seaman's quaff
7 H. H. Munro's pseudonym
8 Biblical liar
9 Zilch
10 Jalopy
11 Menotti hero
12 Worn-out
14 Old fighting vessel
21 Lowly worker
22 Rules: Abbr.
25 Gush forth
26 Hatcher of "Lois & Clark"
27 Happy face
28 Accra's land
29 Bobble
30 Newswoman Tabitha
33 Warship danger
34 Tableland

Puzzle 80 by D. J. DeChristopher

35 At any time
38 Excited
40 Praise
41 "I cannot tell ___"
42 Double
43 Grammy-winning Twain
44 "My Cup Runneth Over" singer, 1967
45 Bridge declaration
46 Beelzebub
47 Savings vehicle, briefly

50 Punjabi prince
51 Screen fave
52 Bake sale order
53 Came to rest
54 New Haven school
58 Composer Rorem

ACROSS

1 Round farm building
5 Hospital fluid
10 Silent assents
14 Riyadh resident
15 Caribbean vacation spot
16 Biblical murder victim
17 Grammatical reptile?
19 Filthy
20 They fit under desks
21 One feuding with the McCoys
23 "All ___ go!"
26 Criminal
27 Hill's opposite
29 Mideast negotiator
33 Kind of exam
37 26-Across items
39 Kenneth with a report
40 New Jersey city next to Hackensack
41 Saddam Hussein, notably
43 Nabisco cookie
44 Helps, as a 26-Across
46 Gulf War missile
47 Library urging
48 City with canals
50 Knots
52 Infatuated
54 Clean a tile floor, maybe
59 Salad pasta

63 Mitchell's Scarlett
64 Landed
65 Riot-causing reptile?
68 Dog in Oz
69 Like some renewable energy
70 Shipped
71 Clairvoyant
72 Fort ___, Fla.
73 Cupid

DOWN

1 Axes
2 Humor with a twist
3 Bowling alley divisions
4 ___ d'art
5 Droop
6 One for the history books
7 Baseball's Bambino
8 Shipper's worry in W.W. I
9 Mrs. Washington
10 Seafaring reptile?
11 Theater award
12 Farmer's place, in song
13 Arctic vehicle
18 Thrift shop condition
22 Ermines and such
24 O. Henry's "The Gift of the ___"
25 Disparages
28 Put into law
30 Taxi rider
31 It's measured in square units

Puzzle 81 by Ed Early

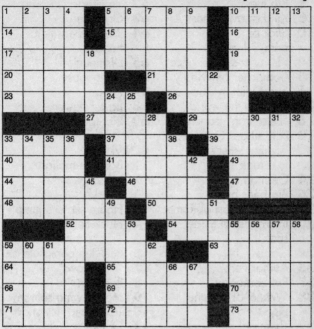

32 Stepped
33 Norwegian king
34 After-bath wear
35 Yemen's chief port
36 Law-practicing reptile?
38 Tentacled sea creature
42 Brainstorm
45 Kind of tissue
49 It's all about me, me, me
51 Target of clean air laws
53 Perturb

55 Temporary attitude
56 Alma ___
57 Maine university town
58 ___ and labor
59 Gymnasts' needs
60 Balm ingredient
61 Summon to court
62 Catalina, e.g.
66 Cigarette stuff
67 Much-maligned federal org.

ACROSS

1 Big mess
6 Kind of awareness
10 Stick of gum, informally
14 Kissinger's boss, once
15 Composer Stravinsky
16 Sport with mallets
17 Dead to the world
18 "Peter Pan" pooch
19 Folk singer Guthrie
20 Fortune-teller's art
23 In a funk
24 German car
25 Big beer buy
27 City southeast of Rome
30 International trade spot
34 Goofs
35 Author Ferber
37 Rubbernecker
38 "Wheel of Fortune" buy
39 Theme of this puzzle
41 Bard's "before"
42 Its mouth is nowhere near its head
44 Feline line
45 High-fiber food
46 Shoreline
48 Martha's Vineyard, e.g.
50 Roger Rabbit, for one
51 ___ B'rith
52 "Norma ___" (Field film)
54 Summer arctic phenomenon

60 Actor Guinness
62 Vegetarian's no-no
63 Sky-blue
64 It comes easily to hand
65 Dismounted
66 Hang loose
67 Rung
68 Easter flower
69 Not for minors

DOWN

1 Barber's motion
2 La ___ (weather worry)
3 Figure skater's jump
4 Black-tie affairs
5 "That's a lie!"
6 Red Sea peninsula
7 "Holy cow!"
8 Burt's ex
9 Médoc wine source
10 Tax expert, for short
11 Oater
12 First name in jazz
13 Golf club
21 Ford folly
22 The Jets and the Sharks
26 Bathroom installation
27 Draws nigh
28 Palmer with an "army"
29 Sam Spade, e.g.
30 Beginning
31 El ___, Tex.
32 Showed again

Puzzle 82 by Nancy Salomon and Sherry O. Blackard

33 Poll revelation
36 Stops up
39 Best man's best friend, often
40 "Dallas" family name
43 Prefix with friendly
45 Charged the quarterback
47 Like some instincts
49 Much of Niger
51 Teensy-weensy

52 Tanners catch them
53 Gobs
55 Where to find a hero
56 It's at your fingertip
57 "Star Trek" helmsman
58 Russian river
59 Doctor's office call
61 Speeder stopper

ACROSS

1 Minnesota's Gov. Ventura
6 Artist Picasso
11 Educ. support group
14 Make permanent, as cartoon drawings
15 Jack who ate no fat
16 Big coffee holder
17 Checked pattern in fabrics
19 "Dollars, taxes," e.g., for Dallas, Texas
20 Ready
21 Flowering plant that climbs
23 Old terr. west of Minnesota
24 Paintings
26 Part of a dental exam
27 "Remembrance of Things Past" novelist
30 Jockey's wear
33 Walk in water
36 Short
38 Isolated
39 Clothes presser
40 First month of el año
41 Integrally divisible by two
42 Writing on the wall, e.g.
43 Cut
44 Requirement
45 Tree with large, oblong leaves
47 Tend to, as a bad lawn

49 Amo, ___, amat (Latin trio)
51 Word before France or Jordan
52 Flub
55 Opened up space (for)
59 The puck stops here?
61 Elderly
62 Classic comic strip by Bud Fisher
64 Note after fa
65 Taking advantage of
66 Top scout
67 Golf ball support
68 Like last year's fashions
69 Washer's partner

DOWN

1 Holy war
2 W.W. II plane ___ Gay
3 Lie in wait
4 They're recited in confessions
5 Ingratiate
6 L.A. clock setting
7 Mil. addresses
8 It may be furrowed
9 Material for a doctor's glove
10 Them
11 Infatuation
12 Steadfast
13 The "I" in "The King and I"
18 Flashing lights

22 Very rear
25 The "T" of TBS
27 Mark Twain, e.g.
28 It doesn't hold water
29 Mother ___
31 Leg's midpoint
32 Cell-phone button
33 Slender one
34 Song for a diva
35 Slowpoke's swimming style
37 From abroad
46 Rehearsal
48 Worn away
50 The March King
52 Poem for the dear departed
53 Winchester, e.g.
54 Direct (to)
55 The majority
56 Burn balm
57 Elevator pioneer
58 Range: Abbr.
60 Open a crack
63 Touchy subject, to some people

ACROSS

1 Joust verbally
5 Tiny amounts
10 Letters stamped on meat
14 Lofty
15 Like seven Ryan games
16 Tidy
17 "So long!"
19 Long hauler
20 Emergency fund, of sorts
21 Key in again
23 Melville's Billy
24 English actress Dame ___ Johnson
25 Day before domenica
28 Readers' haven
31 Writer ___ Tan
32 Largest country in Africa
34 Go Rollerblading
35 Coral construction
37 Slow, in music
39 Leave speechless
40 Monastery head
42 Most 'N Sync fans
44 Before, in poetry
45 Rural outings
47 Crown's makeup, in the Bible
49 Fished for congers
50 Cold-shoulder
51 Make a mummy of
53 Halloween hanging
57 When doubled, a Jim Carrey film
58 "Ta-ta!"
60 Warhead carrier, for short
61 Twangy, as a voice
62 Singer Guthrie
63 Simon ___
64 How some jokes are delivered
65 Not e'en once

DOWN

1 Leveling wedge
2 Strong cotton
3 Steinbeck's "To ___ Unknown"
4 Cuban dance
5 Quick, as a convenience store stop
6 ___ and aahed
7 "___ went thataway!"
8 Auto option, informally
9 Sound system
10 Frees, as a dresser drawer
11 "Ciao!"
12 Wettish
13 End in ___
18 Track tipsters
22 Fraternal fellows
24 ___ Nast (publisher)
25 Singer Vaughan
26 Tiny critter
27 "Toodle-oo!"
28 Reveals
29 Complete switch

Puzzle 84 by Myles Callum

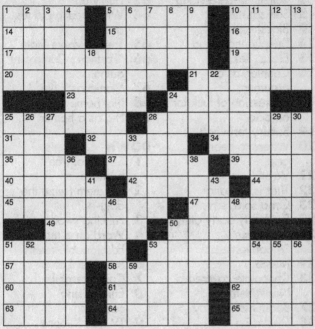

30 Elaine ___ ("Seinfeld" role)
33 Went out with
36 Popeye has big ones
38 Furtively
41 Pull a plow
43 N.F.L. coach Don
46 Supply's partner
48 Kind of band
50 Scandinavian "Salud!"
51 Whitney and Wallach

52 Easily split stuff
53 Señor's emphatic yes
54 Poop out
55 Make eyes at
56 Koh-i-___ diamond
59 Patriotic soc.

ACROSS

1 Bullets, in card slang
5 Self-satisfied
9 Blockheads
14 Deeply engrossed
15 El ___, Tex.
16 Counter, as an argument
17 Expression of luck for an actor
19 Battery terminal
20 Where to hear an aria
21 Wrath
22 That is, in Latin
23 On a sofa, say
25 Fraternity party attire
27 Beethoven's "Moonlight ___"
29 Memo
33 Chocolate-covered Nestlé item
37 Badminton replay
38 Discharge
39 Shoe part connected to the sole
40 In favor of
41 Less crazy
42 Water pipe
43 Sigma follower
44 Scoff at
45 Downhill racer
46 Not alfresco
48 ___ Jemima
50 In the "difficult years"
55 Hayloft locales
58 Do film work
60 Pola of silent films
61 Farewell
62 Hurry up
64 What stealth planes avoid
65 The Hawkeye State
66 "Portnoy's Complaint" author
67 Manicurist's file
68 Not home
69 Hit, as a homer

DOWN

1 Shelter of tree branches
2 ___ diem (seize the day)
3 Fencing swords
4 Word on a maze
5 Fashionable resort
6 Speak evil of
7 Computerphile
8 Enterprising one
9 TV host Kilborn
10 Pay attention
11 Woodwind
12 Bombs that don't explode
13 Proofreader's mark
18 Old German ruler
24 Neither's partner
26 Feed bag item
28 One way to read
30 Universally: Prefix
31 Even
32 Peut-___ (French for "maybe")
33 What gingivitis affects

34 October birthstone
35 Andy Taylor's son, in 60s TV
36 Go on and on with someone
40 1940 Disney film
41 Tranquil
43 Old can material
44 Unknown John
47 Canada's capital
49 Shylock's business
51 Approaches
52 Incandescent
53 Actress Garbo
54 Black billiard ball
55 Not clothed
56 Sandler of "Big Daddy"
57 Hitchhike
59 Dog with a blue-black tongue
63 Mary ___ cosmetics

ACROSS

1. ___ Na Na
4. Samms and Thompson
9. He bugs Bugs
14. Late-night competitor of Jay and Dave
15. Strike back
16. Nary a soul
17. 1957 Disney classic
19. Prime minister before Yitzhak
20. Potpourri scent
21. Rating a 10, say
23. Paranormal letters
24. Wields, as influence
26. Plain-living sect
28. Its primary is primary
33. Question starter
36. Singer Celine
37. Paris's abductee
38. Mansard overhang
40. Mercury or cobalt
43. Croat or Bulgar
44. Blur with tears
46. Blunted weapon
48. Like some glances
49. A daredevil may be living on this
53. Bank deposit?
54. Calm down
58. ___ Paulo
60. Lodge resident
63. Aired over the summer, maybe
64. Hang around for
66. Earl Scruggs's music
68. Use a crowbar on, say
69. Petrol unit
70. Appliance meas.
71. Mormon leader
72. Let up
73. Understand

DOWN

1. Lifted, so to speak
2. Toy Slinky, essentially
3. Discombobulate
4. Built
5. "Braveheart" star Gibson
6. French Sudan, today
7. Sailed through
8. Mill site
9. Backspin or topspin
10. Elton's john
11. Minor problems, so to speak
12. Pulls the plug on
13. Harvest
18. Tar's tale
22. Fuse rating unit
25. Do the crawl
27. "___ a Lady"
29. Weed whacker
30. Chipped in
31. Not fanciful
32. A deadly sin
33. "Just the facts, ma'am" speaker

Puzzle 86 by Randall J. Hartman

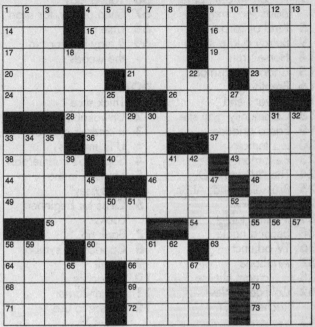

34 Luminous topper
35 Where jetsam goes
39 Marquis's inferior
41 It may have 2 BR's
42 Maui necklaces
45 Comb carrier
47 Left the cocoon
50 Moo goo gai pan pan
51 Fit to consume
52 River of Hesse
55 Many OPEC ministers
56 Nibble on
57 Follow

58 Having escaped a tag
59 M.P.'s quarry
61 "On the Waterfront" director Kazan
62 Dead-end jobs
65 Rock salt may be used on it
67 Before, to Burns

ACROSS

1 Person whose name starts Mc-, maybe
5 Kind of carpet
9 Betray à la a snitch
14 Horse's run
15 Chanel of fashion
16 Breathing
17 Prayer's end
18 Community gym site
19 Frisco gridder
20 ___ tomato
23 Be a monarch
24 The "N" in NCO
25 Brussels's land: Abbr.
28 Indy entry
31 Writing tablet
34 Second name
36 TV adjunct
37 Armbone
38 ___ cream cheese
42 College in New Rochelle, N.Y.
43 Wetland
44 Like notebook paper
45 Feminizing suffix
46 Holy
49 Nickname in the oil biz
50 Money for old age: Abbr.
51 Leave
53 ___ jelly
61 Pretend
62 Spanish 101 verb
63 Sailing
64 Single-handedly
65 Perfect place
66 Young lady
67 Shea player, for short
68 Little pastry
69 It may be worn in the woods

DOWN

1 Thick slice
2 Unwakable state
3 It controls a lot of U.S. imports
4 Soprano's counterpart
5 Monster in the "Odyssey"
6 Class for beginner cooks
7 Bank no.
8 Capricorn's symbol
9 Ill will
10 Unearthly
11 Singer Turner
12 Where to use Easy-Off
13 Mr. Uncool
21 Operating room aide
22 Deprive of weapons
25 Musical Count
26 St. who's fire?
27 Popular civic club
29 Cowgirl Dale
30 250, Roman-style
31 City north of Dallas
32 Take over
33 Whom "my heart belongs to"
35 Abbr. before a 34-Across

Puzzle 87 by Gregory E. Paul

37 Prefix with cycle
39 Key of Prokofiev's first piano concerto
40 Envision
41 "Under the Boardwalk," e.g.
46 Brown-haired
47 Bowling alley machine
48 Surviving
50 Words after two or hole
52 Hobo

53 Blueprint
54 Slippery
55 Chemistry book chapter, with "the"
56 Red vegetable
57 Org. that oversees food stamps
58 Where Japan is
59 Oriole's abode
60 Short race

ACROSS

1 Pesto flavoring
6 Madly in love
10 "That was close!"
14 With a single voice
15 Over again
16 Pro ___
17 Chip dip
18 Rigatoni relative
19 Trojan war suicide
20 Hanna-Barbera production of the 70s and 90s
23 Disney exec Michael
24 Cain's victim
25 Not keeping out the wind
27 5½-point type
32 Big Apple area near TriBeCa
35 Itsy-bitsy
36 Made baskets
37 1939 Academy Award-winning short
40 Makes one out of two
41 "Wheels"
42 Palm fruit
43 Like Eric the Red
44 Hostile intent
46 Close in on
48 Flimflams
52 1955 Disney classic
57 ___ vera
58 Melville tale
59 A-one
60 Clown
61 Golden Triangle country
62 Massey of old films
63 This-and-that dish
64 Either of two wives of Henry VIII
65 Carrying the latest

DOWN

1 Sew loosely
2 Japanese beer brand
3 Arch supports?
4 Tricks of the trade
5 Pacesetter
6 Huxley's "Eyeless in ___"
7 20-, 37- or 52-Across
8 Manages
9 "Had ___ and couldn't keep her" (nursery rhyme line)
10 Baby buggy
11 Traveler to Mecca
12 Common Latin abbr.
13 Sleek, as a floor
21 Uses Dixie diction
22 "Alas and ___"
26 Magical, as elves
28 Good neighbor policy
29 Strain at La Scala
30 Fair sight
31 Sharpness
32 Flabbergast

Puzzle 88 by Manny Nosowsky

33 "___ you don't!"
34 Immediate successor
36 Torah copyist
38 Davis of "Thelma & Louise"
39 TWA rival
44 Maniac
45 Interrupts on the dance floor
47 ___ Gay (W.W. II plane)
49 Wham!
50 Future indicators
51 Waterfall effect
52 Science building features
53 Scads
54 Drop off
55 "That hurt!"
56 Faucet hookup

ACROSS

1 Hollywood favorite
5 Dwelling
10 Walk back and forth
14 Russian legislature
15 Robert's ___ of Order
16 Roarer
17 E-mailed
18 Role for Charlie Chaplin
19 Work units
20 On a long project, perhaps
23 Monopoly properties: Abbr.
24 Extremity
25 Faddish 90s "art"
29 MasterCard alternative
31 Number cruncher, familiarly
34 San Antonio shrine, with "the"
35 Coal holders
36 Cries from creative people
37 Needing a loan
40 Daffy Duck or Donald Duck
41 Black-and-white cookie
42 Wed
43 Superlative suffix
44 "Les Misérables" novelist
45 Parisian brothers
46 Perfect Olympics score

47 Constrictor
48 1976 film about Woody Guthrie
55 Street/sidewalk separator
56 Seaweed
57 Rod, reel, tackle box, etc.
59 Fairy tale opener
60 "___ Park" (1981 best seller)
61 Suburban green
62 Asterisk
63 Tools for duels
64 Sea eagles

DOWN

1 Driver's licenses, in bars
2 Tune for two
3 Prefix with directional
4 Missing a deadline
5 Maestro Toscanini
6 Pats on the back, say
7 Elgar's "King ___"
8 Showroom car
9 Starbucks order
10 Make, as a case
11 Breezy
12 Gear teeth
13 Printer's widths
21 Sag
22 Genetic stuff
25 Kind of treat
26 Choral section
27 Picture card
28 I.R.S. worker

29 Audio's partner
30 Data
31 Preside over
32 Hit, and how!
33 Hearth waste
35 Arctic floater
36 Teenage woe
38 Weight
39 The "R" in R.F.D.
44 Biddy
45 Old-fashioned ones
46 Potato, for one

47 "I ___ for animals"
48 Diamond sacrifice
49 Killer whale
50 Big failure
51 Fairy tale villain
52 Eye up and down
53 Derrière
54 Indicate boredom
55 Nasdaq list: Abbr.
58 T.L.C. givers

ACROSS

1 Where the Seine flows
6 Think hard
11 Highland topper
14 Give forth
15 Kind of coffee
16 Rocks, to a bartender
17 Strong effort in cleaning
19 Cover with graffiti, e.g.
20 Notch's shape
21 Piano player in "Casablanca"
22 Ebb
24 Bygone brand on U.S. highways
26 Medieval laborer
29 Lost color
30 Watering hole
33 Food critic Sheraton
34 Wading bird
36 It has a creamy middle
38 Physicist's alma mater, maybe: Abbr.
39 Fist, so to speak
43 Old telecommunications giant
44 Margarita need
45 Horse's fare
46 Circus safety features
48 Garden tools
51 Say hi to
53 Swamp snapper
54 Colors
58 Bird and King
60 Super-long time
62 Part of Pfc.: Abbr.
63 Yuletide worker
64 Really good one
68 Feel awful
69 Dine at home
70 Ireland, personified
71 Sunbeam
72 Plumb tuckered out
73 Quota of winks

DOWN

1 Toilet paper rolled the "wrong" way, e.g.
2 Wheel turners
3 Unsophisticates
4 Chapel vow
5 Uses a Singer
6 Not so gentle
7 Seam contents
8 Spy's org.
9 Subj. of a 1991 breakup
10 Wool-ites?
11 "Final Jeopardy" feature
12 Professors
13 New Hampshire town on a lake
18 Fun house sound
23 Ending with video
25 Suffix with psych-
27 Nature's alarm clock
28 ___ song
31 Entreats
32 Fellows

Puzzle 90 by Elizabeth C. Gorski

34 Among others
35 Swimming stroke
37 Bouquet
39 Father of three daughters
40 Police, with "the"
41 Certain util.
42 Fab place?
47 Sun. talk
49 Abstains, in brief
50 Earth Day subj.
52 Furby fans
55 Stimulant

56 Happening
57 Shelter adoptee
59 Ginger cookie
61 Babe in the woods
65 Vacation time for Henri
66 A, on the Aare
67 U.S. Open entrant

ACROSS

1 ___ Romeo (sports car)
5 Bottom of a boat
9 Yankee Stadium surface
14 Jump (out), as from a plane
15 Woodwind
16 Main artery
17 Theodore Roosevelt follower, 1912
19 Take to jail
20 Suffix with Gator
21 "___ Man Answers" (Sandra Dee film)
22 1-Down, e.g.
24 Overly common
26 Book before Esth.
27 Black-footed animal
30 Purify ceremonially
35 Not silently
36 More than serious
37 Midmonth date
38 Machine cylinders
39 ___ bourgeois
40 Car scar
41 Coup d'___
42 "Buyer beware" phrase
43 Free-for-all
44 Two five-spots
46 Special Forces headgear
47 French article
48 Amount of hair
50 Arthur Fiedler, e.g.
54 Partner of outs

55 Demolition stuff
58 Supplement
59 Theodore Roosevelt's namesake toy
62 Star in Orion's left foot
63 "Picnic" playwright
64 ___ Major
65 Edgar Bergen's Mortimer ___
66 Tea leaves reader
67 Velcro alternative

DOWN

1 "Waterloo" pop group
2 Praise
3 Manicurist's tool
4 Word before "that" or "there"
5 Forgo a cab
6 Depth charge target
7 The "L" of L.A.
8 Popular jeans
9 January's birthstone
10 Theodore Roosevelt's group
11 "Rule Britannia" songwriter
12 Paint can direction
13 Lacking
18 Stuck
23 Corner map
24 Theodore Roosevelt's moniker
25 High-hatter
27 Aspect
28 Thrill to death

29 Kind of candle
31 "Exodus" author
32 Fred Astaire's sister
33 Basic belief
34 ___ Park, Colo.
36 Dorm room feature
39 Hoosier hoopster
43 Stylike
45 Numerous
46 Drinking spree
49 Blue ___ Mountains
50 "Total Recall" setting

51 Tennis score after deuce
52 Narrowly defeat
53 Elevator man
55 Beach bird
56 Jet Propulsion Lab grp.
57 Pitfall
60 WSW's reverse
61 School transport

ACROSS

1 Victoria's Secret product
4 It's hard on the head
8 Sergeant's command
14 ___ room (place for play)
15 Actress Best
16 Neighbor of Neptune
17 The Monkees' "___ Believer"
18 Librarian's advice
19 Cakes with ground nuts
20 1991 Michael J. Fox film
23 Sneakers brand
24 Swit's TV co-star
25 Says grace
29 Smallest
31 Sandy's bark
33 "This is bad!"
34 1996 Adam Sandler film
38 Reverence
41 Bowl game cheer
42 Miner's find
43 Thumbs-up vote
44 1993 Walter Matthau film
48 Architect Saarinen
49 ___-through
50 Boxer's stat
54 They have upturned noses
56 River fish
59 Skin cream ingredient
60 1999 Johnny Depp film
63 Human
66 Neighbor of Turkmenistan
67 Inventor Whitney
68 Border patrol concern
69 Khartoum's river
70 ___-Xers (boomers' kids)
71 Gracie's comedy partner
72 Some square dancers
73 Work unit

DOWN

1 Kind of gown
2 Eliminate
3 Decorative tree
4 Submarine
5 Writer ___ Rogers St. Johns
6 With everything counted
7 Nickname for Billie Holiday
8 Model T, e.g.
9 Scouting group
10 It might get busted at a concert
11 Little scurrier
12 Common girl's middle name
13 Road curve
21 Corned beef dish
22 Mars, for one
26 Ship-to-shore line?
27 Time long ago

	28	Stadium near the Grand Central Parkway		47	Oscar-winner Patricia
	30	Diamond cover		51	Assert without proof
	32	Not negotiable		52	Picnic carrying case
	35	Compensates		53	Chopping
	36	"Friends" character		55	Teen talk, often
	37	Lascivious look		57	Damascus's land
	38	Years and years		58	"We ___ Overcome"
	39	Songbird		61	Otherwise
	40	Dollar rival		62	Small bills
	45	Cosa Nostra member		63	"Cosmo" or "GQ," e.g.
	46	Up in the air?		64	Bullring yell
				65	Carnival city

ACROSS

1 Does simple arithmetic
5 Aide: Abbr.
9 Cat, informally
14 "I ___ to recall . . ."
15 Gossipy Barrett
16 What treasure hunters want to know
17 Capri, e.g.
18 Heart of the matter
19 Flip chart holder
20 Suffice, and then some
23 Faucet
24 Mai ___ (drink)
25 Budget competitor
27 Society newcomer
30 Shake on it
36 Ceramic-making, e.g.
38 Wanton look
39 Rick's "Casablanca" love
40 Group of key officers
41 London's Big ___
42 Flies alone
43 Tennis great Arthur
44 Parts of a min.
45 Congregational cries
46 Go for a swim, say, during hot weather
49 Bygone car
50 "Now it's clear"
51 "___ the season . . ."
53 Not near
55 Surpass all others
62 Up in years
64 "Tickle-me" character
65 Creme-filled snack
66 Violinmaker who taught Stradivari
67 Per ___ (daily)
68 Huckleberry ___
69 Central American Indians
70 Not crazy
71 Minnesota ___

DOWN

1 "Like, no way!"
2 He loved Lucy
3 Big computer maker
4 Refine, as metal
5 Veronica's guy, in the comics
6 Achy
7 Social slight
8 Curbside cry
9 Jury number, commonly
10 "Now I get it!"
11 Any Grisham novel
12 La ___ tar pits
13 Kennel sound
21 "Here, try some!"
22 Bert of "The Wizard of Oz"
26 Peculiar expression
27 1983 comedy with Mr. T
28 Clear, as a disk
29 Coiffure crisis
31 "Who's Afraid of Virginia Woolf?" dramatist

Puzzle 93 by Nancy Salomon and Louis Hildebrand

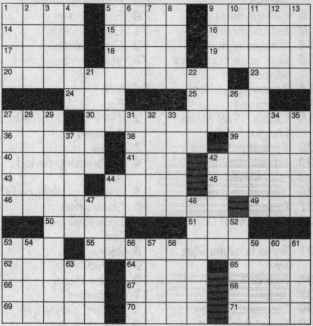

32 Parasitic type
33 Pluperfect, e.g.
34 In unison
35 Rodeo rope
37 Worries
42 Composer Erik
44 Mets' home
47 Hot 1990s computer game
48 In
52 Speak derisively
53 Shaving stuff
54 ___ mater

56 Sneakers brand
57 Charles Lamb's pen name
58 Certain Feds
59 Song for Carmen
60 Superman, most of the time
61 Almost forever
63 Airplane announcement, for short

ACROSS

1 Jerry's ice-cream partner
4 College finals
9 Indian honorific
14 Monterrey hooray
15 Sign in an apartment window
16 Radarange maker
17 Evergreen
18 Classic 1969 Merle Haggard song
20 #1 thing
22 Brontë heroine
23 ___ Moines
24 Vitamin regimen
27 Care for
30 City north of Carson City
31 Try to beat the light, say
34 Festoon's shape
37 Jester
39 Diamond or ruby
40 Sweet deal for a company executive
44 Venusian, e.g.
45 "Mon ___!"
46 Exceed
47 Meals
50 Runs
52 Bluegill fish
53 Et cetera
57 Stir
59 Take five
61 Jazzy Fitzgerald
62 It won't go over well
67 Turn down, as lights

68 "The Sound of Music" lady
69 Hawaiian veranda
70 Eden evictee
71 Chilean range
72 Clever, slangily
73 Visibly embarrassed

DOWN

1 Fab
2 1999–2000 name in the news
3 Cheek
4 Tie-breaking periods: Abbr.
5 Louis IX or Philippe IV
6 Show-offish basketball move
7 Tax
8 Rears
9 Espied
10 Pal for Pierre
11 Distributed
12 "Picnic" playwright
13 Bigmouth, e.g.
19 Go for another tour
21 Musical ability
25 Cabinet department
26 Soon
28 Like lucky castaways
29 Son of 70-Across
32 Golden rule word
33 Chick's sound
34 Petri dish filler
35 It has lines
36 Paper carrier?
38 Boy
41 Sweetie

Puzzle 94 by Monica Krausse

42 Short, ribbed pasta
43 Geological extent
48 1939 film home
49 Detects a rat?
51 Atlanta-to-Tampa dir.
54 Wiser's partner
55 Shade of green
56 Dubbed
57 Soprano Gluck
58 College bigwig
60 Picnic dish
63 Stop

64 English majors get them: Abbr.
65 Big lug
66 Critic's pick?

ACROSS

1 Bygone pay phone amount
5 Hunk
9 Biblical betrayer
14 "Exodus" author
15 Essence
16 Wear away
17 Academic accomplishment, redundantly
20 WSW's reverse
21 1975–76 World Series champs
22 Regions
23 Norma ___ (Sally Field role)
24 Bellicose deity
25 Not many, redundantly
30 Possesses
33 Honor ___ thieves
34 Chuck
35 "Oh, heck!"
36 Mississippi River transport
37 Bullring cheer
38 Semisheer fabric
39 Prom night rental
40 Golden Gate section
41 Printing press gizmo
42 Trains that go clickety-clack
43 Avoid, redundantly
45 Inter ___
46 Disfigure
47 Craft for Sacajawea
49 Drink from a flask
51 Bro's partner
54 Leading character, redundantly
57 Provide, as with some quality
58 Faux pas
59 Pavarotti solo
60 Projection room items
61 Has markers out
62 Brief letter sign-off

DOWN

1 Fancy dresser
2 Wrinkle remover
3 Cheese nibblers
4 Winter hours in N.Y.C.
5 Drive-in feature
6 Burden
7 ___ and sciences
8 Spelling contest
9 Heckler
10 Prods
11 David Copperfield's first wife
12 Summer drinks
13 "Didn't I tell you?"
18 Halloween color
19 Tempts fate
23 Fab Four member
24 Not in class
25 Aesop tale
26 Modern memo
27 A lot of bait
28 Perfect world
29 Back tooth

Puzzle 95 by Randall J. Hartman

30 Japanese verse
31 "Over the Rainbow" composer
32 Dummy Mortimer
35 Organ transplant need
38 Shrew
40 Winter Olympian
43 Places for a 40-Down
44 Mexican pals
45 Invalidate
47 Christmas sweet
48 Right-hand person

49 Pack (away)
50 Diminish
51 What to call a king
52 Mother of Horus
53 Career home runs, e.g.
54 Debussy's "La ___"
55 The Plastic ___ Band, of 60s–70s music
56 Catch red-handed

ACROSS

1 Pedestal topper
5 Oodles
9 Went white
14 "Uh-uh"
15 Carefree adventure
16 Beyond's partner
17 Always
20 Checkers color
21 They're rated in B.T.U.'s
22 Scratch-off game, e.g.
23 ___ -Lorraine
25 ___-mo replay
26 Golf's ___-Ryder Open
28 Act the toady, slangily
34 That's a laugh
37 Branding tool
39 The necktie in a necktie party
40 Sometimes
43 Kind of show
44 El ___ (weather phenomenon)
45 Wrongful act
46 Familiar saying
48 "Hup, two, three, four" caller
50 "Yay, team!"
52 Firstborn
56 Mideast money
61 Absorbed, as a loss
62 P, on a fraternity jacket
63 Practically never
66 Earthy pigment
67 Tusked critter
68 "Zip-___-Doo-Dah"
69 "Miracle on 34th Street" actor John
70 Play material for a kitten
71 Comic Foxx

DOWN

1 The "I" in IV
2 Wooden peg
3 Newspaper opinion pages
4 Spy novelist Deighton
5 Cosmetic ingredient
6 Bozos
7 Friend in the 'hood
8 Jolly Roger depiction
9 Time machine's destination
10 Aid in a felony
11 Zero, on a court
12 At any point
13 Declare false
18 Snack in a shell
19 Kasparov's corner man
24 Is gaga over
25 Rather poky
27 Elvis ___ Presley
29 Neither Rep. nor Dem.
30 Bombed
31 New York gallery district
32 Computerphile
33 Confined, with "up"

Puzzle 96 by Fred Piscop

34 Firefighter, maybe
35 Certain window shape
36 Rancher's concern
38 "Peter Pan" pooch
41 Thumbs-up vote
42 Like soda bottles, in pre-recycling days
47 Small songbird
49 Tickled-pink feeling
51 Sheik's land, in song
53 Chip away at
54 Did a smithy's job

55 Got in shape, with "up"
56 Inside info
57 Victim of Pizarro
58 Stiff and sore
59 Caught in the act
60 Run out of gas
61 Controversial orchard application
64 Feathery wrap
65 Fold, spindle, or mutilate

ACROSS

1 Place for a barbecue
6 Magical being
9 One who's not out on called strikes
13 Lessen
14 Equine color
16 Diva's song
17 Strategic military advantage
20 Wineglass part
21 ___ man out
22 Indian home
23 Suffix with serpent
24 Touchdown makers
25 What a poor winner does
29 Clarinetist Artie
30 Cowboys' home
31 Neck wraps
32 Plummet
36 They're far from the coastline
39 Boxing match results
40 Dweeb
41 Eight-person band
42 "___ funny. Ha, ha!"
43 Pot winners
44 Cats, informally
48 It's a boy
49 Completely wrong
50 "___ Gang" comedies
51 Restaurant handout
55 Hidden agenda
58 Italian money
59 Wood cutter
60 The Atlantic, e.g.
61 Officeholder's office
62 Many, many years
63 Italian food

DOWN

1 "No bid"
2 Touch on
3 3M product
4 Any thing
5 "___ the land of the free . . ."
6 Wear away
7 "___ of the Flies"
8 Auto engine part
9 Cavalry weapon
10 Brunch serving
11 Broadcaster
12 They're covered on diamonds
15 Weirdo
18 Charged particles
19 Cat call
23 Road to Rome
24 Pottery fragment
25 Sand inside a shoe, e.g.
26 Thin
27 "I'm ___ your tricks!"
28 Many, many years
29 "Pardon me"
31 Afrikaners
32 Tracy of the comics
33 Learning system
34 It has no comparison
35 Attention-getters

Puzzle 97 by William A. Ballard

37 Subject of a law of physics
38 Prod
42 Go off in a new direction
43 Tropical root
44 Manhandles
45 Half of an old comedy duo
46 The "U" in UHF
47 Chocolaty
48 Unit of light
50 Kind of 63-Across

51 Flaky mineral
52 After-dark times, in classifieds
53 Tidy
54 Annapolis institution, for short
56 Flowery verse
57 Pinnacle

ACROSS

1 "Do ___ others . . ."
5 Disorganized
11 Dirty campaign stuff
14 Drudge of feudal times
15 District in the Philippines
16 Document or diet ending
17 Ducker of military service
19 DiMaggio stat
20 Dewey, e.g.: Abbr.
21 Debonair "bunny man"
22 "Desperately Seeking Susan" actor Quinn
24 "Date film" classic of 1987
28 Devils
31 "Diana," for one
32 Determinant of utility charges
33 Decreases
37 Disclaimer on a sale tag
38 Dobie Gray's "___ Crowd"
40 Deere product: Abbr.
41 Definite agreement
43 Denizen of an aquarium
44 Divorce lawyer on "L.A. Law"
45 Disagreeable air
46 Dauntless ones
50 Dawn
51 Dander
52 Danube locale: Abbr.
55 Decimal point
56 Difficult jump-rope game
61 Defeater of A.E.S.
62 Detach, as a rind
63 Disney lion
64 "Definitely!"
65 Danish, e.g.
66 Decisive time (or theme of this puzzle)

DOWN

1 Dairy or ranch regulator: Abbr.
2 Doofus-y sort
3 Downhill/uphill conveyance
4 Dash ___ (write quickly)
5 Drivers' fares
6 Drifting above
7 Doze
8 Delve (into)
9 "Down with the bull!"
10 Droll actor in "Ghostbusters"
11 Day after lundi
12 Densely settled
13 Declining, as embers
18 Dated term for "yours"
23 Drinks popular in hot weather
24 Docked animal parts, maybe
25 Did alpine calls
26 Diocletian's 552
27 Djibouti's Gulf of ___

Puzzle 98 by Alan Arbesfeld

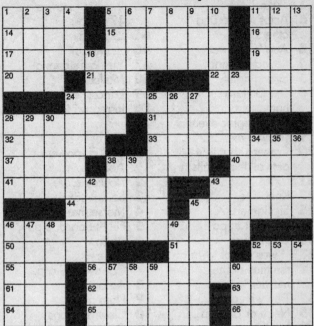

28 Doublet
29 Defunct oil name
30 Duct
34 Dinner scraps
35 Devoted, as friends
36 Duke belongs to it:
    Abbr.
38 Dollywood locale:
    Abbr.
39 Department of State
    chief under Reagan
42 Desiccated
43 Drowsy

45 Describing no more
    than
46 Daughter's cry?
47 Diminish by degrees
48 Devotional ceremonies
49 Dock sight in Galveston
52 Diminutive amount
53 Daily Bruin sch.
54 Dobbin pulls one
57 Dismiss ___ technicality
58 Delivery co.
59 Dice game action
60 Düsseldorf connector

ACROSS

1 "Yikes!"
6 Actor Mineo and others
10 Aug.'s follower
14 Sound thinking
15 Strung tightly
16 The O'Hara homestead
17 Catastrophic event
19 "How sweet ___!"
20 Camera shot that gets all the details
21 Logos
23 Knob site
25 Sicilian erupter
26 Phi ___ Kappa
30 Chauffeurs
33 "I was out of town at the time of the murder," e.g.
35 Tree with cones
36 Neon or oxygen
39 Locale for a 17-Across
43 Underhanded
44 Raise ___ (cause a ruckus)
45 Soup seasoning
46 The South and the Southwest
49 Right away, on a memo
50 Messy dresser
52 Partner of 4-Down
54 Song starting "My country, 'tis of thee"
57 Team heads

62 An arm or a leg
63 It might follow a 17-Across
65 ___ vera
66 ___ Rabbit
67 Vietnam's capital
68 Mailed
69 Princes, e.g.
70 In regard to

DOWN

1 Con Ed power: Abbr.
2 Hockey score
3 Soil: Prefix
4 Morse marks
5 Flight board, e.g.: Abbr.
6 Daze
7 Car owners' org.
8 An apostle
9 Plant part
10 Clowns' props
11 Consumed
12 Kind of ballerina
13 Soviet news service
18 Part of Q.E.D.
22 Deprived (of)
24 Matured, as fruit
26 Lowest voice
27 Airline to Israel
28 Minuscule
29 Lawyers' org.
31 By way of
32 Lt.'s inferior, in the Navy
34 Evil spirits
36 Fellows

37 ___ mater
38 Stair part
40 Newsman Rather
41 Tease
42 "I have an idea!"
46 Cold dessert
47 Ones stringing up shoes
48 Thunder god
50 Photographer's request
51 Scent in furniture polish

53 Alexander, for short
54 "What a shame"
55 Taxis
56 1960s activist's hairdo
58 Detective Charlie
59 Sharpen
60 Supply-and-demand subj.
61 Comical playlet
64 Perfect rating

ACROSS

1 Important exam
6 Serene
10 Pint sellers
14 Concert site
15 Zone
16 "Make it snappy!"
17 Small salamanders
18 Hussy
19 Pro ___
20 Command to a
   sloucher
23 Mutt
25 Mao ___-tung
26 Haunt
27 Nervous
30 Contains
31 Greek theater
32 Stoltz of "Mask"
34 Dog in "Beetle
   Bailey"
38 Park
41 Dry run
42 Wraps up
43 Losing come-out roll
   in craps
44 Madrid Mrs.
45 ___ Tunes (cartoon
   series)
46 Summer attire
50 Hack's workplace
52 Stubborn one
53 Be dead and buried
57 With the bow, in
   music
58 Na+ and Ca++, e.g.
59 "Cheers" mailman
62 Dressed

63 Authentic
64 Influential member of
   a tribe
65 Fictional Jane
66 Writer ___ Stanley
   Gardner
67 Squalid

DOWN

1 Strike out
2 Wrath
3 Bygone cinema
   bonuses
4 Opposed
5 Remain in good
   shape
6 Pitches a tent
7 Get up
8 It begins on Ash
   Wednesday
9 Noted jazz drummer
10 Notre Dame's city
11 Style manual
   concern
12 Spa
13 Fop's footwear
21 Sport ___ (modern
   vehicle)
22 Stomach
   muscles, briefly
23 Take for one's own use
24 Excessive
28 Moron
29 Bearded antelope
30 Top 40 station's play
   list
32 11,000-foot mount in
   Europe

33 Pistol, slangily
34 Cuatro y cuatro
35 Avert
36 Park features
37 Respects the rules
39 Get worked up?
40 D.D.E.'s command, once
44 Good name for a cook
45 There are 2.2 in a kg.
46 "The final frontier"
47 ___-burly

48 "American Beauty" prize
49 ___ Island
50 Ear part
51 Air passenger's request
54 Perpetrator
55 Clinches
56 Vogue competitor
60 Agent from Washington
61 Prepare scrapple, say

ACROSS

1 Tobacco mouthful
5 Potato
9 Commercial makers
14 Swearing-in words
15 ___ Vista (Web search engine)
16 Part of a gay refrain
17 Mozart's "Madamina," e.g.
18 New arrival on a horse farm
19 Nonsensical
20 Fibs of song
23 Movie locations
24 Shakespearean prince
25 High-spirited
28 The "p" in m.p.g.
30 Part of a cowboy's boot
34 Someone ___ (not mine or yours)
35 Give permission
37 Sacagawea coin denomination
38 Boy in a nightgown, in a children's rhyme
41 A Gabor sister
42 Closes in on
43 Cuts down, foodwise
44 Not so much
46 Campers, for short
47 Main course
48 As well
50 Snare
51 Waterspout habitué
59 Capt. Ahab's obsession
60 Tabula ___
61 Bat's home
62 Where Van Gogh cut off his ear
63 Gershwin's "___ Plenty o' Nuttin'"
64 Baby-bouncing place
65 Elvis's blue shoe material
66 Mercedes-___
67 Lost buoyancy

DOWN

1 Anthracite, e.g.
2 Mata ___ (spy)
3 Going strong
4 "How's tricks?"
5 Football 2-pointer
6 Prepares ground for planting
7 Rocky Mountain state
8 Limp watch painter
9 Bamboozled
10 Dentists' tools
11 French Sudan, today
12 Vogue rival
13 Votes against
21 Allows entry
22 Dice roll
25 Gem
26 Advil competitor
27 "___ directed"

28 Twosomes
29 View finders?
31 Bluffer's game
32 Bring together
33 Dodger shortstop of old
35 Many a Balkan
36 Abduct
39 "Vive ___!"
40 Overdoes the criticism
45 Did salon work
47 Imitation
49 Like a 500-pounder

50 1980s–90s ring champ
51 "___ only trying to help"
52 Drive-___
53 After-Christmas event
54 Chicago paper, briefly
55 Wise one
56 Author Richard Henry ___
57 Not odd
58 Smell horrible

ACROSS

1 60s do
5 "Cool!"
9 Tie at a derby?
14 1958 chiller, with "The"
15 Singer Guthrie
16 Melodramatic
17 Baby bear reconnoiterers?
19 President before Polk
20 Person of note?
22 ___ Diavolo (seafood sauce)
23 Puts on an act
26 Conqueror of England, 1066
28 Actress Lena
29 Resorts of sorts
32 Give the heave-ho
33 Cowpoke competitions
36 Klingons and Vulcans
38 Coming-out party?
39 Baby fox carriers?
41 Form filer, for short
44 Platforms
46 Lords and ladies
48 Dundee denizen
50 Charlie Brown expletive
52 Security concern
53 Player who's good with a bat
55 Bishops' subordinates
58 German cry
59 B-52, e.g.

62 Caterpillar competitor
64 Baby bird vegetables?
68 Boo-boo
69 Computer clickers
70 Oscar winner Kazan
71 Medicine measures
72 Said "not guilty," e.g.
73 It's in a pickle

DOWN

1 "N.Y.P.D. Blue" network
2 Winter woe
3 Rip off
4 Really awful
5 One of the Judds
6 Blows one's top
7 Kind of clef
8 Not sleep peacefully
9 Houston player
10 Sauce source
11 Baby moose movers?
12 Met productions
13 Tough boss to work for
18 Comedian Bill, informally
21 Naval Academy grad
23 Escort company
24 Mother Nature's burn balm
25 Baby goat siblings?
27 "Apollo 13" director Howard
30 Blue Ribbon maker
31 In the style of

Puzzle 102 by Nancy Salomon

34 Green-lights
35 Environmentalists' club name
37 That, to Tomás
40 Caroler's syllable
42 Marsh material
43 Questions
45 ___ Industries (defense contractor)
47 Censored
48 Protected from the sun
49 "O tempora! O mores!" orator

51 Piece together, as tape
54 Water servers
56 Sped
57 Press coverage
60 Dudley Do-Right's org.
61 Pop singer Collins
63 Seafood delicacy
65 Actor Wallach
66 Be laid up
67 Mule of song

ACROSS

1 Fellow
5 Contented
9 Noise at a street protest
14 Film part
15 Put on the payroll
16 Mandel of "St. Elsewhere"
17 Aid in crime
18 Look at flirtatiously
19 Make reparations
20 Alternative to briefs
23 Barbie's guy
24 Baseball great Mel
25 Says
27 Russian villas
31 Change, as a hemline
33 Brand of sweetener
34 Leave out
35 Singer Paul
39 First newspapers on the street
42 Like most basketball stars
43 Decorative vases
44 Victorious
45 Chose
47 Beginnings
48 Drunk as a skunk
51 Animal that beats its chest
52 Superman foe ___ Luthor
53 Part of a girl's sock hop attire
60 Believe without question
62 Young Lennon
63 Pulitzer-winner James
64 "Purple" writing
65 Disabled
66 Place for an earring
67 President before Polk
68 Skunk's defense
69 Cenozoic and Paleozoic, e.g.

DOWN

1 Taurus : Bull :: Cancer : ___
2 Penniless person
3 Trebek of "Jeopardy!"
4 Townshend of The Who
5 Haunted house inhabitants
6 Traffic controller
7 Singer Guthrie
8 Stag or hart
9 Celibate
10 Sexy
11 Came to
12 Frisco footballer
13 New drivers, usually
21 Willy Wonka creator Dahl
22 ___ -frutti
26 Choo-choos
27 ___ of gratitude
28 Greenish-blue
29 Select
30 Venerate
31 Change, as the Constitution
32 Jar tops

Puzzle 103 by Peter Gordon

34 Folklore meany
36 Post-It, e.g.
37 Windsor or sheepshank
38 Venomous snakes
40 Perform better than
41 Answering machine signals
46 Waiter's offering
47 First game of a doubleheader
48 Caught some Z's
49 Very sad

50 Praise
51 San Antonio landmark
54 Norway's capital
55 Not working, as a battery
56 Cabbagelike vegetable
57 Dr. Frankenstein's helper
58 Singer McEntire
59 Golf shop purchase
61 Employ

ACROSS

1 In the thick of
5 Fallings-out
10 Nose (out)
14 Chauffeur's spot
15 Ahead of the game
16 In need of patching
17 ___ uproar
18 Food from heaven
19 Old-time oath
20 They're loaded
23 Dan Aykroyd's old show, briefly
24 "What a good boy ___!"
25 Ground-breakers?
26 French composer Erik
28 Bluegrass strings
30 They're loaded
32 Native Alaskan
33 Sound like a siren
35 Uno + dos
36 Possible title for this puzzle
39 Telegram punctuation
42 Words from Wordsworth
43 More boorish
47 They're loaded
49 Per ___ income
50 Some tournaments
51 Garr of "Mr. Mom"
53 Floral ring
54 PBS benefactor
55 They're loaded
59 Poet ___ St. Vincent Millay
61 Earth that's "firma"
62 ___ Hotels (luxury chain)
63 Botch
64 Stream
65 Mideast sultanate
66 Humane org.
67 Pays attention to
68 Good buds

DOWN

1 "Arabian Nights" hero
2 Barely adequate
3 Use the mind's eye
4 Slips into
5 Ladies' men
6 Really dumb
7 ___ for oneself (goes it alone)
8 The sound of music
9 Practice in the ring
10 Ram's ma'am
11 Part of Canis Major
12 Rock for a monument
13 Nonstop
21 ID item
22 Concorde, e.g.
27 Goes on the fritz
29 Attack
30 Whopper juniors?
31 Pie ___ mode
33 Ties the knot with
34 Admiral's affirmative
37 Alternative to smoking

38 Last Supper cup
39 Those who shouldn't live in glass houses?
40 Prepared, as a memo
41 Sea-dwelling
44 Thorny problem
45 Nonstop
46 Cereal fruit
48 City in Kyrgyzstan
49 Frog sounds
51 Wee hour
52 Slipped up

56 Rash reaction?
57 Richard of "Pretty Woman"
58 Cloverleaf feature
60 Santa ___ winds

ACROSS

1 It may be high or low on a car
5 Immediately, to a surgeon
9 Little bits
14 Airport outside Paris
15 Brain tests: Abbr.
16 Book that's read word-for-word
17 Docking spot
18 Waterproof cover
19 Black, on a piano
20 Entry requirement, sometimes
23 Headlight?
24 Little 'un
25 Uncle ___
28 Retaliate
31 Hot springs
34 Bowie's weapon
36 "Mo' Better Blues" director Spike
37 Money man Greenspan
38 Spy
42 Fibster
43 Color
44 Watermelon throwaways
45 "___ Misérables"
46 Popular place
49 Take care of a bill
50 Diving seabird
51 Fair-sized field
53 Buried loot
60 Stored on board

61 Like some testimony
62 Surgery souvenir
63 Lagoon encloser
64 Decorate anew
65 ___ mater
66 Brawl
67 Shake hands for the first time
68 Chatters

DOWN

1 Conks
2 Buffalo's lake
3 Actor Guinness
4 Gift of the Magi
5 Agree out of court
6 Part of a china set
7 Taj Mahal's city
8 Dosage amts.
9 Utilized
10 Brainless one
11 Composer Stravinsky
12 Curve
13 Hog's home
21 Raring to go
22 Wield a wheel
25 Brain protector
26 Comics orphan
27 King with a golden touch
29 Santa's assistants
30 Churchill's sign
31 What a new parent craves
32 Bamboo eater
33 On pins and needles
35 ___-de-lance

37 Space-___ (modern)
39 Auto airflow regulator
40 Over's partner
41 Ad ___ (to the stars): Lat.
46 Football strategy session
47 Memorial Day event
48 American wildcat
50 Fred's dancing sister
52 English paper
53 Love's opposite
54 Matinee hero
55 Test standard
56 Squirrel's home
57 Bruins' sch.
58 Freeway access
59 Historic times
60 On the ___ (fleeing)

ACROSS

1 Bit of parsley
6 Go crazy, slangily
10 "Woe is me!"
14 Historical 1960 John Wayne film, with "The"
15 Bit
16 Hardly the life of the party
17 Headline about lightning hitting a landfill?
19 1996 also-ran
20 Psychic's claim
21 See 2-Down
22 Get, as an idea
24 Gets ore
26 Jiffy
27 Child punishment tool?
33 Afrikaners
34 "Cool!"
35 Noted 1964 convert to Islam
36 Character
37 Offspring
39 Assist a writer
40 The Braves, on scoreboards
41 Aberdeen native
42 First sign of spring
43 What the Little Engine That Could experienced?
47 Leader in a 1972 summit meeting with Nixon
48 Scarlett's third
49 Garden pavilions
53 Faulkner's "___ Lay Dying"
54 Pub quaff
57 Skating jump
58 Student who plays hooky at noon?
61 Pro or con
62 Actor Estrada
63 Bale binder
64 "Hey!"
65 TV rooms
66 Ice cream drinks

DOWN

1 Marquis de ___
2 Sign used in a 21-Across
3 Alternative to steps
4 Mischief-maker
5 Spreads rumors
6 Less flexible
7 "Mambo No. 5" singer ___ Bega
8 Yen
9 Islamabad's country
10 Take into a flying saucer, say
11 Roller coaster part
12 Folk singer Guthrie
13 Viewed
18 Bluefin, e.g.
23 New driver's hurdle
24 Simple
25 Gramm or Grams
27 Wisdom ___
28 "You there?"

29 Right from the factory
30 r's, in geometry
31 Not of this world
32 They may be bottomless
33 Bric-a-___
37 Taught
38 Nanki-___ of "The Mikado"
39 Part of Q.E.D.
41 Wound cover
42 Drawers
44 Egg dish

45 Not the finest homes
46 Musician John
49 [You don't mean THAT!]
50 Allies' foe
51 Last letters, in England
52 Positive
54 Like a desert
55 Actress Turner
56 Snake ___ (60-Down)
59 Writer Anaïs
60 See 56-Down

ACROSS

1 Gather
6 Talk glowingly about one's children, e.g.
10 Doctrines, informally
14 Devastation
15 Prom night transportation
16 Twirl
17 Say four-letter words
18 Makes choices
19 Mrs. Chaplin
20 The rain goes ___
23 Feather
25 Spray can
26 The horse goes ___
29 Blockhead
30 Kind of wrestling
31 Socially challenged
35 Desserts with crusts
37 Cheapskate
40 Red Cross supplies
41 Throat ailment
43 Film director Kazan
45 Ely of Tarzan fame
46 The church bells go ___
50 It's between Mars and Saturn
53 Military barker
54 20-, 26- or 46-Across, e.g.
57 "Blue" or "White" river
58 Frost
59 Mr. Spock portrayer
63 English school since 1440

64 Satan's work
65 Mortimer who was asked "How can you be so stupid?"
66 Method: Abbr.
67 Depend (on)
68 Russian despots

DOWN

1 Cries at fireworks
2 Gaping mouth
3 Caesar's hello
4 Get all sudsy
5 Is frugal
6 Rorschach presentation
7 Like a yellow banana
8 Military vehicle for landing assault troops
9 Absolute truth
10 Some are radioactive
11 Leopard features
12 Sal of "Exodus"
13 Guard dog's greeting
21 Prepare to hit a golf ball
22 Elvis's middle name
23 Braid
24 Inmate who's never getting out
26 The finest
27 1979 nuclear accident site: Abbr.
28 Like oxen pulling a plow

32 Hook up again
33 Pilotless plane
34 Yin's partner
36 Lees
38 "Xanadu" rock group, for short
39 Get the suds off
42 Sandwich bread
44 Anti
47 Lower
48 Phonograph needle's place
49 Sink outlets

50 Tommy Lee or James Earl
51 Agreement
52 Pullover shirts
55 Mop's companion
56 Alternative to Charles de Gaulle
60 "Culpa" starter
61 Hockey's Bobby
62 QB's gains: Abbr.

ACROSS

1 Place for a fire
5 Oklahoma's state tree
11 Hot resort?
14 Water for Juan
15 May who directed "Ishtar"
16 Middle X of X-X-X
17 It's closed for fighting
18 Initial consideration
20 Powers that be
22 Law, in Lyon
23 Church recess
24 It sweeps across the face
27 Requiring sudden death
28 Amateur sports org.
29 Ecclesiastical gathering
31 Buckeyes' sch.
34 Ribosomal ___
36 ___ Rock (Australian tourist site)
39 Possible title for this puzzle
44 Disney theme park
45 Singing cowboy Ritter
46 Wee one
47 Windblown soil
50 "___ the Wild Wind" (DeMille movie)
53 Do library research
55 Unindustrialized
60 Actor Jannings

61 It comes with a charge
62 Flight segment
63 Headquarters
67 Thomas ___ Edison
68 Had dinner
69 Flatware factory worker
70 Boo-boo
71 Hospital unit
72 Somebody
73 London's ___ Park

DOWN

1 Parisian sidewalk sights
2 Sprightly
3 "The ___ of the spheres"
4 George C. Scott's Oscar-winning role
5 Whistle blower
6 Yalie
7 "Our Gang" girl
8 Buffalo Bill's targets: Var.
9 Piglike
10 Belle of the ball
11 Maximally dense
12 Antiquated
13 Longed (for)
19 Singer Jackson
21 Business letter abbr.
25 "Shucks!"
26 Suspend
30 Make a collar
31 Pay dirt
32 Have dinner

33 Like some airport luggage

35 Part of "D.A.": Abbr.

37 Antique auto

38 Speedy flier

40 Gray matter

41 Suffix with Canaan

42 Mannheim mister

43 Crossed (out)

48 Suppress

49 Yom Kippur horn

51 Cornball comebacks

52 Soap ingredient

53 Starting-over place

54 Ham it up

56 Everything ___ place

57 Good news on Wall Street

58 More than miffed

59 Arrange gracefully

64 Antonym: Abbr.

65 Top of the corp. ladder

66 Seabird

ACROSS

1 "___ for the poor"
5 German author Hermann
10 Iridescent gem
14 Lamb : sheep :: kid : ___
15 Crowning points
16 Whitish
17 Horrible boss
18 Unexpected benefits
19 They may be smoked or pickled
20 1974 Mel Brooks comedy
23 Fancy drinking glass
24 Optometrist's interest
25 Common name for sodium hydroxide
26 As well
27 Wettish
30 New moon, e.g.
32 Gumbo ingredient
34 Halloween cry
35 ___ constrictor
36 1959 film with Marilyn Monroe
41 Suffix with Paul
42 To do this is human
43 In for the night
45 Whitish
48 Fix up
50 Susan of "The Partridge Family"
51 Norma ___ (Sally Field role)
52 Raises, as the ante
55 Military greeting
57 Best Picture of 1981
61 It's hard to believe
62 Baby grand, e.g.
63 Guardianship
65 More than annoys
66 Distant planet
67 Particular
68 Apple carrier
69 Divvy up
70 Turner and Danson

DOWN

1 In the past
2 Ships' records
3 ___ Man (classic ad figure)
4 Great buy
5 Fit for living
6 Supply-and-demand subj.
7 Grimy air
8 Have a hunch
9 Think piece
10 ___ page (place for a 9-Down)
11 Spanish dish with rice
12 Bowling spots
13 Apartment dweller
21 A's opposite, in England
22 Bus station
23 1960s Pontiac muscle car
28 "You don't mean me?!"
29 Game played with a straight . . . or a straight face

31 Big laugh
33 French friend
35 Place for a claw
37 World-weariness
38 Before, to a bard
39 Bull-headed
40 Was on the brink
44 Blonde's secret, maybe
45 Extremely cold
46 Libyan expanse
47 Doctor
49 Stumblebum

53 The old man
54 Silence
56 Permissible
58 Take it easy
59 "Herzog" author Bellow
60 Latch ___ (get)
64 Ens' preceders

ACROSS

1 Game of kings and queens
6 Show snide satisfaction
11 Act like
14 Artificial jewelry
15 Winchester, for one
16 Lobster ___ Diavolo
17 Pounce on some mariners' gear
19 In favor of
20 Gusto
21 Off the leash
23 Where Woodstock can be found
27 Used a teaspoon
29 Changes
30 Interlaced
31 Card catalogue listing
32 Fetch
33 Pompous person
36 List ender
37 Really bad
38 "___ first you don't . . ."
39 Kind of room
40 Bowwow
41 Hacienda brick
42 Black belt activity
44 Capital of South Dakota
45 Military school
47 Celebrated Mardi Gras, in a way
48 ___ 6
49 Maintained

50 Victoria's Secret purchase
51 Validate, businesswise
58 Resinous substance
59 Ruin of a statue, perhaps
60 Tennessee footballer
61 Wapiti
62 Live
63 Sonneteer's Muse

DOWN

1 I.R.S. job applicant, maybe
2 Owns
3 Tee preceder
4 Sched. locale
5 Confiscation
6 Hawaiian skirt material
7 Top 10, e.g.
8 "Birth ___ Nation"
9 Actress MacGraw
10 Revelatory
11 Be able to buy some wheels
12 Simple writing
13 Like an ewer
18 "___ Fall in Love"
22 Refinable rock
23 Object of a Latin prayer
24 Cream of the crop
25 Start hammering
26 Carter of sitcoms
27 Make a rustling sound

Puzzle 110 by Richard Silvestri

28 Pint-sized
30 Armistice
32 Spoils of war
34 Buffalo hockey player
35 Spirited horse
37 Rich soil
38 Concept
40 Church dignitary
41 When a show is
broadcast
43 Citrus drink
44 It may be read
45 Stroll

46 Reef material
47 Candidate of 1992
and 1996
49 Sound like a snake
52 CBS competitor
53 Night that "Miami
Vice" was on: Abbr.
54 Christmas buy
55 Call ___ day
56 Betrayer
57 L-P filler

ACROSS

1 Dept. of Labor division
5 Be ill-humored
9 Bloodhound's clue
14 Erupt
15 Shortly
16 Handles the situation
17 Go around the Internet
18 Monopoly equipment
19 Ralph's wife, on "The Honeymooners"
20 Nonstop
23 1970 Kinks hit
24 Rooster's mate
25 Little League coach, often
28 Firefighter, at times
31 Sault ___ Marie
34 Change with the times
36 Broke bread
37 Fisherman's bucketful
38 Nonstop
42 Willy of "Free Willy"
43 Perceive
44 Suitably
45 Hillary Clinton, ___ Rodham
46 ___ tank
49 Sushi fish
50 Instigate litigation
51 Spring bloom
53 Nonstop
60 Main impact
61 Ill-mannered
62 Lasso
63 "Last ___ in Paris"
64 Comparable
65 Submachine guns
66 Out-and-out
67 Sugar source
68 Repressed, with "up"

DOWN

1 Mount in Greek myth
2 It's used with a "giddyup!"
3 Medal recipient
4 More than bad
5 Word before shoe or soap
6 #19 of the Colts
7 ___ Ness
8 Where a cap is found on the body
9 Tackle box gizmo
10 :
11 Grand in scale
12 Bottle part
13 When doubled, an African fly
21 Toward cooler weather, say
22 "Give me an A . . .," e.g.
25 Matt of "The Talented Mr. Ripley"
26 Like a lot
27 "Shall we ___?"
29 Handle the food for a party
30 Rocky Mountain Indian
31 "À votre ___" (toast)
32 Card catalogue entry
33 Kind of alcohol

Puzzle 111 by Gregory E. Paul

35 Kind of meeting at a school
37 Certain jazz
39 Pale-faced
40 Service charge
41 Pokémon card collecting, e.g.
46 Gentleman caller
47 Annapolis student
48 Gung-ho
50 "The Playboy of the Western World" author

52 Pancake topper
53 "Doggone it!"
54 Em, to Dorothy
55 Palestinian
56 Deadly missile
57 Trickle
58 ___ arms (angry)
59 Audition
60 A.C. capacity

ACROSS

1 Poker variation
5 Sources of delight
9 Bashful, e.g.
14 Improve, as one's skills
15 Sector
16 Contest in the West
17 Milo's pal, in a 1989 film
18 Word after body or grand
19 Avoid answering
20 "While I'm away on vacation, would you ___ . . . ?"
23 Object of an old French cheer
24 Gives in to gravity
25 Quick-witted
28 Over there, poetically
30 Surface sheen
32 Battering device
35 "And ___ . . . ?"
38 Designer Cassini
40 Teeny
41 One of two on a brig
42 "And ___ . . . ?"
47 Place to do the samba
48 Editor/suffragist Bloomer
49 Begin a hand
51 Neither's partner
52 Nudge forward
55 Streetcars

58 "And ___?"
61 Stick that's waved
64 Plane prefix
65 Old TV clown
66 Glorify
67 Alka-Seltzer jingle starter
68 Started a gunfight
69 Tropical lizard
70 Political doctrines
71 Capitol Hill worker

DOWN

1 Third place
2 Wreck beyond recognition
3 Bring together
4 Catch sight of
5 Incense scent
6 Paris airport
7 Informal affirmatives
8 Pago Pago's place
9 Put on one's Sunday best
10 Made a tapestry
11 Cavity fillers' org.
12 Like a sunset
13 Any Hatfield, to a McCoy
21 Foot that goes clop
22 Hideous
25 How some stocks sell
26 Coke competitor
27 "___ Remember" (1960 song)
29 Like a morning meadow
31 Addition solution

Puzzle 112 by Patrick Jordan

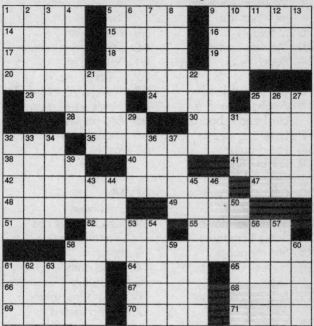

32 Mr. Bean portrayer Atkinson
33 Crockett's last stand
34 Cabbie's counter
36 Neighbor of Md.
37 Honey drink
39 Hairstyling goop
43 Attack verbally
44 Painter Chagall
45 Does a swab's job
46 Not (a one)
50 Kappa follower
53 Giraffelike beast

54 Combats of honor
56 New Zealand native
57 Measured, with "up"
58 Tyler and Taylor's go-between
59 Place for a king and queen
60 1993 Emmy-winner Chad
61 Dog command
62 Chopper
63 Middle X or O

ACROSS

1 What an umbrella may provide
6 Moolah
10 Mama's partner
14 Dead, as an engine
15 Gallic girlfriend
16 Appliance with a cord and a board
17 Hole-___
18 Head-butts
19 Former Speaker Gingrich
20 Office fasteners
22 "Trick" joint
23 Symbol of slowness
24 Some Romanovs
25 Stir-fry pan
28 Former Detroit auto inits.
29 Belgian composer Jacques
31 Safe to eat
33 Not rigid
37 Gaucho's weapon
38 Neighbor of Egypt
40 Docking spot
41 Vegetable with a head
43 Went ape
45 "Kiss me, ___"
46 Norm: Abbr.
47 Opposite of NNW
48 Embezzlement, e.g.
51 Battery terminal
53 Rock's partner

54 They're seen in air traffic control towers
59 Nay sayer
60 Dinner from a bucket
61 Foil maker
62 Chicken site
63 "Psycho" actress Miles
64 Members of a pride
65 Sea eagles
66 Locked (up)
67 Raises some interest?

DOWN

1 Pass over
2 Czech tennis ace Mandlikova
3 Each
4 Sand drifts
5 Unending
6 Scampi seasoning
7 Memo from a dot-com, maybe
8 Not having much body
9 Actress Harper
10 Fires
11 "Gladiator" setting
12 Major nation
13 Pays to play
21 King Arthur's home
24 Gore-___ (fabric)
25 "Dragnet" star
26 What the nose knows
27 Prefix with hertz
29 Round-the-world traveler Nellie

Puzzle 113 by Marjorie Berg

30 One with a lot to offer?
32 Reverse springs
33 J. Edgar Hoover's org.
34 Computer units
35 Hawaiian neckwear
36 One-named Art Deco designer
39 ___ de France
42 Jazz man
44 Eccentric
46 Speak sharply to

48 Not do original drawings
49 "Employee of the Month," e.g.
50 Pop-rocker John
51 Deck out
52 "Dallas" matriarch Miss ___
54 Invitation request
55 Toward shelter
56 Computer image
57 Frog's home
58 Back talk

ACROSS

1 "Macbeth" quintet
5 Distort
9 Place for a mirrored ball
14 Smith Brothers unit
15 Actress Spelling
16 Poland Spring competitor
17 Object of a classic pursuit
19 43-Across division
20 Rice University mascot
21 The life of ___
22 Tee off
23 S. & L. offerings
24 Lupino of "High Sierra"
25 Elvis or Fabian, once
26 Childbirth
31 Kind of wool or drum
34 Some drafts
35 Rocky pinnacle
36 Didn't give way
37 Eric Clapton classic
39 Jim-dandy
40 Before, to Burns
41 Haughty pose
42 Tack on
43 Hellish literary work
47 Aardvark's meal
48 Brian of Roxy Music
49 Shriver of tennis
52 Photo finish
54 Family name at Indy
56 In need of salting, perhaps
57 Little green man
58 You can't touch this
60 Embellish
61 Deer sir
62 Gumbo ingredient
63 Heavenly gift
64 ___ -poly
65 Part of MOMA's address

DOWN

1 Kind of committee
2 Jam-pack
3 Trucker's expense
4 Le Carré character
5 Big step
6 Eucalyptus-eating animals
7 Iroquoian Indian
8 Cunning
9 The Roaring 20s and others
10 Chekhov's first play
11 Playing card without a match
12 Blanchett of "Elizabeth"
13 ___ close to schedule
18 Give the third degree
25 Brainstorm
26 Fourposter, e.g.
27 Final authority
28 Wright wing?
29 Poor dog's portion
30 "Jurassic Park" beast, for short
31 Get rid of

Puzzle 114 by Randall J. Hartman

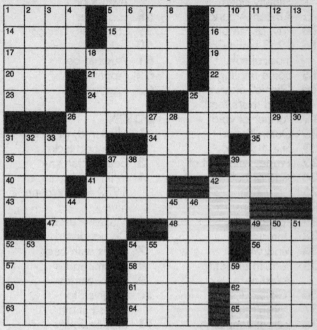

32 Hatcher of "Lois & Clark"
33 One mile, for Denver
37 Golf positions
38 Compass creation
39 "___ Given Sunday"
41 One of a bug's pair
42 Be nuts over
44 Trainee or detainee
45 Peyote
46 The "E" in E = mc²
49 Hard to please
50 Squirreled-away item

51 Sinatra classic
52 Hat-tipper's word
53 "Betsy's Wedding" star
54 The Beatles' "Back in the ___"
55 Cold war winner
59 Mafia figure

ACROSS

1 Slightly open
5 African-American
10 Pay, as the bill
14 1953 Leslie Caron musical role
15 Spine-tingling
16 "Picnic" playwright
17 "And that's that!"
19 Partner of void
20 Outer: Prefix
21 See 4-Down
22 Evade, with "out of"
24 Kind of bag
25 ___ weevil
26 ___ corpus
29 Routine
33 Unreactive
34 Madam
35 Peak in ancient Palestine
36 "Go, ___!"
37 Doesn't just diet
38 School zone sign
39 Former Atlanta arena
40 Second voice
41 Spin
42 When both hands are together
44 Treasure locales
45 Open to the breeze
46 Wedding cake feature
47 Carry all over the place
50 Throws a shot
51 Bandleader Brown
54 Come into view

55 Not plan A or B, or even X or Y
58 ___ mater
59 "Farewell, François"
60 Exhort
61 Adult-to-be
62 Approvals
63 Egg holder

DOWN

1 Sheltered, at sea
2 Give bad luck
3 Beefy actor Ray
4 With 21-Across, a 1970 John Wayne film
5 Makes soused
6 Do not disturb
7 Suffix with buck
8 Geom. figure
9 Index entries
10 It's given to Regis Philbin
11 Responsibility
12 Look at lustfully
13 Be a snitch
18 Parade sight
23 Lodge member
24 Michael Crichton novel, with "The"
25 Greet ceremoniously
26 Make a pass at
27 Prefix with meter
28 Betting game
29 What's not used
30 Places for heros
31 Call off, at Cape Canaveral

Puzzle 115 by Nick Grivas

32 Cat calls
34 Favorable forecast
37 Referee's demand
41 "We hold ___ truths . . ."
43 Item with a clip or a pin
44 Like oranges and lemons
46 Student getting one-on-one help
47 Bed board
48 ___ slaw

49 It's where the heart is
50 Letters before omegas
51 Folk tales and such
52 Work units
53 "Leave it," to a typesetter
56 Summer drink
57 Ice melter

ACROSS

1 Two smackers?
5 "___ la Douce"
9 Is eliminated from competition
14 Yearn (for)
15 Contemptible one
16 Take over
17 Mason's wedge
18 Italian lake
19 Hawaiian party site
20 1932 novel of crime and race by 40-Across
23 British biscuit
25 Berlin bar need
26 One-on-one sport
27 From a personal standpoint
30 Slump
32 Genesis victim
33 Symbol of sturdiness
35 Mind terribly
40 See 20- and 57-Across
43 Hung around
44 ___ -de-sac
45 Cutting part
46 Q-U connection
48 Kind of film
50 It may react with an acid
54 Swiss canton
56 Fish that's split for cooking
57 Fictional county, locale of 20-Across
61 Hearty breakfast dish

62 MOMA artist
63 "Bus Stop" playwright
66 Cheri of "Saturday Night Live"
67 Dash
68 Hoops tournament org.
69 Bells the cat
70 "Auld Lang ___"
71 Dinero

DOWN

1 ___ Vegas
2 German pronoun
3 In myth she was changed into a nightingale
4 From the very beginning
5 Dermatologist's concern
6 Kind of vegetable
7 Ike's mate
8 Poster boy
9 Lollapalooza
10 ___ orange
11 Dawn
12 Delete
13 Maliciousness
21 Washington, e.g.: Abbr.
22 Usually
23 Bandleader Artie and others
24 Biblical length
28 Packs a lot in

29 Edible 6-Down
31 Hair goop
34 Popular fast-food chain
36 Outlining
37 Marathoner's trait
38 The "N" of UNCF
39 Unable to escape
41 Ending with cash or bombard
42 "___ Wiedersehen"
47 Swaps
49 Nile reptile

50 "I swear . . .!"
51 Feeder of the body's organs
52 Winter sight at Tahoe
53 ___ nous
55 Where Soave comes from
58 Yard sale tag
59 Ladd or Alda
60 Soave, e.g.
64 Guy's honey
65 "Dig in!"

ACROSS

1 Hertz competitor
5 Mature
10 Play parts
14 1/500 of the Indianapolis 500
15 Wear away
16 ___ cheese (salad topping)
17 Animal skin
18 Valley ___, Pa.
19 Wild pig
20 Where to get scared
23 Org. with secrets
26 "___ a small world . . ."
27 Second of two
28 Still rumpled, as a bed
30 Wineglass features
32 Where to get jarred
34 Insane
37 Child most likely to be spanked
38 ___ de Janeiro
39 Satisfy a hankering
40 Hankering
41 Where to get dizzy
44 Hoity-toity sorts
46 Debit's partner
47 "Little ___ Annie"
50 Decorated war pilot
51 Place to recuperate
52 Gentle alternative to 20-, 32- and 41-Across
56 Shaking chill
57 Computer operators
58 Greasy
62 Full house, e.g.
63 Crème de la crème
64 Quote as an example
65 Bartenders tender them
66 Echolocation
67 Baby goats

DOWN

1 Piece of band equipment
2 Compete
3 Down with the flu
4 Son of Adam and Eve
5 Opponent in an argument
6 Shackles
7 Harbor
8 Perimeter
9 Christmas tree shedding
10 Monastery heads
11 Influence
12 Hardly the prim sort
13 More certain
21 Campaign worker
22 Boars Head product
23 Small compartment
24 Become accustomed (to)
25 Jordan's capital
29 Liable
30 Leaves harbor
31 Gait faster than a walk

33 Test taker's dirty secret
34 Hotel cleaners
35 Just clear of the ocean floor
36 Altanta-based airline
39 "What ___ Is" (1988 #1 country hit)
41 Languages
42 Plaintiff
43 Carolina ___ (little songster)
44 Rips to bits
45 Opponent's vote

47 University of Nebraska campus site
48 Magnificent
49 Wrinkly fruit
50 Major blood carrier
53 Nobel Peace Prize city
54 Bridle strap
55 Loading area
59 Caesar's three
60 Inc., in Britain
61 "You bet!"

ACROSS

1. ___ Lee cakes
5. Nifty
9. Places for plaques
14. Sit (down)
15. "This round's ___"
16. Duck
17. Charitable donations
18. Brain wave
19. Moses' mount
20. John Denver sang it in 1975
23. French sea
24. "___ out!" (ump's call)
25. Dis's opposite
26. School zone caution
28. Posture problem
30. Piercing places
32. Shakespeare's was "mortal"
33. Steamed (up)
35. Boozer
36. Make ___ dash for
37. Gwen Verdon sang it in 1966
41. "Out with it!"
42. Nod from offstage, maybe
43. Toupee, slangily
44. Inn inventory
45. Lip service?
47. Kind of list
51. Word before and after "oh"
52. Hobbyist's place
53. "Take out the trash," repeatedly
55. Xmas time: Abbr.
56. Elvis Presley sang it in 1962
60. Calf-length skirts
61. Cuddly "Return of the Jedi" creature
62. Pierce player on "M*A*S*H"
63. In a rut
64. Small, medium or large
65. Like the diver's end of the pool
66. Illicit cab
67. Act the worrywart
68. Tacks on

DOWN

1. Jerks
2. Completely off-base
3. The Joker portrayer Cesar
4. Church alcove
5. Boom or zoom
6. Stand the test of time
7. U.S.A. part: Abbr.
8. Pendant gem shape
9. "Fuzzy Wuzzy ___ fuzzy"
10. Gung-ho
11. Wanting company
12. 1997 Jim Carrey comedy
13. Reagan's long-range plan?: Abbr.

Puzzle 118 by Nancy Salomon and Sherry O. Blackard

21 Laid-back
22 Break time
27 Vintage
29 "But of course!"
31 Silly sorts
32 Bum off of
34 Heart
37 Boisterous fun
38 Tied
39 Brand in a bar
40 Elbow
41 Looker's leg

46 Catch some Z's
48 Mixed up
49 Had to have
50 Tidbits for Fido
52 Somewhat dark
54 Cockeyed
57 Nervous twitches
58 Simple Simon
59 Zapata's "zip"
60 Flavor enhancer,
     briefly

ACROSS

1 A property may have one on it
5 Sound of a fall
10 Robed
14 Singer Arnold
15 Piece of garlic
16 Tiptop
17 NATO's first supreme commander
19 Bone parallel to the radius
20 Stage actress Caldwell
21 General Motors line, for short
22 Deodorant type
24 They'll show you the world
26 Done, in Dijon
27 Dickens's orphan in "Great Expectations"
28 Tropical plant with a trunklike stem
32 Military capability
35 Stead
36 Polite turndown
37 Russian orbiter
38 Ship navigation aid
39 Uzbekistan's ___ Sea
40 Leafy shelter
42 Massachusetts's nickname
44 H_2O at 0°
45 Radio amateurs
46 Stranger in a strange land?
50 Win back one's losses
53 Lions and tigers
54 Cause for sudden death
55 "There oughta be ___!"
56 Academic enclave
59 Not yours or theirs
60 Swab the deck again
61 Old piano tunes
62 Ibsen's "___ Gynt"
63 Tickle pink
64 Fortuneteller's opening

DOWN

1 Host Gibbons
2 Numbskull
3 1950s Ford flop
4 Bill ___, the Science Guy
5 Lug around
6 Walks like a workhorse
7 Areas on weather maps
8 "___ Maria"
9 Wirehair, e.g.
10 It has a big head
11 Hang (around)
12 ___ Domini
13 University V.I.P.
18 More meddlesome
23 It's next to nothing
25 Spring event
26 "___ Jacques" (children's song)
28 Bale binder
29 Yeats's land
30 Kind of admiral
31 Woman of habit?

Puzzle 119 by Dave and Diane Epperson

32 ___ song (cheaply)
33 "___, old chap"
34 Leaves out
36 Catch in the act
38 Part of a biblical plague
40 Dracula, for one
41 Genetically related organisms
43 St. Anthony's cross
46 Diviner's deck
47 "___ a dark and stormy night . . ."

48 Start of a long battle
49 Short-winded
50 Wheelchair access
51 Author Wiesel
52 Sugar source
53 Film "sleeper" of 1978
57 Speed: Abbr.
58 "Either you say it ___ will"

ACROSS
1 "You missed a ___!"
5 Hilo hello
10 Summer place
14 Heather Headley title role on Broadway
15 Lions' locks
16 Concluded
17 2000 runner
19 Alternative to hot pants
20 Go astray
21 They're on tap in taprooms
22 Coats with gold
23 Stir up
24 Humor that's not funny
26 Classic Chevy
29 Broadway aunt
30 ___ dog (backwoods animal)
31 Game for the asocial
36 What 55-Across is to 17-Across
39 Toppled, in a way
40 Reply to the Little Red Hen
41 "Off with you!"
42 Frank
44 Part of a freight train
48 ___ on (orders to attack)
49 Ill-gotten gains
50 Prego competitor
51 Part of a litter
54 Sparkling wine center
55 See 36-Across

58 Rung
59 Restaurateur of song
60 Brezhnev's land
61 Famous alter ego
62 Got smart, with "up"
63 Ravioli filler

DOWN
1 Solomon
2 Jetty
3 Locker room emanation
4 Driveway material
5 Aviator Earhart
6 RCA or Columbia
7 Burden
8 "___ a Rebel" (1962 #1 hit)
9 Straight-grained wood
10 Chris Rock, for one
11 1950s Indians All-Star Bobby
12 Darns
13 Rainbow maker
18 Famous Dartmoor facility
22 Garbo of "Anna Christie"
23 Dude's place?
24 First course, maybe
25 Notorious Idi
26 Like shrimp during shipping
27 Infiltrator
28 Langston Hughes, e.g.
29 Dollars and Deutsche marks

Puzzle 120 by Ed Early

31 Echo analyzer
32 Choreographer de Mille
33 Monopoly token
34 5¢/gallon, e.g.
35 Head of state in Kuwait
37 Vestige
38 Where Red Delicious apples originated
42 Like a London jurist
43 Some hosp. rooms
44 Jiffy

45 Robust
46 Functioned
47 Rubbish
48 50-Across, e.g.
50 McGwire stats
51 Sit for a photograph
52 ___ Minor
53 Overly familiar, maybe
55 Hee's follower
56 Whitney of gin fame
57 Ruin, with "up"

ACROSS

1 Lump of cream, for example
5 Open a bit
9 Man with a fable
14 Debauchee
15 Wowser
16 Lollipop flavor
17 Really happy, as an angel?
20 ___ dish
21 Al or Tipper
22 When said three times, a 1970 war movie
23 Sault ___ Marie
25 Without principles
27 Really happy, as a kid in March?
33 "Garfield" dog
34 H.S. junior's test
35 Concur
40 Tony-winner Moore
42 7, on a phone
43 Tailless hoppers
44 Really bother
45 They have their pluses and minuses
47 Currier's partner in lithography
48 Really happy, as a meteorologist?
51 Auto trim
55 Unit of energy
56 Raise, as kids
57 "Two Years Before the ___"
61 "Measure twice, cut once," e.g.

65 Really happy, as a mountaineer?
68 Teatime treat
69 Bulrush, e.g.
70 Remove from a mother's milk
71 Monsieur: Paris :: ___ : Madrid
72 Isn't keeping up with bills
73 Zippo

DOWN

1 Tight hold
2 Sole
3 Bump from office
4 Southernmost city of ancient Palestine
5 Pub order
6 Father of Analytical Psychology
7 Choir voice
8 German industrial region
9 Paleontologist's estimate
10 A Muse
11 Relish
12 "Lohengrin," e.g.
13 Kind of code
18 Ars longa, ___ brevis
19 Miami basketball team
24 Debatable "skill"
26 Vegetarians eschew it (NOT chew it)
27 "Where the heart is"
28 Concept
29 Coated with gold
30 Savory jelly

Puzzle 121 by Richard Hughes

31 Pope John Paul II's real first name
32 "___ skin off my nose!"
36 Submerging
37 Sitarist Shankar
38 Garden with a snake
39 Start of North Carolina's motto
41 Part of a molecule
46 Take to court
49 Nautilus captain
50 Sketch

51 Angry
52 From now on
53 Betray, in a way
54 Maine college town
58 60s do
59 Fret
60 You, to the Amish
62 Region
63 Happy
64 ___ St. Vincent Millay
66 For each
67 Newsman Bradley et al.

ACROSS

1 On the ocean
6 Andy's radio partner
10 Dish that sticks to your ribs
14 Hunky-dory
15 1993 film in which Kevin Kline played the president
16 Chair-raising experience?
17 Miami sights
18 Kind of hygiene
19 Singer Redding
20 Don Shula or Knute Rockne
23 "___ Misérables"
25 Doc for a boxer
26 Expenditure
27 Single-celled protozoa
30 Place to have a pint
31 Less common
32 Mickey's creator
34 Comics canine
38 Scold severely
41 Cheers for banderilleros
42 Bitter drinks
43 Seashore
44 Insect in a colony
45 Goodness
46 On the train
50 Luau food
52 "___ Haw"
53 Rosa Parks Day
57 Bread spread
58 "Oh, that'll happen!"
59 Heart outlet

62 Blueprint
63 Intent look
64 Plane seating division (and the key to this puzzle's theme)
65 Change for a twenty
66 Sought damages
67 Part of a ruble

DOWN

1 Killer snake
2 U.S. Airways competitor
3 Like buffet restaurants
4 Ticklish doll guy
5 In addition
6 Building brick
7 French radical murdered in his bathtub
8 White House office shape
9 Events with no empty seats
10 Make a film
11 Horribly wreck
12 "Fear of Flying" writer Jong
13 Wishy-___
21 Attachments to VCR's
22 Chicago athlete
23 Key ___
24 Correspondence that may come with attachments
28 Apiary residents
29 High school elective
30 In addition

32 Whip mark
33 Homer Simpson's dad
34 ___ about (approximately)
35 Ira Levin play
36 Matter of dispute
37 Cosmetician Lauder
39 Lipstick holders
40 Here, in France
44 Radius's place
45 The Henry who founded the Tudor line
46 Take in, as a stray cat

47 "Beauty and the Beast" beauty
48 Indian ___
49 Ages and ages
50 Trophy
51 Killed, slangily
54 Rebecca and Isaac's eldest
55 Spice holder
56 Fly without a co-pilot
60 Mao ___-tung
61 Interview

ACROSS

1 Arm bones
6 Tiny swab
10 Rat-___
14 "___ We All?" (old show tune)
15 With the bow, in music
16 Falls behind
17 Cores
18 Christmas song
19 Money in Milano
20 Witch's phrase, in "Macbeth"
23 Dolt
24 Alliance since 1948: Abbr.
25 Washington's ___ Sound
27 Pep rally cry
30 Tennis champ Ilie
32 Resolutely
35 Bricks measure
36 End of beach season, to many
41 Sheep-ish one
42 Impart, as values
43 Pathetic bumbler
46 Polite turndown
50 Beginners
51 Summer hours in Pa.
53 Baton Rouge sch.
54 Piece of unfinished business
59 It goes to waist
60 Deserving a C
61 Integrates
62 ___ fruit
63 Nutrient in spinach
64 Skirt style
65 Boxer's punching spot
66 Ditto
67 Midterms and finals

DOWN

1 Disheveled
2 Bach piece
3 Partner of cease
4 The "I" in IHOP: Abbr.
5 "___ Long Way to Tipperary"
6 Lecture follower, briefly
7 Gaits slower than gallops
8 Cake decorator
9 Game on horseback
10 Nearly
11 Follow too closely
12 Consents to
13 Mao ___-tung
21 Wandering
22 Raises
26 Care for
28 Old name for Tokyo
29 ___ Lingus
30 Former Speaker Gingrich
31 Corroded
33 Moist, as a cellar
34 Method: Abbr.
36 For fear that
37 Jackie Gleason catchphrase, with "And"

Puzzle 123 by Elizabeth C. Gorski

38 Sleeping bags
39 "Telephone Line" rock grp.
40 Carrier to Amsterdam
44 Troop movement
45 Request
47 French writer ___ de Tocqueville
48 Concurrence
49 Disarranges, as the hair
51 England's ___ Downs

52 Unengaging speaking voice
55 Egyptian fertility goddess
56 "Heartburn" author Ephron
57 Coll. senior's hurdle
58 Anger, with "up"
59 Hamburger helper?

ACROSS

1 ". . . and carry ___ stick"
5 Concerning
9 With 69-Across, locales for this puzzle's theme
14 Mugger repellent
15 Ensure the failure of
16 Divination deck
17 "Who ___?" (knock response)
18 History test answer
19 Make giddy with delight
20 "Kitty Foyle" Oscar winner
23 Vice president with a "Jr." in his name
24 Brouhaha
25 Over: Fr.
28 ___ Spumante
31 Baby bottle topper
33 U.N.C. is in it
36 Word from the wise
38 Where birds fly in the fall
41 What "it" plays
42 Pittsburgh product
43 Brown-nose
46 A.M.A. members
47 "Ripe" stage of life
48 Jacob's twin
50 6-pointers
51 Altar avowal
53 Dishes
58 TV staple since 1969
61 Have dinner at home

64 Seasoned sailor
65 57-Down request
66 Draw ___ in the sand
67 Notion
68 About 30% of the earth's land
69 See 9-Across
70 Burn with a branding iron
71 Be "it"

DOWN

1 Old computer
2 Actor Rathbone
3 Cake topper
4 Very beginning
5 State of the Union, e.g.
6 Fly high
7 Dog in Oz
8 Alpha's opposite
9 Some bodybuilders' body builders
10 Cronies
11 Lyricist Gershwin
12 Barracks bed
13 Summer on the Seine
21 Piece of history
22 1999–2000 "Dame" on Broadway
25 Looked in (on)
26 Stress symptom, they say
27 Projection booth items
29 "Later!"
30 "___ at the office"
32 Cpl.'s inferior
33 Yachtsman's neckwear

Puzzle 124 by Chris Sallade

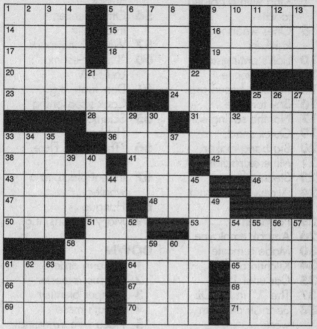

34 Was capable of
35 Half of Miss Muffet's dish
37 Capital I's?
39 ___ -la-la
40 Cleanliness regimens
44 Agents from D.C.
45 Eminem, e.g.
49 Nth deg.
52 Caravan's spot
54 Rich tapestry
55 Flirt with
56 Goosebump-raising

57 The turf in "surf and turf"
58 Wash-up spot
59 Fabricated
60 Philosopher Zeno of ___
61 Swab target
62 In the style of
63 Personal quirk

ACROSS

1 King with a golden touch
6 Ones wearing knickers
10 Lion's antithesis
14 Sports venue
15 Mideast-based grp.
16 Say for sure
17 Not the sailing sort
19 Quick snack
20 Big bang maker
21 Mine extraction
22 Steamroll
24 Access the Internet, with "on"
25 Postpone
26 Amtrak employee
30 Made a movie
34 Kitchen or den
35 Car until 1957
37 The "L" in AWOL
38 Spanish museum work
39 Squirrels' homes
41 Diva's song
42 Put on a happy face
44 Confident
45 Obsolescent phone feature
46 "What's ___ you?"
48 Drill instructor, usually
50 They "just want to have fun" in a 1984 song
52 Ruin

53 "The Satanic Verses" author
56 Office seeker, informally
57 Wide of the mark
60 "L' ___ c'est moi": Louis XIV
61 Don Juan, e.g.
64 Cook's seasoning
65 Scientologist ___ Hubbard
66 "The Magic Flute," e.g.
67 In that place, to a whaler
68 Hangup
69 Mary Poppins, e.g.

DOWN

1 Drive-in order
2 Big rug exporter
3 Bumper blemish
4 What's more
5 Place with swinging doors
6 Rounded part
7 N.Y.P.D. alert
8 Mower maker
9 Back of the neck
10 Samuel Gompers, e.g.
11 Tel ___, Israel
12 Dish (out)
13 ___ Fox
18 FedEx notation
23 Moon man Armstrong
24 Stage star
25 "The Cat in the Hat" writer

Puzzle 125 by Gregory E. Paul

26 Clean a blackboard
27 Actress Shearer
28 Cry after a catch
29 Supports for specs
31 Newswoman Shriver
32 Poland Spring competitor
33 Handed out, as cards
36 Roll call reply
40 Billy Graham delivery
43 Novelist Bagnold

47 Gives the third degree
49 Cider unit
51 Live's companion
53 Downtime
54 Four Corners state
55 Sweeping story
56 Engine knock
57 Dutch cooker
58 Forest plant
59 Skirmish
62 ___ fault (overmuch)
63 ___-Locka, Fla.

ACROSS

1 Door frame upright
5 Muslim's journey
9 Mosque officials
14 Kind of arguments
15 "Typee" sequel
16 KwaZulu-___ province, South Africa
17 Airport/hotel connection
18 Take to ___ (reprimand)
19 Sales clerk's minimum
20 Faces up to expected hardship
23 Tappan ___ Bridge
24 Le ___ Soleil (Louis XIV)
25 Soapmaking need
26 Snake with a nasty bite
29 Reindeer herder
32 Promgoers: Abbr.
34 Emotes
40 Muscle quality
41 Prefix with center
42 1997 Peter Fonda title role
43 Falls for a scam
48 Kipling novel
49 Shirt brand
50 Start of the 16th century
51 Ex of Frank and Artie
54 Singer Zadora
56 Moon vehicle
58 Takes in recent events
64 Sicily's "kicker"
65 Act on, as advice
66 Gung-ho quality
68 Constellation with a belt
69 Linen color
70 "Beetle Bailey" boob
71 Part of SST
72 Carpentry class
73 Thumbs-up

DOWN

1 Scribble
2 Riyadh resident
3 Shin-covering skirt
4 Football charge
5 Chair facing Regis Philbin, with "the"
6 Latin 101 verb
7 Kid
8 Ace topper
9 Ask
10 Stake-driving hammer
11 Bikini, for one
12 Brit's buddy
13 Candidate list
21 Snakelike swimmers
22 Pear variety
26 "Hamlet" has five
27 Come in third
28 Elizabeth of "La Bamba"
30 "That was close!"
31 RC competitor
33 Social rebuff
35 "Champagne music" maestro

Puzzle 126 by Bill Zais

36 Therapeutic kind of bath
37 Western film actor Jack
38 Nevada Sen. Harry
39 Himalayan legend
44 Not really sing
45 Leave out
46 Hid from pursuers
47 First place?
51 "So long"
52 In ___ fertilization
53 Once more

55 Contents of some urns
57 Certain soprano
59 "The Time Machine" people
60 Kind of support
61 Decorated cop, say
62 Half a fortnight
63 "___ Smile" (Hall & Oates hit)
67 Moviedom's Myrna

ACROSS

1 Hunter in the night sky
6 Gush
10 "Get out!"
14 AM/FM device
15 Artificially jazz (up)
16 ___ vault
17 Where Elsie looks for a husband?
19 Water pitcher
20 Guileful
21 Actress Judith
22 World Cup sport
24 "National Velvet" author Bagnold
25 Knickknack
26 Like the word of God
29 "No, it doesn't make you look fat," maybe
32 747, e.g.
33 Entices
34 Cut off, as branches
35 Watch amorously
36 Throws, as dice
37 One-time divorce mecca
38 Clodhopper
39 Drying ovens
40 Mr. Spock's forte
41 It's yellow and crusty
43 Full of modern gadgetry
44 Complete change of course
45 Superman accessory
46 Birthplace of St. Francis

48 Kind of grapes
49 Civil War inits.
52 Tetched in the head
53 Phone message from Elsie's friends?
56 Buddies
57 Rework, as stories
58 Quarrel
59 German battleship Graf ___
60 Poet Teasdale
61 Some blondes

DOWN

1 Sun and moon, for example
2 Julia of "The Addams Family"
3 Without purpose
4 Squeaky wheel's need
5 Convention V.I.P.
6 Scrap paper?
7 Dawdling
8 Squeeze (out)
9 Divers' wear
10 Coined money
11 Where Elsie gets educated?
12 Not aweather
13 Dakotas, once: Abbr.
18 Greedy
23 Table scraps
24 White-tailed eagle
25 Signed I.O.U.'s
26 Thread holder
27 Low end of the food chain

Puzzle 127 by Sherry O. Blackard and Lyell Rodieck

28 What Elsie's child develops at the gym?
29 Trash
30 Like some Greek columns
31 Memorable time
33 Yacht club site
36 Whims
37 Mechanical learning
39 Burden
40 Take the words out of one's mouth?

42 Idle
43 Thieves' booty
45 Terra ___
46 Peaks near Bern
47 Camay, for one
48 Ado
49 Zoo feature
50 Ugly putdown
51 Pub offerings
54 Nabokov novel
55 Hue's partner

ACROSS

1 Nerd's friend
5 Sonia of "Moon Over Parador"
10 Bears' hands
14 Lucy's partner
15 Fished for morays
16 Raison d'___
17 Shrinking Asian sea
18 Hotelier Helmsley
19 Locale
20 Classic pickup line #1
23 Murder mystery plot device
24 Doesn't proceed openly
25 Nickel-and-dime org.?
28 Pitt of "Meet Joe Black"
29 Grab (onto)
30 Leave stranded in the Arctic, say
32 Alehouse
35 Classic pickup line #2
39 Sault ___ Marie
40 Rabbit relatives
41 Gymnast Korbut
42 Fridge posting
43 Talisman
45 Extreme cruelty
48 Apple gadget
50 Modern pickup line
55 Skirt that's not for the modest
56 Venus' flytrap feature

57 Honolulu's island
58 Sugar source
59 Fur trader John Jacob
60 Wrestling finales
61 "Shave ___ haircut"
62 Ill-tempered
63 Schedule position

DOWN

1 Greeting for a mate
2 Architect Saarinen
3 Biblical birthright seller
4 Idle
5 Wisconsin college city
6 Smells to high heaven
7 Among the clouds
8 Rowlands of "Hope Floats"
9 1949 Tracy/Hepburn film
10 Rang out
11 Courtyards
12 Inflict
13 Anchor store at many malls
21 Have the deed to
22 Senseless
25 Words said while holding the nose
26 Blind part
27 Player's turn
28 "Rouge" and "noir"
30 50s Hungarian leader Nagy
31 Mediocre mark

Puzzle 128 by Myles Callum

32 Campaign effort
33 Exhort
34 Conquer
36 TV's "___ Line Is It Anyway?"
37 End of a challenge
38 1960s–70s Motown hitmakers
42 Mr. Khrushchev
43 Angioplasty target
44 ___ culpa
45 Disney's Lion King
46 Green card holder

47 Had supper
48 Rugby kicks
49 Insider's vocabulary
51 Seine tributary
52 Follow furtively
53 "Say it isn't so!"
54 Kick out

ACROSS

1 Peanut, in the South
7 Kitten's plaything
11 Magazine with a fold-in back cover
14 Richly decorated
15 Eminently draftable
16 Intense anger
17 Gab
19 TV room
20 A weather's opposite
21 Winning tic-tac-toe row
22 College application part
24 Piece next to a knight
26 Core group
28 Sound from a moving train
32 Winter forecast
33 On guard
34 Explosive stuff
36 Hardly neatniks
37 Dress with a flared bottom
39 Uncles, in Cuba
40 Doctors' org.
41 Les États-___
42 Base stealer Lou
43 Darned
47 Novelists Ferber and O'Brien
48 Feedbag fill
49 Town square
51 Make a goof
52 Radio operators
56 Captain's journal
57 Important person
61 Bird that gives a hoot
62 French 101 verb
63 Aviator Earhart
64 Driving range peg
65 Calendar units
66 Stagecoach robber

DOWN

1 "Naked Maja" painter
2 Spoken
3 Give the ___-over
4 Pastry shops
5 When the French fry
6 Seized again
7 Toy that goes "around the world"
8 Santa ___, Calif.
9 ___ room (place to play games)
10 In an unprotected manner
11 Torso
12 Zone
13 Contradict
18 Oxen connector
23 ___ Lanka
25 Halloween's mo.
26 Shade of blue
27 Big garden size
28 Ascend
29 Top-notch lawyer
30 Chubby Checker's dance
31 Word repeated before "Who's there?"

Puzzle 129 by Peter Gordon

32 Health resort
35 Sound of disappointment
37 "My Way" songwriter
38 Commits perjury
39 Sanitation workers
41 Not specified
42 Sandwich that usually contains mayo
44 Axlike tool
45 Time past
46 It grows every time you get a shot

49 Parcel of land
50 Actor Rob
51 Meagerly maintains, with "out"
53 "___ Lang Syne"
54 Early 12th-century date
55 Three-person card game
58 Actress Hagen
59 Weep
60 Singer Sumac

ACROSS

1 Literary lioness
5 Titicaca, por ejemplo
9 Person with a handle
13 People to hang with
14 Wear down
16 Edison's middle name
17 "The jig __!"
18 Cliffs __ (study aids)
19 Exclamation after "What are you waiting for?"
20 December singer?
23 Not play fair
24 Blazed a trail
25 Hollywood Indian's word
28 Young __ (tads)
29 Friend of François
31 Deviate from a direct course
34 __ dictum
36 Dean's world
38 Nick at __
39 Like Cheerios
41 With 12-Down, a modern idler
42 No longer chic
44 Winner's crown
46 Bat wood
47 "How about that!"
48 Songwriter Coleman et al.
49 Gridiron divs.
50 Boo follower
52 Word with house or mouth
54 Fast-food addict?

60 Drop off
61 Triangular formation
62 The Crimson Tide, for short
63 Take down __ (humble)
64 __ acid (soap ingredient)
65 They have pull
66 Kind of monster
67 Caen's river
68 Cherry variety

DOWN

1 Colossal, filmwise
2 Punishment unit
3 Talk like a tosspot
4 Savory jelly
5 One who blossoms in spring?
6 Bouquets
7 Reached
8 Poems with "To" in their titles
9 Training group
10 Sunday brunch regular?
11 Sermon topic
12 See 41-Across
15 PC "oops" key
21 Cage's "Leaving Las Vegas" co-star
22 "Put __ on it!"
25 Accord maker
26 Drama awards since 1955
27 Helper with sprains and bruises?

29 Duffer's dream
30 Tomboyish one?
32 Had a bug
33 Jericho features
35 No. on a business card
36 Downed
37 Outback runner
40 Enzyme suffix
43 Lots
45 Urgent notation
48 Hardly a Mensa candidate

51 Horseshoe-shaped letter
52 Leer-y one?
53 Moneybags
54 Pueblo Indian
55 Widmark's role in "Kiss of Death"
56 Move, in Realtor lingo
57 Rainy day rarity
58 Many Feds
59 Yin's complement
60 Nobelist Hammarskjöld

SOLUTIONS

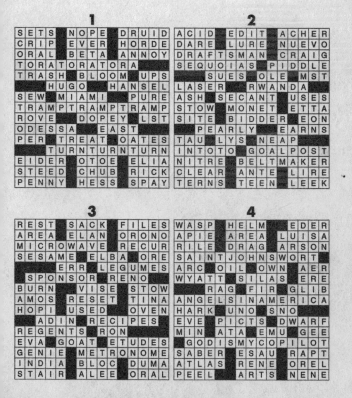

1

S	E	T	S		N	O	P	E		D	R	U	I	D
C	R	I	P		E	V	E	R		H	O	R	D	E
O	R	A	L		B	E	T	A		A	N	N	O	Y
T	O	R	A	T	O	R	A	T	O	R	A			
T	R	A	S	H		B	L	O	O	M		U	P	S
			H	U	G	O			H	A	N	S	E	L
S	E	W		M	I	A	M	I			P	U	R	E
T	R	A	M	P	T	R	A	M	P	T	R	A	M	P
R	O	V	E		D	O	P	E	Y		L	S	T	
O	D	E	S	S	A			E	A	S	T			
P	E	R		T	R	E	A	T		O	A	T	E	S
			T	U	R	N	T	U	R	N	T	U	R	N
E	I	D	E	R		O	T	O	E		E	L	I	A
S	T	E	E	D		C	H	U	B		R	I	C	K
P	E	N	N	Y		H	E	S	S		S	P	A	Y

2

A	C	I	D		E	D	I	T		A	C	H	E	R
D	A	R	E		L	U	R	E		N	U	E	V	O
D	R	A	F	T	S	M	A	N		C	R	A	I	G
S	E	Q	U	O	I	A	S		P	I	D	D	L	E
			S	U	E	S		O	L	E		M	S	T
L	A	S	E	R			R	W	A	N	D	A		
A	S	H		S	E	C	A	N	T		U	S	E	S
S	T	O	W		M	O	N	E	T		E	T	T	A
S	I	T	E		B	I	D	D	E	R		E	O	N
			P	E	A	R	L	Y		E	A	R	N	S
T	A	U		L	Y	S		N	E	A	P			
I	N	T	O	T	O		G	O	A	L	P	O	S	T
N	I	T	R	E		B	E	L	T	M	A	K	E	R
C	L	E	A	R		A	N	T	E		L	I	R	E
T	E	R	N	S		T	E	E	N		L	E	E	K

3

R	E	S	T		S	A	C	K		F	I	L	E	S
A	R	E	A		E	L	A	N		O	R	O	N	O
M	I	C	R	O	W	A	V	E		R	E	C	U	R
S	E	S	A	M	E		E	L	B	A		O	R	E
			E	R	R		L	E	G	U	M	E	S	
	S	P	O	N	S	O	R		R	E	N	O		
B	U	R	N		V	I	S	E		S	T	O	W	
A	M	O	S		R	E	S	E	T		T	I	N	A
H	O	P	I		U	S	E	D		O	V	E	N	
	A	D	I	N		R	E	C	I	P	E	S		
R	E	G	E	N	T	S		R	O	N				
E	V	A		G	O	A	T		E	T	U	D	E	S
G	E	N	I	E		M	E	T	R	O	N	O	M	E
I	N	D	I	A		B	L	O	C		D	U	M	A
S	T	A	I	R		A	L	E	E		O	R	A	L

4

W	A	S	P		H	E	L	M			E	D	E	R
A	P	I	E		A	R	E	A		L	U	I	S	A
R	I	L	E		D	R	A	G		A	R	S	O	N
S	A	I	N	T	J	O	H	N	S	W	O	R	T	
A	R	C		O	I	L		O	W	N		A	E	R
W	Y	A	T	T		S	I	L	A	S		E	R	E
			R	A	G		F	I	R		G	L	I	B
A	N	G	E	L	S	I	N	A	M	E	R	I	C	A
H	A	R	K		U	N	O			S	N	O		
E	V	E		P	I	C	T	S		D	W	A	R	F
M	I	N		A	T	A		E	M	U		G	E	E
	G	O	D	I	S	M	Y	C	O	P	I	L	O	T
S	A	B	E	R		E	S	A	U		R	A	P	T
A	T	L	A	S		R	E	N	E		O	R	E	L
P	E	E	L		A	R	T	S		N	E	N	E	

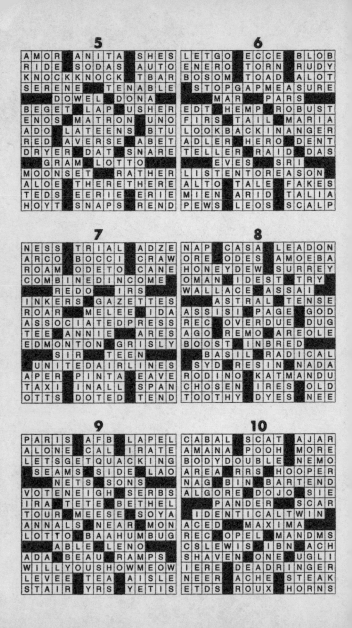

5

A	M	O	R		A	N	I	T	A		S	H	E	S
R	I	D	E		S	O	D	A	S		A	U	T	O
K	N	O	C	K	K	N	O	C	K		T	B	A	R
S	E	R	E	N	E			T	E	N	A	B	L	E
			D	O	W	E	L		D	O	N	A		
B	E	G	E	T		L	A	P		U	S	H	E	R
E	N	O	S		M	A	T	R	O	N		U	N	O
A	D	O		L	A	T	E	E	N	S		B	T	U
R	E	D		A	V	E	R	S	E		A	B	E	T
D	R	Y	E	R		D	A	T		S	N	A	R	E
		G	R	A	M		L	O	T	T	O			
M	O	O	N	S	E	T			R	A	T	H	E	R
A	L	O	E		T	H	E	R	E	T	H	E	R	E
T	E	D	S		E	E	R	I	E		E	R	I	E
H	O	Y	T		S	N	A	P	S		R	E	N	D

6

L	E	T	G	O		E	C	C	E		B	L	O	B
E	N	E	R	O		T	O	R	N		R	U	D	Y
B	O	S	O	M		T	O	A	D		A	L	O	T
	S	T	O	P	G	A	P	M	E	A	S	U	R	E
			M	A	R			P	A	R	S			
E	D	T		H	E	M	P		R	O	B	U	S	T
F	I	R	S		T	A	I	L		M	A	R	I	A
L	O	O	K	B	A	C	K	I	N	A	N	G	E	R
A	D	L	E	R		H	E	R	O		D	E	N	T
T	E	L	L	E	R		R	A	I	D		D	A	S
			E	V	E	S			S	R	I			
L	I	S	T	E	N	T	O	R	E	A	S	O	N
A	L	T	O		T	A	L	E		F	A	K	E	S
M	I	E	N		A	R	I	D		T	A	L	I	A
P	E	W	S		L	E	O	S		S	C	A	L	P

7

N	E	S	S		T	R	I	A	L		A	D	Z	E
A	R	C	O		B	O	C	C	I		C	R	A	W
R	O	A	M		O	D	E	T	O		C	A	N	E
C	O	M	B	I	N	E	D	I	N	C	O	M	E
			R	E	D	O			I	R	S			
I	N	K	E	R	S		G	A	Z	E	T	T	E	S
R	O	A	R		M	E	L	E	E		I	D	A	
A	S	S	O	C	I	A	T	E	D	P	R	E	S	S
T	E	E		A	N	N	I	E		A	R	E	S	
E	D	M	O	N	T	O	N		G	R	I	S	L	Y
			S	I	R			T	E	E	N			
	U	N	I	T	E	D	A	I	R	L	I	N	E	S
A	P	E	R		P	I	N	T	A		E	A	V	E
T	A	X	I		I	N	A	L	L		S	P	A	N
O	T	T	S		D	O	T	E	D		T	E	N	D

8

N	A	P		C	A	S	A		L	E	A	D	O	N
O	R	E		O	D	E	S		A	M	O	E	B	A
H	O	N	E	Y	D	E	W		S	U	R	R	E	Y
O	M	A	N		I	D	E	S	T		T	R	Y	
			W	A	L	L	A	C	E		A	S	S	A	I
	A	S	T	R	A	L			T	E	N	S	E	
A	S	S	I	S	I		P	A	G	E		G	O	D
R	E	C		O	V	E	R	D	U	E		D	U	G
A	G	O		R	E	M	O		A	R	E	O	L	E
B	O	O	S	T		I	N	B	R	E	D			
			B	A	S	I	L		R	A	D	I	C	A	L
S	Y	D		R	E	S	I	N		N	A	D	A	
R	O	D	I	N	O		K	A	T	M	A	N	D	U
C	H	O	S	E	N		I	R	E	S		O	L	D
T	O	O	T	H	Y		D	Y	E	S		N	E	E

9

P	A	R	I	S		A	F	B		L	A	P	E	L
A	L	O	N	E		C	A	L		I	R	A	T	E
L	E	T	S	G	E	T	Q	U	A	C	K	I	N	G
	S	E	A	M	S		S	I	D	E		L	A	O
			N	E	T	S		S	O	N	S			
V	O	T	E	N	E	I	G	H		S	E	R	B	S
I	R	A		T	E	T	E		B	E	T	H	E	L
T	O	U	R		M	E	E	S	E		S	O	Y	A
A	N	N	A	L	S		N	E	A	R		M	O	N
L	O	T	T	O		B	A	A	H	U	M	B	U	G
			A	B	L	E		L	E	N	O			
A	D	A		B	E	A	U		R	A	M	P	S	
W	I	L	L	Y	O	U	S	H	O	W	M	E	O	W
L	E	V	E	E		T	E	A		A	I	S	L	E
S	T	A	I	R		Y	R	S		Y	E	T	I	S

10

C	A	B	A	L		S	C	A	T		A	J	A	R
A	M	A	N	A		P	O	O	H		M	O	R	E
B	O	D	Y	D	O	U	B	L	E		N	E	M	O
A	R	E	A		R	R	S		H	O	O	P	E	R
N	A	G		B	I	N		B	A	R	T	E	N	D
A	L	G	O	R	E		D	O	J	O		S	I	E
			P	A	N	D	E	R			S	C	A	R
	I	D	E	N	T	I	C	A	L	T	W	I	N	
			A	C	E	D		M	A	X	I	M	A	
R	E	C		O	P	E	L			M	A	N	D	M	S
C	S	L	E	W	I	S		I	B	N		A	C	H
S	H	A	V	E	N		O	N	E			U	G	L	I
I	E	R	E		D	E	A	D	R	I	N	G	E	R
N	E	E	R		A	C	H	E		S	T	E	A	K
E	T	D	S		R	O	U	X		H	O	R	N	S

11

M	O	M	S		C	O	R	N		R	A	V	E	S
A	L	O	E		O	L	E	O		E	R	A	S	E
T	I	N	A		R	A	T	E		C	A	U	S	E
H	O	O	V	E	R	V	I	L	L	E		D	O	N
			E	L	I	S	E		A	I	D	E		
M	A	D	R	I	D			P	O	P	O	V	E	R
E	M	U		S	O	D	A	S		T	R	I	P	E
G	O	L	F		R	E	H	A	B		A	L	E	S
A	R	L	E	S		B	A	T	I	K		L	E	E
N	E	S	T	E	R	S			R	I	P	E	S	T
			V	E	N	I		M	E	D	E	A		
A	N	I		S	P	L	I	T	S	V	I	L	L	E
C	E	L	L	O		A	C	H	E		R	E	E	F
T	I	L	E	R		T	R	E	E		U	N	I	T
S	L	E	D	S		S	O	L	D		P	A	S	S

12

B	E	A	M		P	H	I		A	P	P	E	A	R
I	T	S	A	T	R	A	P		R	E	G	I	M	E
T	H	E	D	O	O	R	S		G	R	A	N	T	S
			A	M	F	M		M	E	T		S	R	I
S	H	A	M	E		O	R	A	N		S	T	A	N
T	U	N	E	I	N	N	E	X	T	W	E	E	K	
P	A	T			H	I	D			A	M	I		
		C	A	R	O	L	C	H	A	N	N	I	N	G
			G	A	R		O	D	E			I	O	S
	S	O	N	G	O	F	T	H	E	S	O	U	T	H
T	I	N	T		R	O	S	E		A	L	M	A	Y
A	L	I		T	A	X		R	O	U	E			
M	O	Z	A	R	T		R	E	N	T	A	C	O	P
P	E	E	W	E	E		I	N	T	E	R	I	O	R
A	D	D	L	E	D		G	T	O		Y	A	P	S

13

O	B	I	T		M	A	L	E	S		C	R	I	B
N	O	S	H		A	B	A	S	E		O	I	S	E
A	X	L	E		V	O	I	C	E		R	C	A	S
	Y	E	S	T	E	R	D	A	Y	S	N	E	W	S
			A	I	N	T			P	A	C	E		
S	H	O	U	T		S	D	I		H	A	S	A	T
T	E	T	R	A	S		E	S	C			P	S	I
A	T	H	I	N	G	O	F	T	H	E	P	A	S	T
R	U	E			T	R	E		A	V	O	W	A	L
S	P	R	A	T		B	R	R		E	R	N	I	E
			X	I	I	I		A	A	R	E			
A	N	C	I	E	N	T	H	I	S	T	O	R	Y	
H	A	L	O		L	A	U	D	S		V	I	V	E
S	I	A	M		E	L	L	E	N		E	T	E	S
O	L	D	S		T	S	A	R	S		R	A	S	P

14

A	C	T	S		P	L	U	M		E	A	G	L	E
S	H	O	P		R	O	S	E		P	L	E	A	D
P	I	Q	U	E	E	X	P	E	R	I	E	N	C	E
E	L	U	D	E	S		S	T	U	D		T	E	N
N	E	E		R	E	V		S	E	E	D			
			L	O	N	E	R		S	M	E	A	R	S
B	A	L	I		C	R	U	D		I	M	B	U	E
I	W	I	T	N	E	S	S	A	C	C	O	U	N	T
T	O	R	M	E		E	T	C	H		N	Y	E	S
S	L	E	U	T	H		S	H	I	P	S			
			S	W	A	B		A	T	E		A	S	A
T	I	E		O	L	E	G		C	R	U	S	T	Y
U	N	D	E	R	T	H	E	W	H	E	T	H	E	R
B	R	I	S	K		A	R	E	A		N	E	N	E
S	E	E	P	S		N	E	S	T		E	N	O	S

15

U	R	S	A		M	O	S	H	E		P	A	L	L
S	A	I	S		E	A	T	E	N		A	R	I	A
E	G	G	S		A	T	I	L	T		I	T	E	M
R	U	N	O	F	T	H	E	M	I	L	L			
			C	A	L		S	E	R	E		P	A	M
C	A	P	I	T	O	L		T	E	A		A	V	E
A	R	E	A		A	I	R			P	U	R	E	R
B	O	L	T	O	F	L	I	G	H	T	N	I	N	G
L	U	T	E	S			D	O	E		S	A	G	E
E	S	E		A	D	S		B	L	A	T	H	E	R
T	E	D		K	I	C	K		I	W	O			
		D	A	S	H	O	F	P	E	P	P	E	R	
W	I	F	E		B	E	R	E	A		P	O	P	E
I	D	O	L		A	M	E	N	D		E	R	I	E
T	A	X	I		R	E	A	D	S		D	E	C	K

16

T	A	O	S		E	S	S	A	Y		A	D	E	S
E	L	B	A		R	E	E	S	E		M	I	K	E
E	T	O	N		N	A	T	A	L		I	N	E	Z
T	H	I	G	H	S	L	A	P	P	I	N	G		
H	E	S		I	T	S				D	O	D	O	S
E	A	T	A	T		A	P	T	S			O	A	R
			T	U	E	S	D	A	Y		I	N	F	O
	L	I	P	S	M	A	C	K	I	N	G			
T	R	O	T		T	O	T	T	E	R	S			
I	D	O		L	O	G	E			W	O	M	A	N
M	A	P	L	E			M	C	I		A	W	E	
	H	E	A	R	T	P	O	U	N	D	I	N	G	
R	I	O	T		O	R	A	L	S		A	L	I	A
A	C	L	U		S	A	R	A	H		V	E	N	T
D	E	E	P		E	M	E	R	Y		E	D	G	E

17

F	A	C	E	T		A	P	E	S		P	A	P	A
A	W	A	S	H		H	A	L	O		U	S	E	R
T	A	K	E	I	T	E	A	S	Y		T	I	R	E
E	Y	E		N	E	A	R		B	L	A	S	T	S
			G	I	L	D		S	E	A	L			
S	P	L	I	C	E		S	H	A	D	I	N	G	S
W	A	I	V	E		M	A	I	N		D	O	R	A
A	N	N	E		M	A	L	E	S			O	P	E	N
M	I	D	I		A	I	L	S		K	N	E	A	D
I	N	A	T	I	Z	Z	Y		H	E	I	S	T	S
			A	T	E	E		L	A	I	T			
P	A	T	R	O	L		S	I	R	S		I	S	A
E	R	I	E		T	O	N	E	I	T	D	O	W	N
A	G	E	S		O	D	I	N		E	A	T	A	T
T	O	R	T		V	E	T	S		R	Y	A	N	S

18

S	H	A	Y		C	H	A	S	E		B	A	B	E
H	O	B	O		R	E	L	A	Y		L	E	O	N
A	L	L	U	V	I	A	L	D	E	P	O	S	I	T
D	Y	E		O	N	L	Y			L	O	O	S	E
			D	I	G	S		S	C	A	M	P	E	R
P	A	R	A	D	E		S	L	A	T	S			
O	V	E	R			O	P	A	R	T		P	I	S
P	O	I	N	T	O	F	I	N	T	E	R	E	S	T
E	N	D		A	L	O	N	G			A	R	E	A
			T	H	I	N	E		T	O	T	T	E	R
M	A	C	H	I	N	E		P	O	L	E			
O	W	L	E	T		S	A	R	A			S	O	T
D	A	Y	L	I	G	H	T	S	A	V	I	N	G	S
U	S	D	A		Y	O	U	T	H		C	O	L	A
S	H	E	W		M	I	D	A	S		E	W	E	R

19

P	R	O	P		A	F	R	O		S	C	A	M
R	E	P	O		A	L	I	E	N		H	O	N	E
O	L	E	S		F	I	R	S	T	R	O	U	N	D
F	I	R	S	T	B	A	S	E		E	E	R	I	E
S	T	A	L	K		S	T	A	F	F		T	E	A
			Q	O	M		S	T	L	U	K	E		
M	I	A		S	I	R	E		A	N	I	S	E	S
E	N	D	S		S	E	C	O	N	D	R	A	T	E
S	E	C	O	N	D	D	O	W	N		I	N	A	N
A	Z	A	L	E	A		N	E	E	R		S	T	D
		M	I	S	T	E	D		L	O	S			
G	O	P		T	E	N	T	S		A	P	E	R	S
U	S	A	G	E		T	H	I	R	D	R	A	I	L
T	H	I	R	D	P	R	I	Z	E		I	T	S	A
S	E	G	O		A	E	R	E	O		T	M	E	N
Y	A	N	G		W	E	D	S		Z	E	S	T	

20

L	A	R	G	E		R	I	N	D		I	D	E	S
A	L	O	U	D		A	R	I	A		G	E	R	E
M	U	S	E	D		D	O	G	C	O	L	L	A	R
A	M	E	R	I	C	A	N	H	E	R	O			
			R	E	A	R			T	O	N	E	R	
S	A	D	I	S	M		C	O	D	E		A	V	E
A	X	E	L			I	R	R	I	G	A	T	E	S
Y	E	L	L	O	W	S	U	B	M	A	R	I	N	E
E	M	P	A	T	H	I	E	S			C	O	S	T
R	A	H		H	O	S	T		E	T	H	N	O	S
S	N	I	D	E				E	A	V	E			
			O	R	G	A	N	G	R	I	N	D	E	R
L	I	F	E	S	A	V	E	R		D	E	I	C	E
E	V	E	R		S	I	T	E		O	M	A	H	A
T	E	D	S		P	S	S	T		L	Y	S	O	L

21

T	S	A	R		S	W	E	D	E		E	Q	U	I
O	L	G	A		E	A	T	I	N		R	U	S	S
P	E	A	C	H	E	S	A	N	D	C	R	E	A	M
P	E	T	E	R	S			N	U	R	S	E		
E	V	E	R	S		E	M	E	R	Y		N	T	H
D	E	S		S	T	A	R	E		A	B	O	O	
			C	A	P	O	N		A	L	E	U	T	
S	A	L	T	A	N	D	P	E	P	P	E	R		
H	A	B	I	T		A	U	N	T	S				
U	N	D	O		B	U	T	T	E		A	S	P	
P	E	I		E	L	S	E	S		P	E	S	T	O
		C	U	R	I	E		S	E	N	S	E	S	
M	E	A	T	A	N	D	P	O	T	A	T	O	E	S
C	U	T	E		D	U	E	N	A		E	R	L	E
I	R	E	S		S	P	R	A	T		R	T	E	S

22

B	A	S	S	O		G	E	R	E		L	I	M	B
E	A	T	E	R		U	N	I	T		O	V	A	L
D	R	A	W	B	R	I	D	G	E		N	A	S	A
S	E	S	S	I	O	N		A	S	S	E	N	T	S
				T	I	E	D			E	R	A	S	E
J	A	V	A		L	A	U	R	E	L	S			
O	R	O	N	O			S	A	K	E		M	O	O
J	E	W	E	L	I	N	T	H	E	C	R	O	W	N
O	S	S		D	R	I	P			T	U	L	L	E
			P	H	A	L	A	N	X		T	E	S	S
A	T	S	E	A			N	O	V	A				
F	A	I	N	T	E	D		N	I	G	E	R	I	A
T	U	R	N		P	I	E	F	I	L	L	I	N	G
E	P	E	E		I	D	E	A		O	L	D	I	E
R	E	N	D		C	O	L	T		W	E	S	T	S

23

B	A	A	L		C	H	U	M		D	E	L	T	A
A	C	R	E		A	O	N	E		E	V	E	R	T
S	H	E	A		T	R	I	M		S	I	S	A	L
H	E	A	V	E	N	S	T	O	B	E	T	S	Y	
			E	L	I	E				E	R	A		
M	C	M		U	P	S	T	A	R	T		T	A	E
A	H	E	A	D			A	I	L		A	R	T	S
J	E	E	P	E	R	S	C	R	E	E	P	E	R	S
O	A	S	T		O	A	K		X	E	N	I	A	
R	T	E		C	O	N	S	O	R	T		D	A	Y
			E	A	T			P	U	R	E			
L	A	N	D	S	A	K	E	S	A	L	I	V	E	
P	A	S	T	E		S	A	N	S		I	D	E	A
O	C	T	E	T		A	L	E	E		T	O	T	S
T	E	A	R	S		P	E	R	T		E	L	S	E

24

F	I	A	T	S		J	I	L	L		R	U	B	E
A	N	G	I	E		I	D	E	A		U	S	E	R
C	H	A	S	E	C	H	E	V	Y		S	U	E	R
E	O	N		D	R	A	M		E	T	H	A	N	E
S	T	A	B	B	E	D		S	T	A	B	L	E	D
			E	E	E		S	U	T	R	A			
F	I	E	N	D	S		A	N	E		R	O	A	D
A	W	A	C	S		I	N	K		A	B	A	C	I
B	O	T	H		I	R	T		A	W	A	K	E	N
				J	A	C	K	O		W	A	R		
R	E	S	O	L	E	S		G	A	R	A	G	E	S
A	L	T	H	E	A		A	R	I	D		A	L	P
T	U	R	N		G	O	R	E		T	I	P	P	E	R
E	D	E	N		E	R	L	E		N	I	E	C	E
D	E	W	Y		S	O	O	N		G	E	S	T	E

25

D	I	R	E		S	T	O	I	C		C	O	I	F
U	S	E	R		N	A	R	C	O		A	U	D	I
C	L	E	A	R	A	N	C	E	C	E	N	T	E	R
T	E	D		E	R	G	S		K	A	N	S	A	S
			O	L	E	O		C	A	R	Y			
C	A	L	A	I	S		R	A	T	S		V	I	E
O	D	O	R	S		R	E	D	O		S	A	R	A
W	A	R	E	H	O	U	S	E	O	U	T	L	E	T
E	G	A	D		M	I	T	T		M	A	I	N	E
D	E	N		P	E	N	S		B	I	N	D	E	R
			G	A	L	S		C	L	A	D			
A	M	A	L	I	E		K	O	O	K		S	A	M
D	E	P	A	R	T	M	E	N	T	S	T	O	R	E
A	M	E	S		T	O	N	I	C		A	F	A	R
M	O	S	S		E	P	O	C	H		B	A	B	E

26

R	A	D	A	R		S	A	S	S		P	R	O	P
A	N	O	D	E		O	R	C	A		I	A	M	A
S	T	U	D	M	U	F	F	I	N		E	T	E	S
H	E	R		A	L	A	S		D	E	C	E	N	T
			T	I	E	R		F	I	N	E	S	S	E
T	H	E	O	N	E		C	R	E	D	O			
M	I	N	U	S		H	A	I	G		F	R	A	T
A	L	O	G		C	A	M	E	O		C	O	M	A
N	O	S	H		A	S	P	S		R	A	T	O	N
				C	E	R	T	S		P	O	K	E	R	S
P	A	R	O	L	E	E		L	I	T	E			
A	X	I	O	M	S		B	E	T	H		S	A	P
S	I	N	K		S	W	E	E	T	I	E	P	I	E
S	A	K	I		E	Y	E	D		R	E	A	D	E
E	L	S	E		S	E	T	S		A	L	T	E	R

27

S	A	L	A	D		C	A	P	E		S	P	O	T
U	V	U	L	A		A	R	I	A		A	L	O	E
M	I	K	E	H	A	M	M	E	R		R	A	Z	E
O	V	E	R	L	I	E		S	P	I	N	E	S	
			T	I	L	L	E	D		A	S	E		
	I	D	E	A	S		Y	E	T	I		T	R	E
C	O	R	D		H	E	M	A	N		R	E	X	
A	N	I		R	E	A	S	O	N	S		I	L	E
N	I	L		A	K	R	O	N		S	P	A	S	
S	A	L		B	E	E	R		A	R	T	S	Y	
			T	E	A		M	E	M	B	E	R		
A	V	E	R	T	S		C	E	R	A	M	I	C	
J	O	A	N		S	I	N	G	L	E	F	I	L	E
A	T	M	S		T	R	E	E		N	E	C	K	S
R	E	S	T		S	A	G	E		T	R	E	A	T

28

S	P	A	S		D	A	R	K		E	J	E	C	T
T	A	N	K		E	B	O	N		N	O	R	M	A
O	P	I	E		L	E	V	I		C	Y	N	I	C
W	E	S	T	S	I	D	E	S	T	O	R	E		
E	R	E	C	T			S	H	A	R	I			
			H	A	L	O		R	E	D	F	I	R	
R	A	E		R	E	N	E	E		E	I	N	E	
A	N	N	I	E	G	E	T	Y	O	U	R	G	U	M
S	T	U	N		S	C	E	N	T		S	P	Y	
	P	I	F	F	L	E		S	T	I	R			
			R	O	M	E	O		C	A	S	T	E	
M	A	N	O	F	L	A	M	A	N	C	H	U		
D	E	A	R	E		L	I	M	A		C	A	R	R
A	R	I	E	L		A	V	E	C		O	R	E	O
D	A	N	D	Y		T	E	N	S		R	Y	E	S

29

V	I	B	E	S		L	A	S	S		E	D	E	N
E	R	A	S	E		O	N	T	O		N	O	D	E
R	O	B	O	T		B	E	A	M		I	N	G	A
A	N	Y		B	R	O	W	N	B	A	G	G	E	R
		B	E	A	U	S			R	I	M			
A	T	O	N	C	E		O	P	E	R	A	B	L	E
C	R	O	O	K		S	T	A	R	S		R	O	N
H	U	M	S		M	E	T	R	O		H	O	O	T
E	S	E		B	E	R	E	T		D	O	W	S	E
S	T	R	A	I	N	E	R		B	E	R	B	E	R
		L	B	S		S	E	T	A	E				
B	A	C	K	B	R	E	A	K	E	R		A	P	T
R	I	L	E		O	R	C	A		O	A	T	E	R
A	D	I	N		O	M	I	T		I	R	E	N	E
G	A	P	E		M	A	D	E		T	E	R	S	E

30

T	A	T	E	R		S	A	R	I		A	M	I	E
I	N	U	R	E		I	R	O	N		J	I	N	X
A	N	N	A	L		L	O	P	S		A	L	O	E
R	A	I	S	E	S	O	M	E	I	B	R	O	W	S
A	S	C	E	N	T			A	S	T	I			
			T	A	J			U	N	B	O	R	N	
M	E	M	O		R	E	Z	A		G	I	G	U	E
A	S	I	G	H	T	F	O	R	S	O	R	E	I	S
I	S	T	L	E		F	E	E	T		D	E	N	T
D	E	T	E	S	T			S	O	S				
			S	U	B	S			C	H	A	S	E	D
I	N	T	H	E	B	L	I	N	K	O	F	A	N	I
M	A	Y	O		F	A	T	E		V	O	L	G	A
A	M	P	S		U	R	I	S		E	U	L	E	R
M	E	E	T		L	E	N	S		S	L	Y	L	Y

31

A	C	T	S		R	E	N	O		I	O	N	I	C
M	O	E	T		A	V	E	C		I	V	A	N	A
P	O	L	O	S	H	I	R	T		N	O	V	A	S
S	P	L	I	T		D	O	O	M	S		A	P	T
		S	C	A	L	E		P	E	I		H	I	E
M	A	O		T	E	N	N	I	S	S	H	O	E	S
A	L	F	R	E	S	C	O			A	T	E		
W	I	F	E			E	V	E		R	A	Z	E	
			N	A	G		E	S	C	O	R	T	E	D
B	A	S	E	B	A	L	L	C	A	P		T	D	S
R	U	E		S	P	A		A	R	E	N	A		
A	L	T		A	E	S	O	P		R	I	C	K	S
N	A	T	A	L		S	K	I	J	A	C	K	E	T
D	I	E	G	O		O	R	S	O		H	E	R	D
S	T	R	O	M		S	A	M	E		E	R	R	S

32

O	M	A	R		S	H	A	M	E		S	P	A	T
F	I	L	E		S	A	L	A	D		C	A	P	O
F	R	I	G	H	T	W	I	G	S		E	N	I	D
			R	A	S		T	I	E		P	I	S	A
C	A	S	E	R			C	L	U	T	C	H	Y	
A	S	H	T	R	A	Y	S		S	H	E	B		
M	I	O		Y	I	E	L	D		F	R	U	M	P
E	A	C	H		R	A	O	U	L		S	T	A	R
O	N	K	E	Y		R	O	P	E	S		T	R	A
			T	A	M	P		P	E	N	O	L	O	G	Y
H	A	R	V	A	R	D			N	I	N	E	S	
E	L	O	I		O	E	D		H	I	E			
A	L	O	E		A	L	A	R	M	C	L	O	C	K
R	I	P	S		M	I	N	E	O		O	P	I	E
T	E	S	T		S	A	L	T	S		W	E	A	N

33

S	O	B	S		S	W	I	S	H			A	B	S
P	R	O	P		T	E	S	L	A		P	L	O	T
A	S	I	F		A	L	L	Y	S	H	E	E	D	Y
C	O	N		P	Y	L	E		B	U	N	G	E	E
E	N	G	A	R	D	E		B	E	L	A			
			K	I	R	S	T	I	E	A	L	L	E	Y
E	F	F	I	G	Y		H	A	N	S		I	R	E
W	E	A	N			L	E	S			T	O	G	A
O	T	C		S	K	I	T		F	M	I	N	O	R
K	A	T	E	A	N	D	A	L	L	I	E			
			A	M	E	S		E	Y	E	S	O	R	E
B	I	G	T	O	E		O	M	A	N		F	A	X
A	L	I	M	A	C	G	R	A	W		V	A	N	E
L	I	F	E		A	R	E	N	A		I	G	O	R
M	E	T		P	R	O	S	Y		P	E	N	T	

34

G	A	Z	E	B	O		A	C	E	D		C	I	A
O	L	I	V	E	R		M	A	C	E		A	N	D
N	E	G	A	T	E		I	N	R	E		M	A	D
			G	H	O	S	T	B	U	S	T	E	R	S
I	R	M	A		A	Y	E			E	R	O	O	
S	E	A	B	A	S	S		R	A	E	D	A	W	N
R	A	M	O	N	A			B	R	I	T			
	P	A	R	T	Y	C	R	A	S	H	E	R	S	
			E	N	O	S		L	E	M	O	N	S	
E	G	G	E	D	O	N		D	E	L	I	M	I	T
X	R	A	Y		G	O	I			S	E	T	S	
H	O	M	E	W	R	E	C	K	E	R	S			
A	V	E		H	E	A	T		Q	U	I	T	I	T
L	E	T		I	D	L	E		U	B	O	A	T	S
E	R	E		P	S	S	T		I	S	N	T	O	K

35

```
S E A T   S E T T O   S C O T
A L O E   T R O O P   P A L O
L E N A   P R O N E   E R I N
E V E R L A S T I N G L O V E
      D A T       F U L L E R
S W A R M   V I L L A S
O H I O   S A M O A N   R C A
P E R P E T U A L M O T I O N
H E Y   B A N G L E   E C O N
      T O R T E S   S M O K E
U R G E N T       G O P
B O U N D L E S S E N E R G Y
O U R S   I R A T E   R E M O
A G U E   N I K E S   E B A Y
T E S S   G E S T E   D A N O
```

36

```
B A M A   N E A T O   F A D S
A C E S   O X L I P   E L E A
W H A T O N E L E T S D O W N
D E L I C A C Y   I N O U Y E
      E M S   A M I R
  S T I L E   A G I T A T O R
P O R N O   I L E S   O S U
A M I S T E R I N M U N I C H
I M P   V E S T   S O L A R
R E S I D E N T   E M B E R
      G E N E   P G A
T H E N E T   T E R I Y A K I
A E S O P F A B L E L O S E R
N E A R   U R A L S   W I N K
G L U E   L I R A S   L A O S
```

37

```
D A R K   C O M P   A L T O
A L O E   P R E O P   L E A N
W O O D B A R R E L   T A X I
N U T S O     T A B A S C O
    P A P E R C A R T O N
I O W A   D R A Y E D
G L A S S J A R   M U F T I
E L L I O T T   O R A T I O N
T A T A R   S T O N E J U G
    D O M A I N   S I R E
  A L U M I N U M C A N
D I V I D E S   O S A G E
E M U S   P L A S T I C B A G
P O L E   M I X U P   A L M A
T S A R   M E E K   N E E D
```

38

```
F L A G G   S A H L   A G R A
I O N I A   O N E I   S E E P
J O A N V A N A R K   L O C A
I N T   O L A   D E P A R T S
    S T A R S   W I N G I T
D E B U T S   O P I A T E
A G R E E   D R E S S   R A T
L A Y S   V E R N E   B A B A
I D A   D E M O N   O R F E O
  N A R R O W   K N O T T S
D E F E A T   S H O T S
A L E R T E D   O O H   R E B
M I R A   B O A T P E O P L E
P O R T   R C A S   G I M M E
S T Y E   A S H Y   O L S O N
```

39

```
P R O P   R A F T   C A P O N
H O P I   A R L O   A L E V E
D O E R   R E A M   S I R E D
S T L O U I S P A S T E U R
      U P T O   T H E N
C A M E B Y   F O E S   W A C
A M A T O   E I R E   E R G O
F O R T W A Y N E R O G E R S
E R I E   D E E D   M O N E T
S E E   C L O D   M A S S E S
      S O A P   R O N A
S A N D I E G O R I V E R A
R U L E D   N A D A   I D O L
R I V A L   E M I L   N I L E
S T A K E   R E N E   G E L S
```

40

```
C A A N   A S A P   G H A N A
A S T O   L U L U   R E L A X
F I T S   I G O T   I M A G E
F A I T H D A N I E L S
E N C R E   R E N A L   H A L
    A L E C   R E N E G E
C B S   G R O P E   T R A P
H O P E A G A I N S T H O P E
A D E N   T E T R A   N E W
S E L D O M   R O N S
E S T   S A L S A   Y E A S T
  S W E E T C H A R I T Y
B A S I E   M E T A   E R O S
A M O N G   O V E R   N E R O
T A N G O   N E S T   E D E N
```

41

```
F A N G . S L I P . H A S N T
O G E E . H E R A . E R N I E
G E O R G I A O N M Y M I N D
Y E S M E N . N A B . . F E D
. . . A L B . S M A L L F R Y
O P E N T O E . A S I A . . .
P A L . N R A . F L U N K . .
T W O S L E E P Y P E O P L E
. . F L U N K . . . . . . . .
S N I P E . E E L . . T E E .
. A W H O . N E W B O R N . .
S T A R D U S T . A A A . . .
C R T . A C H . S A R O N G .
H O A G Y C A R M I C H A E L
M O L T O . R E I N . O H I O
O N L O W . S W A G . P U L P
```

42

```
O F A L L . P L E A . B A C H
R A D I O . R Y E S . E C H O
C H O P S T I C K S . S T I R
A D S . T I N E . . F O U L S
. . . M I N C E M E A T P I E
D I N E T T E . A X I S . . .
I D E A . E R I N . K A T . .
B L E N D E R S E T T I N G S
S Y D . A N A T . C O U P . .
. . S N U G . A N N E X E S .
G R A T E F U L D E A D . . .
L E V I S . Y A W N . S A W .
U P O N . W H I P S T I T C H
E R I K . W A N T . E N E M Y
D O D O . W I G S . S A T E S
```

43

```
P E S T . A C T S . J A M E S
A L O E . S O U P . O P E R A
N I N A . H E R R . S P R A Y
T O A S T E D B A G E L . . .
S T R E W . I N T . A F A R .
. . . O R A N G E J U I C E .
C H A P . A L E . A D O R N .
R O S E T T A . E U G E N I E
A L I A S . O F T . D A D E .
B L A C K C O F F E E . . . .
S Y N E . A R F . D O Z E R .
. . T O D A Y S P U Z Z L E .
V A L I D . T E A S . O T I S
C R I M E . E A R S . N O T E
R I P E R . D R A T . E P E E
```

44

```
S A L A D . E A C H . D E E D
E C O L E . L V I I . E R M A
A L O O F . P I G G Y B A C K
M U S T R E A D . H O T T E A
. . . A N S . A S U . O E R .
C A T T Y C O R N E R . . . .
M I R O S . E T A . L A V A .
O D E R . H A V E S . O T I S
N E X T . O R E . B L O C S .
. . . B U L L Y P U L P I T .
C S A . U S O . E U R . . . .
A L G O R E . A S T R I N G S
D O G G Y B A G S . I V O R Y
R O I L . O D I E . T E T O N
E P E E . Y E N S . O S A G E
```

45

```
M A M A . A B A C K . F A T S
O D O R . N I X O N . A B E T
D O U B L E T I M E . L O R E
E R N I E . S O M E . L U M P
L E T T E R . M A S C O T . .
. . . E R I N . . A W F U L .
C H A R . G E E Z E R . A N A
H A T . C O M M A N D . C I T
A R T . A R O U N D . F E T E
T E E N S . E U R O . . . . .
. . N E A R E R . P U R P L E
P A T E . O V E R . S T E A L
A V I D . P A R A D E R E S T
P O O L . E D U C E . A L S O
A N N E . R E N E W . N E O N
```

46

```
S W A P . T S P S . P H O N O
A A R E . H A U T . R U M O R
W I L D S W I N E . E N N U I
S T O I C A L . M U G G I N G
. . . C O R O T . T A U . . .
C O U N T R Y B U M P K I N .
S H I R E . P O R E . Y O U .
T I L E . C L E A N . D O W N
A L E . A N A S . F I T A S .
T I R E S O M E P E R S O N .
. . . A P T . T E N E T . . .
S H U S H E S . A S A R U L E
A O R T A . A F R I K A N E R
B A G E L . P A L L . C I A O
E X E R T . S T Y E . T S K S
```

47

L	A	N	A		D	A	D	A			L	I	T	E	R
I	R	O	N		I	G	O	R			E	A	R	T	H
S	K	A	T	E	S	O	N	T	H	I	N	I	C	E
T	S	H	I	R	T			T	I	E		M	H	O
			C	E	E	S		E	L	E	E			
G	O	E	S	I	N	H	A	R	M	S	W	A	Y
A	P	R			D	A	M		S	T	E	N	O	S
S	T	A	P	H		H	E	W		A	R	G	U	E
P	I	T	I	E	S		N	A	P		S	R	A	
	C	O	U	R	T	S	D	I	S	A	S	T	E	R
			S	E	E	P		L	Y	R	E			
A	L	P		L	I	T		C	A	C	H	E	D	
W	A	L	K	S	A	T	I	G	H	T	R	O	P	E
E	M	A	I	L		E	R	I	E		E	R	I	C
D	A	N	D	Y		S	E	N	D		T	A	C	K

48

T	E	C	H		C	A	R	E	W		W	R	E	N
O	G	R	E		A	N	O	D	E		R	A	T	E
W	R	A	P	A	R	T	I	S	T		I	N	R	E
N	E	Z		R	T	E	S		R	A	G	G	E	D
	S	T	E	W	A	R	D		S	A	S	H		
			R	B	I		H	I	G	H	T	O	P	S
S	E	M	I		P	L	O	T		E	S	T	O	P
P	L	A	N	T		A	M	I		S	T	I	L	E
A	M	I	G	O		M	E	N	S		U	S	E	D
R	O	L	L	O	V	E	R		E	L	F			
			E	L	I	S		S	N	I	F	F	L	E
C	R	E	A	S	E		D	U	A	D		L	O	S
H	E	R	D		W	R	E	S	T	S	T	O	P	S
I	N	G	E		E	E	R	I	E		A	R	E	A
P	O	O	R		D	A	N	E	S		L	A	Z	Y

49

T	I	F	F		C	H	I	L	I		W	I	S	P
E	V	I	L		P	A	N	A	M		I	D	E	A
R	A	R	E	E	A	R	T	H	M	E	T	A	L	S
I	N	S	E	T			S	T	U	N		H	I	S
			T	R	A	P	S		I	N	A	F	O	G
I	S	L		L	A	W	S		E	M	I			
S	T	A	R		L	E	I	S		E	T	H	E	L
M	E	D	I	U	M	A	R	T	I	L	L	E	R	Y
S	P	Y	O	N		T	E	E	N		Y	A	L	E
			T	U	B		D	A	F	T		D	E	S
	K	I	S	S	E	R		M	O	O	L	A		
T	E	D		E	Y	E	D		L	O	C	H	S	
W	E	L	L	D	O	N	E	O	L	D	C	H	A	P
O	N	E	A		N	E	A	T	O		K	E	N	O
S	E	R	B		D	E	R	B	Y		A	S	S	T

50

L	A	S	S		T	R	A	M	S		C	R	I	B
I	T	T	O		S	E	N	A	T		A	I	D	A
T	R	A	P		U	N	A	M	I		L	O	O	N
C	A	S	H	A	N	D	C	A	R	R	Y			
H	I	E		L	A	S	T		S	E	X	T	E	T
I	N	S	E	A	M		M	I	A			A	T	E
			T	R	I	E	D	A	N	D	T	R	U	E
I	P	S	O		D	U	G			O	T	I	S	
D	O	W	N	A	N	D	D	I	R	T	Y			
E	R	A		R	O	Y			E	A	S	I	E	R
A	T	T	A	I	N		C	A	D	S		G	R	O
			S	A	F	E	A	N	D	S	O	U	N	D
X	R	A	Y		O	L	D	I	E		M	A	A	M
Y	O	R	E		O	B	E	S	E		A	N	N	A
Z	E	S	T		D	A	T	E	R		R	A	I	N

51

C	O	M	A		S	C	A	R		M	O	R	E	S
O	P	A	L		C	O	M	O		O	V	E	R	T
L	E	N	S		A	M	O	S		T	A	B	L	E
A	S	Y	O	U	L	I	K	E	I	T		S	E	W
			N	E	C		B	M	O	C				
C	A	R	E	D		S	L	O	B		L	A	I	T
H	I	A	T	U	S		O	W	E		A	O	N	E
A	S	T	H	E	W	O	R	L	D	T	U	R	N	S
I	L	I	A		A	B	E		S	E	S	T	E	T
N	E	O	N		M	E	N	D		P	E	A	R	Y
			E	N	I	D		U	P	I				
A	R	T		A	S	I	L	A	Y	D	Y	I	N	G
G	O	R	E	S		E	A	R	L		O	R	A	L
E	V	E	N	T		N	I	T	E		L	O	V	E
S	E	E	D	Y		T	R	E	S		K	N	E	E

52

J	A	Z	Z		S	L	A	P			I	N	D	I	A
I	S	E	E		C	U	T	E			N	E	E	D	S
B	A	R	N		A	M	O	R			V	A	L	E	S
	P	O	O	R	R	E	P	U	T	A	T	I	O	N
			A	C	T			H	I	S					
O	C	T	A	V	E		A	K	I	N		D	E	R
G	R	I	M	E		A	B	I	E		D	O	T	E
L	A	T	E	N	I	G	H	T	F	L	I	G	H	T
E	V	A	N		B	R	O	S		A	R	M	O	R
D	E	N		T	S	A	R		U	N	E	A	S	Y
			E	R	E			R	N	A					
C	O	N	J	U	N	C	T	I	V	I	T	I	S
A	L	O	E	S		R	A	V	E		A	N	T	I
T	I	N	C	T		A	L	A	I		P	E	A	R
S	O	O	T	Y		B	E	L	L		E	Z	R	A

53

```
T H A W   M A Y A   N E P A L
H U G E   U B E R   O V I N E
E T A L   F E L T   D I E T S
O U R L I T T L E S E C R E T
      K R I S     H A T
D I A N A   M A U L   E D S
A L C O T T   A G T   I N O N
B E T W E E N Y O U A N D M E
A D E N   T A B   P E S T E R
T E D   R O B E   R O O S T
    M E N     W A I F
M Y L I P S A R E S E A L E D
A S I D E   B I D S   R A T E
L E V I N   E D G E   A V O N
T R Y S T   L E E S   S E N T
```

54

```
M A S T   C H E F   L A D L E
O U C H   H E R E   A F O O T
O G R E   L A N A   S A N T O
S E A S   O V E R S T R A I N
E R G O   R E S     E S E
      N I A N T I C   W R A P
R E C A L L   H O T   E A S E
A T O L L   Y E N   F L U T E
I R A S   D A M   C O L L A R
L E T O   E P I T H E T
      R O E   N R A   O A S T
S C R I M M A G E S   A V O W
A R O S E   A W N S   L A M E
R I P E N   R A T E   M I M E
A B Y S S   E Y E D   S L E D
```

55

```
R A R E   M A O   S O D O M
A V E R   L U L U   C R E D O
M A I N   A S I T   H E L E N
P I N O C C H I O   I O U
A L I   H E Y   F O S S I L S
G E N R E S   S L A M   S A T
E D G A R   S H U T   S E X Y
    P I S T A C H I O
C A R T   P O R K   S A N T A
U T E   H I V E   B U R I A L
R E S T A T E   S E Z   G P S
    U R N   P E T R U C H I O
E L L I S   I G O R   A T O R
M O T T O   P O K Y   P I C A
O L S E N   E S E   S E A N
```

56

```
C E L T S   F E R N   B I C S
A L O N E   A P I E   O R A L
F A N T A S T I C V O Y A G E
E N G   B A T C H   L I N E D
      N I L E     C D S
    I N C R E D I B L E H U L K
B L O O D   R O A R   N A E
A I R S   C L O W N   S T I R
B U M   S O O N   B A I R N
A M A Z I N G S T O R I E S
      E L K   E T A L
B A S R A   T A L O N   M S G
I M P O S S I B L E D R E A M
A M I E   I D L E   O H A R A
S O N S   P E E R   N O T I N
```

57

```
C I G S   S H O A L   S C A M
A S E A   A O R T A   T R U E
P E A C H T R E E S T R E E T
P E R S E I D S   T R A W L S
      A R E   S N I P
A L G O R E   S H A M   A A H
M A R A T   S P A M   O K R A
E M O R Y U N I V E R S I T Y
N E W S   P A C E   E L L I E
D R S   L I K E   T H O L E S
      F I N E   C R I
S A H A R A   N E A R E A S T
T H E C A R T E R C E N T E R
I S N T   M A T T E   D O V E
R O S S   S I S S Y   S M E E
```

58

```
E R A S E   M A S S   F A S T
L A T E X   A L O E   O R M E
S W E A T   N E S T   O D O R
    B E A N C O U N T E R S
A L B E R T A   P A W N E E
M O R E N O   P A S T E
A G O   A N S E L   A B S
N O O D L E C A S S E R O L E
S K I   A L O N G   Z A G
    R Y A N S   O O L O N G
A P P E A L   A R T I S T S
B L O C K L E T T E R S
N A S T   P L O W   I T A L Y
E T T E   R A G A   P E K O E
R E E D   O M A R   S N A P S
```

59

A	L	E	C		O	H	A	R	A		D	A	U	B
C	A	R	L		R	O	G	E	R		U	R	S	A
E	L	I	A		A	S	T	O	R		P	A	N	E
S	O	C	R	A	T	E	S		I	S	O	B	A	R
		I	C	E	D		A	V	O	N				
V	A	P	O	R	S		C	O	A	S	T	E	R	S
O	Z	O	N	E		M	A	R	L	O		L	A	P
I	T	I	S		S	O	R	T	S		H	I	D	E
L	E	N		A	N	I	T	A		S	A	T	I	N
A	C	T	S	S	O	R	E		A	E	N	E	I	D
			T	I	R	E		B	R	A	D			
S	Q	U	E	A	K		S	A	T	S	C	O	R	E
A	U	R	A		E	L	A	T	E		U	L	A	N
R	O	A	D		L	I	V	E	R		F	I	N	D
I	D	L	Y		S	E	E	D	Y		F	O	G	S

60

G	M	A	T		M	E	S	A	S		B	E	S	S
N	O	D	E		A	S	L	I	P		U	N	I	T
A	C	R	E		N	A	O	M	I		M	I	D	I
W	H	E	N	Y	O	U	G	E	T	O	L	D	E	R
S	A	M	B	A			E	S	N	E				
			E	P	S	O	M		H	I	G	H	E	R
A	S	T	A		C	R	I	T	I	C		A	M	Y
J	U	S	T	T	H	I	S	O	N	E	T	I	M	E
O	L	A		H	O	G	T	I	E		O	R	E	S
B	A	R	R	I	O		A	L	S	O	P			
			U	N	L	V			N	I	T	R	O	
G	O	A	S	K	Y	O	U	R	M	O	T	H	E	R
R	I	C	H		A	T	S	E	A		O	R	C	A
A	N	T	E		R	E	T	A	G		F	O	O	L
S	K	I	D		D	R	A	M	S		F	E	N	S

61

B	E	D		A	R	E	A		M	A	B	E	L	L
R	U	E		L	O	L	L		A	M	A	L	I	E
A	C	T		A	B	U	T		T	O	S	S	E	D
C	H	E	E	S	E	D	A	N	I	S	H			
E	R	R	S		R	E	R	U	N		L	O	U	
R	E	S	E	A	T		C	E	I	L	I	N	G	
			D	O	U	B	L	E	D	U	T	C	H	
I	L	I	A	D		R	O	E		A	G	E	E	S
	B	O	D	Y	E	N	G	L	I	S	H			
	M	C	E	N	R	O	E		T	O	A	S	T	S
S	O	S		S	N	E	E	R		L	U	R	E	
	W	H	I	T	E	R	U	S	S	I	A	N		
R	E	D	E	Y	E		R	O	D	E		T	U	T
A	T	O	D	D	S		I	D	E	A		E	M	U
G	E	T	S	E	T		E	E	L	S		S	A	P

62

A	P	A	R		E	N	D	U	E		B	A	T
D	A	N	E		T	O	O	T	L	E		E	V	E
M	R	I	N	B	E	T	W	E	E	N		F	E	N
	A	M	O	O		M	R	P	E	E	P	E	R	S
A	D	A		W	H	E	Y			A	L	S	O	
L	I	T	T	L	E		S	C	U	L	L	E	R	
I	G	O	R		R	E	M	A	I	N				
M	R	A	N	D	M	R	S	N	O	R	T	H		
	S	E	T	T	E	E		A	R	U	T			
I	N	R	O	A	D	S		M	A	D	A	M	E	
N	O	U	N		A	M	A	N		V	I	A		
M	R	S	O	L	E	A	R	Y		T	I	E	D	
A	R	T		M	R	S	R	O	B	I	N	S	O	N
T	I	L		N	O	T	O	N	E		O	T	R	A
E	S	E		S	O	W	E	D		N	Y	S	E	

63

H	B	O	M	B		G	A	I	T		H	A	R	K
A	R	N	I	E		O	R	C	A		E	T	U	I
H	E	A	D	H	U	N	T	E	R		D	O	L	L
A	W	N		O	R	G	Y		P	I	G	P	E	N
			H	O	G	S		S	A	M	E			
A	L	C	O	V	E		S	A	P	P	H	I	R	E
V	A	L	U	E		M	I	L	E		O	D	E	S
A	D	E	S		S	O	L	A	R		P	E	A	T
S	L	O	E		Q	U	A	D		S	P	A	D	E
T	E	N	H	O	U	R	S		R	E	E	S	E	S
			O	L	I	N		A	U	E	R			
E	A	G	L	E	S		A	C	T	S		E	S	P
S	L	I	D		H	I	G	H	H	A	T	T	E	R
P	O	L	E		E	R	I	E		W	H	A	L	E
N	E	A	R		D	E	N	S		S	U	L	L	Y

64

T	A	C	O	S		D	O	R	M		U	M	P	S
A	L	E	P	H		A	D	E	E		T	I	L	E
R	O	D	E	O		M	O	A	N		O	L	I	N
T	H	E	C	O	L	O	R	P	U	R	P	L	E	
S	A	D		E	O	N			I	I	I			
			O	D	S		I	C	E	P	A	C	K	S
S	L	A	Y		E	R	A	S	E		E	E	E	
W	I	L	L	I	A	M	O	F	O	R	A	N	G	E
I	S	M		C	L	I	N	E		I	T	S	A	
M	I	S	D	I	A	L	S		W	A	R			
			H	E	N		C	A	N		A	C	T	
L	O	N	G	J	O	H	N	S	I	L	V	E	R	
L	O	U	T		O	R	E	O		M	O	I	R	E
A	P	S	E		C	A	R	T		A	R	L	E	N
W	E	E	D		K	N	E	E		L	E	A	S	T

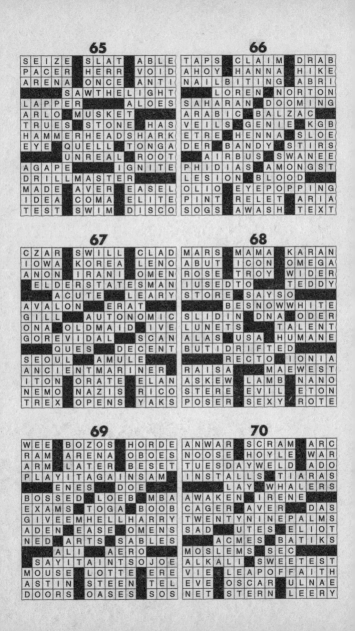

65

S	E	I	Z	E		S	L	A	T		A	B	L	E
P	A	C	E	R		H	E	R	R		V	O	I	D
A	R	E	N	A		O	N	C	E		A	N	T	I
		S	A	W	T	H	E	L	I	G	H	T		
L	A	P	P	E	R			A	L	O	E	S		
A	R	L	O		M	U	S	K	E	T				
T	R	U	E	S		S	T	O	N	E		H	A	S
H	A	M	M	E	R	H	E	A	D	S	H	A	R	K
E	Y	E		Q	U	E	L	L		T	O	N	G	A
			U	N	R	E	A	L		R	O	O	T	
A	G	A	P	E				I	G	N	I	T	E	
D	R	I	L	L	M	A	S	T	E	R				
M	A	D	E		A	V	E	R		E	A	S	E	L
I	D	E	A		C	O	M	A		E	L	I	T	E
T	E	S	T		S	W	I	M		D	I	S	C	O

66

T	A	P	S		C	L	A	I	M		D	R	A	B
A	H	O	Y		H	A	N	N	A		H	I	K	E
N	A	I	L	B	I	T	I	N	G		A	B	R	I
			L	O	R	E	N		N	O	R	T	O	N
S	A	H	A	R	A	N		D	O	O	M	I	N	G
A	R	A	B	I	C		B	A	L	Z	A	C		
V	E	I	L	S		G	E	N	I	E		K	G	B
E	T	R	E		H	E	N	N	A		S	L	O	E
D	E	R		B	A	N	D	Y		S	T	I	R	S
			A	I	R	B	U	S		S	W	A	N	E	E
P	H	I	D	I	A	S		A	M	O	N	G	S	T
L	E	S	I	O	N		B	L	O	O	D			
O	L	I	O		E	Y	E	P	O	P	P	I	N	G
P	I	N	T		R	E	L	E	T		A	R	I	A
S	O	G	S		A	W	A	S	H		T	E	X	T

67

C	Z	A	R		S	W	I	L	L		C	L	A	D
I	O	W	A		K	O	R	E	A		L	E	N	O
A	N	O	N		I	R	A	N	I		O	M	E	N
	E	L	D	E	R	S	T	A	T	E	S	M	A	N
			A	C	U	T	E		L	E	A	R	Y	
A	V	A	L	O	N			E	R	A	T			
G	I	L	L		A	U	T	O	N	O	M	I	C	
O	N	A		O	L	D	M	A	I	D		I	V	E
G	O	R	E	V	I	D	A	L		S	C	A	N	
			Q	U	E	S		D	E	C	E	N	T	
S	E	O	U	L		A	M	U	L	E				
A	N	C	I	E	N	T	M	A	R	I	N	E	R	
I	T	O	N		O	R	A	T	E		E	L	A	N
N	E	M	O		N	A	Z	I	S		R	I	C	O
T	R	E	X		O	P	E	N	S		Y	A	K	S

68

M	A	R	S		M	A	M	A		K	A	R	A	N
A	B	U	T		I	C	O	N		O	M	E	G	A
R	O	S	E		T	R	O	Y		W	I	D	E	R
I	U	S	E	D	T	O			T	E	D	D	Y	
S	T	O	R	E		S	A	Y	S	O				
			B	E	S	N	O	W	W	H	I	T	E	
S	L	I	D	I	N		D	N	A		O	D	E	R
L	U	N	E	T	S			T	A	L	E	N	T	
A	L	A	S		U	S	A		H	U	M	A	N	E
B	U	T	I	D	R	I	F	T	E	D				
			R	E	C	T	O		I	O	N	I	A	
R	A	I	S	A		M	A	E	W	E	S	T		
A	S	K	E	W		L	A	M	B		N	A	N	O
S	T	E	R	E		E	V	I	L		E	T	O	N
P	O	S	E	R		S	E	X	Y		R	O	T	E

69

W	E	E		B	O	Z	O	S		H	O	R	D	E
R	A	M		A	R	E	N	A		O	B	O	E	S
A	R	M		L	A	T	E	R		B	E	S	E	T
P	L	A	Y	I	T	A	G	A	I	N	S	A	M	
			E	N	E	S		D	O	E				
B	O	S	S	E	D		L	O	E	B		M	B	A
E	X	A	M	S		T	O	G	A		B	O	O	B
G	I	V	E	E	M	H	E	L	L	H	A	R	R	Y
A	D	E	N		E	A	S	E		O	M	E	N	S
N	E	D		A	R	T	S		S	A	B	L	E	S
			A	L	I			A	E	R	O			
S	A	Y	I	T	A	I	N	T	S	O	J	O	E	
M	O	U	S	E		L	O	T	T	E		E	R	E
A	S	T	I	N		S	T	E	E	N		T	E	L
D	O	O	R	S		O	A	S	E	S		S	O	S

70

A	N	W	A	R		S	C	R	A	M		A	R	C
N	O	O	S	E		H	O	Y	L	E		W	A	R
T	U	E	S	D	A	Y	W	E	L	D		A	D	O
I	N	S	T	A	L	L	S		T	I	A	R	A	S
			L	A	Y		W	H	A	L	E	R	S	
A	W	A	K	E	N		I	R	E	N	E			
C	A	G	E	R		A	V	E	R		D	A	S	
T	W	E	N	T	Y	N	I	N	E	P	A	L	M	S
S	A	D		U	T	E	S		E	L	I	O	T	
			A	C	M	E	S		B	A	T	I	K	S
M	O	S	L	E	M	S		S	E	C				
A	L	K	A	L	I		S	W	E	E	T	E	S	T
V	I	E		L	E	A	P	O	F	F	A	I	T	H
E	V	E		O	S	C	A	R		U	L	N	A	E
N	E	T		S	T	E	R	N		L	E	E	R	Y

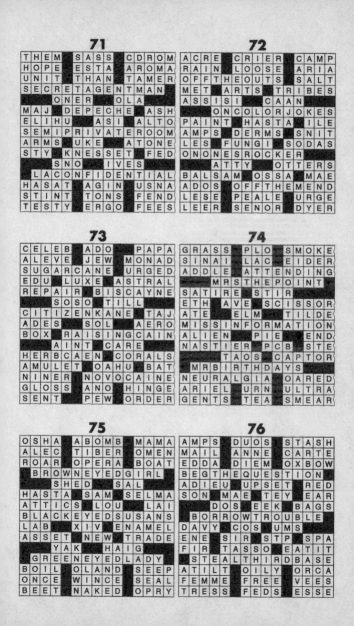

71

T	H	E	M		S	A	S	S		C	D	R	O	M
H	O	P	E		E	S	T	A		A	R	O	M	A
U	N	I	T		T	H	A	N		T	A	M	E	R
S	E	C	R	E	T	A	G	E	N	T	M	A	N	
		O	N	E	R			O	L	A				
M	A	J		D	E	P	E	C	H	E		A	S	H
E	L	I	H	U		A	S	I		A	L	T	O	
S	E	M	I	P	R	I	V	A	T	E	R	O	O	M
A	R	M	S		U	K	E		A	T	O	N	E	
S	T	Y		K	N	E	S	S	E	T		F	E	D
			S	N	O		I	V	E	S				
L	A	C	O	N	F	I	D	E	N	T	I	A	L	
H	A	S	A	T		A	G	I	N		U	S	N	A
S	T	I	N	T		T	O	N	S		F	E	N	D
T	E	S	T	Y		E	R	G	O		F	E	E	S

72

A	C	R	E		C	R	I	E	R		C	A	M	P
R	A	I	N		L	O	O	S	E		A	R	I	A
O	F	F	T	H	E	O	U	T	S		S	A	L	T
M	E	T		A	R	T	S		T	R	I	B	E	S
A	S	S	I	S	I			C	A	A	N			
		O	N	C	O	L	O	R	J	O	K	E	S	
P	A	I	N	T		H	A	S	T	A		I	L	E
A	M	P	S		D	E	R	M	S		S	N	I	T
L	E	S		F	U	N	G	I		S	O	D	A	S
	O	N	O	N	E	S	R	O	C	K	E	R		
			A	T	T	Y			O	T	T	E	R	S
B	A	L	S	A	M		O	S	S	A		M	A	E
A	D	O	S		O	F	F	T	H	E	M	E	N	D
L	E	S	E		P	E	A	L	E		U	R	G	E
L	E	E	R		S	E	N	O	R		D	Y	E	R

73

C	E	L	E	B		A	D	O		P	A	P	A	
A	L	E	V	E		J	E	W		M	O	N	A	D
S	U	G	A	R	C	A	N	E		U	R	G	E	D
E	D	U		L	U	X	E		A	S	T	R	A	L
R	E	P	A	I	R		B	I	S	C	A	Y	N	E
		S	O	S	O		T	I	L	L				
C	I	T	I	Z	E	N	K	A	N	E		T	A	J
A	D	E	S		S	O	L			A	E	R	O	
B	O	X		R	A	I	S	I	N	G	C	A	I	N
		A	I	N	T		C	A	R	E				
H	E	R	B	C	A	E	N		C	O	R	A	L	S
A	M	U	L	E	T		O	A	H	U		B	A	T
N	I	N	E	R		N	O	V	O	C	A	I	N	E
G	L	O	S	S		A	N	O		H	I	N	G	E
S	E	N	T			P	E	W			O	R	D	E	R

74

G	R	A	S	S		P	L	O		S	M	O	K	E
S	I	N	A	I		L	A	C		E	I	D	E	R
A	D	D	L	E		A	T	T	E	N	D	I	N	G
			M	R	S	T	H	E	P	O	I	N	T	
S	A	T	I	R	E		S	T	I	R				
E	T	H		A	V	E		S	C	I	S	S	O	R
A	T	E			E	L	M			T	I	L	D	E
M	I	S	S	I	N	F	O	R	M	A	T	I	O	N
A	L	I	E	N		P	I	E			E	N	D	
N	A	S	T	I	E	R		P	C	B		S	T	E
			T	A	O	S		C	A	P	T	O	R	
	M	R	B	I	R	T	H	D	A	Y	S			
N	E	U	R	A	L	G	I	A		O	A	R	E	D
A	R	I	E	L		U	R	N		U	L	T	R	A
G	E	N	T	S		T	E	A		S	M	E	A	R

75

O	S	H	A		A	B	O	M	B		M	A	M	A
A	L	E	C		T	I	B	E	R		O	M	E	N
R	O	A	R		O	P	E	R	A		B	O	A	T
	B	R	O	W	N	E	Y	E	D	G	I	R	L	
		S	H	E	D			S	A	L				
H	A	S	T	A		S	A	M		S	E	L	M	A
A	T	T	I	C	S		L	O	U		L	A	I	
B	L	A	C	K	E	Y	E	D	S	U	S	A	N	S
L	A	B		X	I	V		E	N	A	M	E	L	
A	S	S	E	T		N	E	W		T	R	A	D	E
			Y	A	K		H	A	I	G				
	G	R	E	E	N	E	Y	E	D	L	A	D	Y	
B	O	I	L		O	L	A	N	D		S	E	E	P
O	N	C	E		W	I	N	C	E		S	E	A	L
B	E	E	T		N	A	K	E	D		O	P	R	Y

76

A	M	P	S		D	U	O	S		S	T	A	S	H
M	A	I	L		A	N	N	E		C	A	R	T	E
E	D	D	A		D	I	E	M		O	X	B	O	W
B	E	G	T	H	E	Q	U	E	S	T	I	O	N	
A	D	I	E	U		U	P	S	E	T		R	E	D
S	O	N		M	A	E		T	E	Y		E	A	R
		D	O	S		E	E	K		B	A	G	S	
	B	O	R	R	O	W	T	R	O	U	B	L	E	
D	A	V	Y		C	O	S		U	M	S			
E	N	E		S	I	R		S	T	P		S	P	A
F	I	R		T	A	S	S	O		E	A	T	I	T
	S	T	E	A	L	T	H	I	R	D	B	A	S	E
A	T	I	L	T		O	I	L	Y		O	R	C	A
F	E	M	M	E		F	R	E	E		V	E	E	S
T	R	E	S	S		F	E	D	S		E	S	S	E

77

P	A	D	S		P	R	I	S	M		W	E	D	S
L	I	O	N		H	A	R	T	E		I	T	A	L
A	R	N	O		O	N	E	A	T		S	U	M	O
Z	E	N		O	T	I	S	R	E	D	D	I	N	G
A	D	A	G	I	O			T	O	R	O			
		F	O	L	S	O	M		R	A	M	J	E	T
O	P	A	L	S		D	E	N	I	M		O	R	O
L	O	R	D		S	O	N	I	C		S	H	A	M
D	O	G		A	U	R	A	L		S	E	N	S	E
S	H	O	G	U	N		T	E	S	T	E	D		
		O	D	D	S			M	U	S	E	U	M	
P	A	T	T	I	A	U	S	T	I	N		N	B	A
A	L	U	M		N	E	P	A	L		A	V	O	N
L	I	R	A		C	R	A	T	E		T	E	A	S
L	A	N	D		E	S	S	E	S		A	R	T	E

78

L	S	A	T		P	I	A	F		E	F	L	A	T
A	C	T	A		O	L	L	A		Q	U	O	T	H
T	A	B	C	O	L	L	A	R		U	N	C	L	E
E	L	A	I	N	E		N	I	P	A	T			
L	A	T	T	I	C	E		N	A	B		A	P	E
Y	R	S		C	A	B	C	A	L	L	O	W	A	Y
			M	E	T	R	O		L	E	S	A	G	E
S	P	A	Y			O	N	A			L	Y	E	S
C	O	H	O	S	T		A	N	G	L	O			
A	R	A	B	C	O	U	N	T	R	Y		F	I	R
R	E	B		H	E	N		S	A	R	D	I	N	E
		A	U	D	I	O			B	I	E	R	C	E
A	T	A	L	L		C	R	A	B	C	A	K	E	S
R	E	L	I	T		E	A	V	E		R	I	S	E
B	L	I	T	Z		F	L	E	D		E	N	T	S

79

T	I	L	T		A	L	E	S		A	L	O	E	S
A	R	I	A		D	O	Z	E		T	A	S	T	E
C	O	R	N		V	A	I	L		E	N	S	U	E
O	N	A	G	A	I	N	O	F	F	A	G	A	I	N
			O	N	C	E			U	S	E			
O	F	T		T	E	R	M	I	T	E		N	A	P
P	A	R	I	S			O	R	O		L	O	C	A
E	V	E	R	Y	N	O	W	A	N	D	T	H	E	N
R	O	A	R		O	R	E			E	D	I	T	S
A	R	T		S	T	A	R	T	U	P		T	O	Y
			D	I	E			O	N	O	S			
I	N	F	I	T	S	A	N	D	S	T	A	R	T	S
T	A	L	E	S		C	O	A	T		R	E	A	L
A	M	I	G	O		I	N	T	O		A	L	P	O
L	E	T	O	N		D	E	E	P		N	Y	S	E

80

E	S	P		J	I	G	S			A	N	W	A	R
O	L	E	G		A	G	R	A		N	O	R	M	A
N	A	N	A		G	O	O	K		A	T	E	A	T
	W	A	L	P	U	R	G	I	S	N	A	C	H	T
			L	E	A				T	I	N	K	L	Y
S	T	G	E	O	R	G	E	S	D	A	Y			
P	E	R	O	N		H	R	O	S	S		M	M	E
E	R	I	N			A	R	R			K	I	E	V
W	I	N		C	A	N	O	E		T	E	N	S	E
			S	O	L	A	R	N	E	W	Y	E	A	R
I	S	T	H	M	I				D	I	E			
P	A	N	A	M	E	R	I	C	A	N	D	A	Y	
A	T	O	N	E		A	D	A	M		U	L	A	N
S	A	T	I	N		J	O	K	E		P	I	L	E
S	N	E	A	D		A	L	E	S		T	E	D	

81

S	I	L	O		S	E	R	U	M		N	O	D	S
A	R	A	B		A	R	U	B	A		A	B	E	L
C	O	N	J	U	G	A	T	O	R		V	I	L	E
K	N	E	E	S		H	A	T	F	I	E	L	D	
S	Y	S	T	E	M	S		T	H	U	G			
			D	A	L	E		A	R	A	F	A	T	
O	R	A	L		G	U	N	S		S	T	A	R	R
L	O	D	I		I	R	A	Q	I		O	R	E	O
A	B	E	T	S		S	C	U	D		R	E	A	D
V	E	N	I	C	E		T	I	E	S				
			G	A	G	A		D	A	M	P	M	O	P
M	A	C	A	R	O	N	I		O	H	A	R	A	
A	L	I	T		I	N	S	T	I	G	A	T	O	R
T	O	T	O		S	O	L	A	R		S	E	N	T
S	E	E	R		M	Y	E	R	S		E	R	O	S

82

S	N	A	F	U		S	E	L	F		C	H	E	W
N	I	X	O	N		I	G	O	R		P	O	L	O
I	N	E	R	T		N	A	N	A		A	R	L	O
P	A	L	M	R	E	A	D	I	N	G		S	A	D
			A	U	D	I			C	A	S	E		
N	A	P	L	E	S		O	P	E	N	P	O	R	T
E	R	R	S		E	D	N	A		G	A	P	E	R
A	N	I		G	L	A	S	S	E	S		E	R	E
R	I	V	E	R		M	E	O	W		B	R	A	N
S	E	A	C	O	A	S	T		I	S	L	A	N	D
			T	O	O	N		B	N	A	I			
R	A	E		M	I	D	N	I	G	H	T	S	U	N
A	L	E	C		M	E	A	T		A	Z	U	R	E
Y	O	Y	O		A	L	I	T		R	E	L	A	X
S	T	E	P		L	I	L	Y		A	D	U	L	T

83

```
J E S S E   P A B L O   P T A
I N K I N   S P R A T   U R N
H O U N D S T O O T H   P U N
A L L S E T   S W E E T P E A
D A K   A R T   X R A Y
    P R O U S T   S I L K S
W A D E   B R I E F   L O N E
I R O N   E N E R O   E V E N
S I G N   S E V E R   N E E D
P A P A W   R E S E E D
    A M A S   A I R   E R R
M A D E R O O M   G O A L I E
O L D   M U T T A N D J E F F
S O L   U S I N G   E A G L E
T E E   P A S S E   D R Y E R
```

84

```
S P A R   I O T A S   U S D A
H I G H   N O H I T   N E A T
I M O U T A H E R E   S E M I
M A D M O N E Y   R E T Y P E
        B U D D   C E L I A
S A B A T O   B O O K C L U B
A M Y   S U D A N   S K A T E
R E E F   T A R D O   S T U N
A B B O T   T E E N S   E R E
H A Y R I D E S   T H O R N S
    E E L E D   S H U N
E M B A L M   S K E L E T O N
L I A R   A D I O S A M I G O
I C B M   N A S A L   A R L O
S A Y S   D R I L Y   N E E R
```

85

```
A C E S   S M U G   C L O D S
R A P T   P A S O   R E B U T
B R E A K A L E G   A N O D E
O P E R A   I R E   I D E S T
R E S T I N G   T O G A
    S O N A T A   N O T E
G O O B E R   L E T   E M I T
U P P E R   F O R   S A N E R
M A I N   T A U   D E R I D E
S L E D   I N D O O R
    A U N T   T E E N A G E
B A R N S   A C T   N E G R I
A D I E U   S H A K E A L E G
R A D A R   I O W A   R O T H
E M E R Y   A W A Y   S W A T
```

86

```
S H A   E M M A S   E L M E R
T E D   R E A C T   N O O N E
O L D Y E L L E R   G O L D A
L I L A C   I D E A L   E S P
E X E R T S   A M I S H
    N E W H A M P S H I R E
W H O   D I O N   H E L E N
E A V E   M E T A L   S L A V
B L E A R   E P E E   S L Y
    B O R R O W E D T I M E
    B L O O D   S E D A T E
S A O   S K I E R   R E R A N
A W A I T   B L U E G R A S S
F O R C E   L I T R E   B T U
E L D E R   E A S E D   S E E
```

87

```
S C O T   S H A G   R A T O N
L O P E   C O C O   A L I V E
A M E N   Y M C A   N I N E R
B A C O N L E T T U C E A N D
    R U L E   N O N
B E L   R A C E C A R   P A D
A L I A S   V C R   U L N A
S M O K E D S A L M O N A N D
I O N A   F E N   L I N E D
E S S   B L E S S E D   O X Y
    I R A   E X I T
P E A N U T B U T T E R A N D
L E T O N   E S T A   A S E A
A L O N E   E D E N   M I S S
N Y M E T   T A R T   P A T H
```

88

```
B A S I L   G A G A   P H E W
A S O N E   A N E W   R A T A
S A L S A   Z I T I   A J A X
T H E A D D A M S F A M I L Y
E I S N E R   A B E L
    D R A F T Y   A G A T E
S O H O   W E E   S C O R E D
T H E U G L Y D U C K L I N G
U N I T E S   C A R   D A T E
N O R S E   M A L I C E
    N E A R   B U N K O S
L A D Y A N D T H E T R A M P
A L O E   O M O O   S U P E R
B O Z O   L A O S   I L O N A
S T E W   A N N E   N E W S Y
```

89

```
IDOL  ABODE  PACE
DUMA  RULES  LION
SENT  TRAMP  ERGS
TIEDUPFORDAYS
      RRS  END
TATTOO  VISA  CPA
ALAMO  BINS  AHAS
STRAPPEDFORCASH
TOON  OREO  UNITE
EST  HUGO  FRERES
     TEN  BOA
BOUNDFORGLORY
CURB  ALGAE  GEAR
ONCE  GORKY  LAWN
STAR  EPEES  ERNS
```

90

```
PARIS  FOCUS  TAM
EXUDE  IRISH  ICE
ELBOWGREASE  MAR
VEE  SAM  RECEDE
ESSO  SERF  PALED
   TAPROOM  MIMI
IBIS  OREO  MIT
KNUCKLESANDWICH
ITT  SALT  OATS
NETS  WEEDERS
GREET  CROC  HUES
LARRYS  EON  PVT
ELF  KNEESLAPPER
AIL  EATIN  IRENA
RAY  SPENT  FORTY
```

91

```
ALFA  HULL  GRASS
BAIL  OBOE  AORTA
BULLMOOSE  RUNIN
ADE  IFA  SINGERS
    TRITE  NEH
FERRET  LUSTRATE
ALOUD  DIRE  IDES
CAMS  PETIT  DENT
ETAT  ASIS  MELEE
TENBUCKS  BERETS
    UNE  TRESS
MAESTRO  INS  TNT
ADDTO  TEDDYBEAR
RIGEL  INGE  URSA
SNERD  SEER  SNAP
```

92

```
BRA  HAIL  ATEASE
REC  EDNA  URANUS
IMA  READ  TORTES
DOCHOLLYWOOD
AVIA  ALDA  PRAYS
LEAST  ARF  UHOH
HAPPYGILMORE
AWE  RAH  ORE  YEA
GRUMPYOLDMEN
EERO  SEE  REACH
SNOBS  BASS  ALOE
SLEEPYHOLLOW
MORTAL  IRAN  ELI
ALIENS  NILE  GEN
GEORGE  GALS  ERG
```

93

```
ADDS  ASST  TABBY
SEEM  RONA  WHERE
ISLE  CRUX  EASEL
FILLTHEBILL  TAP
     TAI  AVIS
DEB  SEALTHEDEAL
CRAFT  LEER  ILSA
CADRE  BEN  SOLOS
ASHE  SECS  AMENS
BEATTHEHEAT  REO
     ISEE  TIS
FAR  TAKETHECAKE
OLDER  ELMO  OREO
AMATI  DIEM  FINN
MAYAS  SANE  FATS
```

94

```
BEN  ORALS  SAHIB
OLE  TOLET  AMANA
FIR  SILVERWINGS
FAVE  EYRE  DES
ONEADAY  NURSE
   RENO  SPEEDUP
ARC  FOOL  STONE
GOLDENPARACHUTE
ALIEN  DIEU  TOP
REPASTS  GOES
  BREAM  ANDSOON
ADO  REST  ELLA
LEADBALLOON  DIM
MARIA  LANAI  EVE
ANDES  SWIFT  RED
```

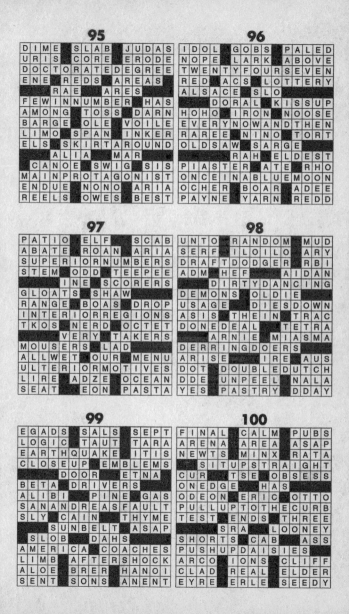

95

```
D I M E   S L A B   J U D A S
U R I S   C O R E   E R O D E
D O C T O R A T E D E G R E E
E N E   R E D S   A R E A S
      R A E   A R E S
F E W I N N U M B E R   H A S
A M O N G   T O S S   D A R N
B A R G E   O L E   V O I L E
L I M O   S P A N   I N K E R
E L S   S K I R T A R O U N D
    A L I A   M A R
  C A N O E   S W I G   S I S
M A I N P R O T A G O N I S T
E N D U E   N O N O   A R I A
R E E L S   O W E S   B E S T
```

96

```
I D O L   G O B S   P A L E D
N O P E   L A R K   A B O V E
T W E N T Y F O U R S E V E N
R E D   A C S   L O T T E R Y
A L S A C E   S L O
      D O R A L   K I S S U P
H O H O   I R O N   N O O S E
E V E R Y N O W A N D T H E N
R A R E E   N I N O   T O R T
O L D S A W   S A R G E
      R A H   E L D E S T
P I A S T E R   A T E   R H O
O N C E I N A B L U E M O O N
O C H E R   B O A R   A D E E
P A Y N E   Y A R N   R E D D
```

97

```
P A T I O   E L F   S C A B
A B A T E   R O A N   A R I A
S U P E R I O R N U M B E R S
S T E M   O D D   T E E P E E
      I N E   S C O R E R S
G L O A T S   S H A W
R A N G E   B O A S   D R O P
I N T E R I O R R E G I O N S
T K O S   N E R D   O C T E T
      V E R Y   T A K E R S
M O U S E R S   L A D
A L L W E T   O U R   M E N U
U L T E R I O R M O T I V E S
L I R E   A D Z E   O C E A N
S E A T   E O N   P A S T A
```

98

```
U N T O   R A N D O M   M U D
S E R F   I L O I L O   A R Y
D R A F T D O D G E R   R B I
A D M   H E F   A I D A N
      D I R T Y D A N C I N G
D E M O N S   O L D I E
U S A G E   D I E S D O W N
A S I S   T H E I N   T R A C
D O N E D E A L   T E T R A
      A R N I E   M I A S M A
D E R R I N G D O E R S
A R I S E   I R E   A U S
D O T   D O U B L E D U T C H
D D E   U N P E E L   N A L A
Y E S   P A S T R Y   D D A Y
```

99

```
E G A D S   S A L S   S E P T
L O G I C   T A U T   T A R A
E A R T H Q U A K E   I T I S
C L O S E U P   E M B L E M S
      D O O R   E T N A
B E T A   D R I V E R S
A L I B I   P I N E   G A S
S A N A N D R E A S F A U L T
S L Y   C A I N   T H Y M E
    S U N B E L T   A S A P
  S L O B   D A H S
A M E R I C A   C O A C H E S
L I M B   A F T E R S H O C K
A L O E   B R E R   H A N O I
S E N T   S O N S   A N E N T
```

100

```
F I N A L   C A L M   P U B S
A R E N A   A R E A   A S A P
N E W T S   M I N X   R A T A
    S I T U P S T R A I G H T
C U R   T S E   O B S E S S
O N E D G E   H A S
O D E O N   E R I C   O T T O
P U L L U P T O T H E C U R B
T E S T   E N D S   T H R E E
    S R A   L O O N E Y
S H O R T S   C A B   A S S
P U S H U P D A I S I E S
A R C O   I O N S   C L I F F
C L A D   R E A L   E L D E R
E Y R E   E R L E   S E E D Y
```

101

C	H	A	W		S	P	U	D		A	D	M	E	N
O	A	T	H		A	L	T	A		T	R	A	L	A
A	R	I	A		F	O	A	L		S	I	L	L	Y
L	I	T	T	L	E	W	H	I	T	E	L	I	E	S
			S	E	T	S			H	A	L			
J	A	U	N	T	Y		P	E	R		S	P	U	R
E	L	S	E	S		S	A	Y	O	K		O	N	E
W	E	E	W	I	L	L	I	E	W	I	N	K	I	E
E	V	A		N	E	A	R	S		D	I	E	T	S
L	E	S	S		R	V	S		E	N	T	R	E	E
			T	O	O			T	R	A	P			
I	T	S	Y	B	I	T	S	Y	S	P	I	D	E	R
W	H	A	L	E		R	A	S	A		C	A	V	E
A	R	L	E	S		I	G	O	T		K	N	E	E
S	U	E	D	E		B	E	N	Z		S	A	N	K

102

A	F	R	O		N	E	A	T		A	S	C	O	T
B	L	O	B		A	R	L	O		S	O	A	P	Y
C	U	B	S	C	O	U	T	S		T	Y	L	E	R
			C	O	M	P	O	S	E	R		F	R	A
F	A	K	E	S	I	T		N	O	R	M	A	N	
O	L	I	N		S	P	A	S		O	U	S	T	
R	O	D	E	O	S		A	L	I	E	N	S		
D	E	B		K	I	T	B	A	G	S		C	P	A
		R	I	S	E	R	S		N	O	B	L	E	S
S	C	O	T		R	A	T	S		L	E	A	K	
H	I	T	T	E	R		P	R	I	E	S	T	S	
A	C	H		W	A	R	P	L	A	N	E			
D	E	E	R	E		C	H	I	C	K	P	E	A	S
E	R	R	O	R		M	I	C	E		E	L	I	A
D	O	S	E	S		P	L	E	D		D	I	L	L

103

C	H	A	P		G	L	A	D		C	H	A	N	T
R	O	L	E		H	I	R	E		H	O	W	I	E
A	B	E	T		O	G	L	E		A	T	O	N	E
B	O	X	E	R	S	H	O	R	T	S		K	E	N
			O	T	T			U	T	T	E	R	S	
D	A	C	H	A	S		A	L	T	E	R			
E	Q	U	A	L		O	M	I	T		A	N	K	A
B	U	L	L	D	O	G	E	D	I	T	I	O	N	S
T	A	L	L		U	R	N	S		O	N	T	O	P
			O	P	T	E	D		O	N	S	E	T	S
S	T	E	W	E	D		A	P	E					
L	E	X		P	O	O	D	L	E	S	K	I	R	T
E	A	T	U	P		S	E	A	N		A	G	E	E
P	R	O	S	E		L	A	M	E		L	O	B	E
T	Y	L	E	R		O	D	O	R		E	R	A	S

104

A	M	I	D		R	I	F	T	S		E	D	G	E
L	I	M	O		O	N	E	U	P		W	O	R	N
I	N	A	N		M	A	N	N	A		E	G	A	D
B	I	G	S	P	E	N	D	E	R	S		S	N	L
A	M	I		H	O	E	S		F	A	T	C	A	T	S
B	A	N	J	O	S		W	A	I	L		T	R	E	S
A	L	E	U	T		M	O	N	E	Y	B	A	G	S
			S	T	O	P		O	D	E	S		R	U	D	E	R
T	Y	C	O	O	N	S		C	A	P	I	T	A
O	P	E	N	S		T	E	R	I		L	E	I
N	E	A		H	I	G	H	R	O	L	L	E	R	S
E	D	N	A		T	E	R	R	A		O	M	N	I
R	U	I	N		C	R	E	E	K		O	M	A	N
S	P	C	A		H	E	E	D	S		P	A	L	S

105

B	E	A	M		S	T	A	T		D	R	I	B	S
O	R	L	Y		E	E	G	S		R	O	G	E	T
P	I	E	R		T	A	R	P		E	B	O	N	Y
S	E	C	R	E	T	P	A	S	S	W	O	R	D	
			H	A	L	O			T	O	T			
S	A	M		G	E	T	E	V	E	N		S	P	A
K	N	I	F	E		L	E	E		A	L	A	N	
U	N	D	E	R	C	O	V	E	R	A	G	E	N	T
L	I	A	R		H	U	E		S	E	E	D	S	
L	E	S		H	O	T	S	P	O	T		P	A	Y
			A	U	K			A	C	R	E			
	H	I	D	D	E	N	T	R	E	A	S	U	R	E
L	A	D	E	D		O	R	A	L		S	C	A	R
A	T	O	L	L		R	E	D	O		A	L	M	A
M	E	L	E	E		M	E	E	T		Y	A	P	S

106

S	P	R	I	G		F	L	I	P		A	L	A	S
A	L	A	M	O		I	O	T	A		B	O	R	E
D	U	M	P	S	T	R	U	C	K		D	O	L	E
E	S	P		S	U	M		H	I	T	U	P	O	N
			M	I	N	E	S		S	E	C			
T	H	E	P	A	R	E	N	T	S	T	R	A	P	
B	O	E	R	S		N	E	A	T		A	L	I	
R	O	L	E		S	P	A	W	N		E	D	I	T
A	T	L		S	C	O	T		A	R	I	E	S	
C	H	O	O	C	H	O	O	S	T	R	A	I	N	
			M	A	O		R	H	E	T	T			
G	A	Z	E	B	O	S		A	S	I		A	L	E
A	X	E	L		L	U	N	C	H	S	T	R	A	Y
S	I	D	E		E	R	I	K		T	W	I	N	E
P	S	S	T		D	E	N	S		S	O	D	A	S

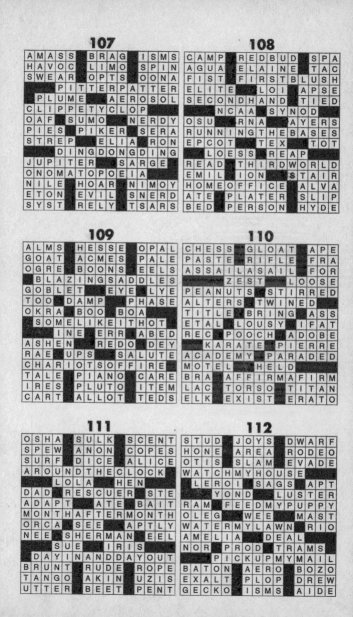

107

```
A M A S S   B R A G   I S M S
H A V O C   L I M O   S P I N
S W E A R   O P T S   O O N A
      P I T T E R P A T T E R
  P L U M E     A E R O S O L
C L I P P E T Y C L O P
O A F   S U M O     N E R D Y
P I E S   P I K E R   S E R A
S T R E P   E L I A   R O N
    D I N G D O N G D I N G
J U P I T E R     S A R G E
O N O M A T O P O E I A
N I L E   H O A R   N I M O Y
E T O N   E V I L   S N E R D
S Y S T   R E L Y   T S A R S
```

108

```
C A M P   R E D B U D   S P A
A G U A   E L A I N E   T A C
F I S T   F I R S T B L U S H
E L I T E   L O I   A P S E
S E C O N D H A N D   T I E D
      N C A A   S Y N O D
O S U   R N A     A Y E R S
R U N N I N G T H E B A S E S
E P C O T   T E X   T O T
    L O E S S   R E A P
R E A D   T H I R D W O R L D
E M I L   I O N   S T A I R
H O M E O F F I C E   A L V A
A T E   P L A T E R   S L I P
B E D   P E R S O N   H Y D E
```

109

```
A L M S   H E S S E   O P A L
G O A T   A C M E S   P A L E
O G R E   B O O N S   E E L S
  B L A Z I N G S A D D L E S
G O B L E T   E Y E   L Y E
T O O   D A M P   P H A S E
O K R A   B O O   B O A
  S O M E L I K E I T H O T
    I N E   E R R   A B E D
A S H E N   R E D O   D E Y
R A E   U P S   S A L U T E
C H A R I O T S O F F I R E
T A L E   P I A N O   C A R E
I R E S   P L U T O   I T E M
C A R T   A L L O T   T E D S
```

110

```
C H E S S   G L O A T   A P E
P A S T E   R I F L E   F R A
A S S A I L A S A I L   F O R
          Z E S T   L O O S E
P E A N U T S   S T I R R E D
A L T E R S   T W I N E D
T I T L E   B R I N G   A S S
E T A L   L O U S Y   I F A T
R E C   P O O C H   A D O B E
    K A R A T E   P I E R R E
A C A D E M Y   P A R A D E D
M O T E L   H E L D
B R A   A F F I R M A F I R M
L A C   T O R S O   T I T A N
E L K   E X I S T   E R A T O
```

111

```
O S H A   S U L K   S C E N T
S P E W   A N O N   C O P E S
S U R F   D I C E   A L I C E
A R O U N D T H E C L O C K
    L O L A   H E N
D A D   R E S C U E R   S T E
A D A P T   A T E   B A I T
M O N T H A F T E R M O N T H
O R C A   S E E   A P T L Y
N E E   S H E R M A N   E E L
      S U E   I R I S
  D A Y I N A N D D A Y O U T
B R U N T   R U D E   R O P E
T A N G O   A K I N   U Z I S
U T T E R   B E E T   P E N T
```

112

```
S T U D   J O Y S   D W A R F
H O N E   A R E A   R O D E O
O T I S   S L A M   E V A D E
W A T C H M Y H O U S E
    L E R O I   S A G S   A P T
      Y O N D   L U S T E R
R A M   F E E D M Y P U P P Y
O L E G   W E E   M A S T
W A T E R M Y L A W N   R I O
A M E L I A   D E A L
N O R   P R O D   T R A M S
    P I C K U P M Y M A I L
B A T O N   A E R O   B O Z O
E X A L T   P L O P   D R E W
G E C K O   I S M S   A I D E
```

113

S	H	A	D	E		G	E	L	T		P	A	P	A
K	A	P	U	T		A	M	I	E		I	R	O	N
I	N	O	N	E		R	A	M	S		N	E	W	T
P	A	P	E	R	C	L	I	P	S		K	N	E	E
		S	N	A	I	L		T	S	A	R	S		
W	O	K		A	M	C		B	R	E	L			
E	D	I	B	L	E		F	L	E	X	I	B	L	E
B	O	L	A		L	I	B	Y	A		P	I	E	R
B	R	O	C	C	O	L	I		L	O	S	T	I	T
			K	A	T	E		S	T	D		S	S	E
T	H	E	F	T		A	N	O	D	E				
R	O	L	L		R	A	D	A	R	B	L	I	P	S
A	N	T	I		S	L	O	P		A	L	C	O	A
C	O	O	P		V	E	R	A		L	I	O	N	S
E	R	N	S		P	E	N	T		L	E	N	D	S

114

A	C	T	S		S	K	E	W		D	I	S	C	O
D	R	O	P		T	O	R	I		E	V	I	A	N
H	O	L	Y	G	R	A	I	L		C	A	N	T	O
O	W	L		R	I	L	E	Y		A	N	G	E	R
C	D	S		I	D	A		I	D	O	L			
			B	L	E	S	S	E	D	E	V	E	N	T
S	T	E	E	L		A	L	E	S		T	O	R	
H	E	L	D		L	A	Y	L	A		A	O	N	E
E	R	E		A	I	R	S		A	N	N	E	X	
D	I	V	I	N	E	C	O	M	E	D	Y			
			A	N	T	S			E	N	O		P	A	M
M	A	T	T	E		U	N	S	E	R		I	C	Y
A	L	I	E	N		S	A	C	R	E	D	C	O	W
A	D	O	R	N		S	T	A	G		O	K	R	A
M	A	N	N	A		R	O	L	Y		N	Y	N	Y

115

A	J	A	R		B	L	A	C	K		F	O	O	T
L	I	L	I		E	E	R	I	E		I	N	G	E
E	N	D	O	F	S	T	O	R	Y		N	U	L	L
E	X	O		L	O	B	O		W	E	A	S	E	L
		T	O	T	E		B	O	L	L				
H	A	B	E	A	S		W	O	R	K	A	D	A	Y
I	N	E	R	T		B	A	W	D		N	E	B	O
T	E	A	M		F	A	S	T	S		S	L	O	W
O	M	N	I		A	L	T	O		T	W	I	R	L
N	O	O	N	T	I	M	E		C	H	E	S	T	S
			A	I	R	Y		T	I	E	R			
S	C	H	L	E	P		P	U	T	S		L	E	S
L	O	O	M		L	A	S	T	R	E	S	O	R	T
A	L	M	A		A	D	I	E	U		U	R	G	E
T	E	E	N		Y	E	S	E	S		N	E	S	T

116

L	I	P	S		I	R	M	A		L	O	S	E	S
A	C	H	E		T	O	A	D		U	S	U	R	P
S	H	I	M		C	O	M	O		L	A	N	A	I
	L	I	G	H	T	I	N	A	U	G	U	S	T	
S	C	O	N	E		E	I	S		E	P	E	E	
H	U	M	A	N	L	Y		S	A	G				
A	B	E	L		O	A	K		R	E	S	E	N	T
W	I	L	L	I	A	M	F	A	U	L	K	N	E	R
S	T	A	Y	E	D		C	U	L		E	D	G	E
				R	S	T		F	E	A	T	U	R	E
B	A	S	E		U	R	I		S	C	R	O	D	
Y	O	K	N	A	P	A	T	A	W	P	H	A		
G	R	I	T	S		D	A	L	I		I	N	G	E
O	T	E	R	I		E	L	A	N		N	C	A	A
D	A	R	E	S		S	Y	N	E		G	E	L	T

117

A	V	I	S		R	I	P	E	N		A	C	T	S
M	I	L	E		E	R	O	D	E		B	L	E	U
P	E	L	T		F	O	R	G	E		B	O	A	R
	H	A	U	N	T	E	D	H	O	U	S	E		
C	I	A		I	T	S		L	A	T	T	E	R	
U	N	M	A	D	E		S	T	E	M	S			
B	U	M	P	E	R	C	A	R	S		M	A	D	
B	R	A	T		R	I	O		S	A	T	E		
Y	E	N		T	I	L	T	A	W	H	I	R	L	
		S	N	O	B	S		C	R	E	D	I	T	
O	R	P	H	A	N		A	C	E		S	P	A	
M	E	R	R	Y	G	O	R	O	U	N	D			
A	G	U	E		U	S	E	R	S		O	I	L	Y
H	A	N	D		E	L	I	T	E		C	I	T	E
A	L	E	S		S	O	N	A	R		K	I	D	S

118

S	A	R	A		N	E	A	T		W	A	L	L	S
P	L	O	P		O	N	M	E		A	V	O	I	D
A	L	M	S		I	D	E	A		S	I	N	A	I
S	W	E	E	T	S	U	R	R	E	N	D	E	R	
M	E	R		Y	E	R		D	A	T		S	L	O
S	T	O	O	P		E	A	R	S		C	O	I	L
		H	E	T		S	O	T		A	M	A	D	
H	E	Y	B	I	G	S	P	E	N	D	E	R		
G	I	V	E		C	U	E		R	U	G			
A	L	E	S		K	I	S	S		D	E	A	N	S
M	A	N		D	E	N		N	A	G		D	E	C
	R	E	T	U	R	N	T	O	S	E	N	D	E	R
M	I	D	I	S		E	W	O	K		A	L	D	A
S	T	U	C	K		S	I	Z	E		D	E	E	P
G	Y	P	S	Y		S	T	E	W		A	D	D	S

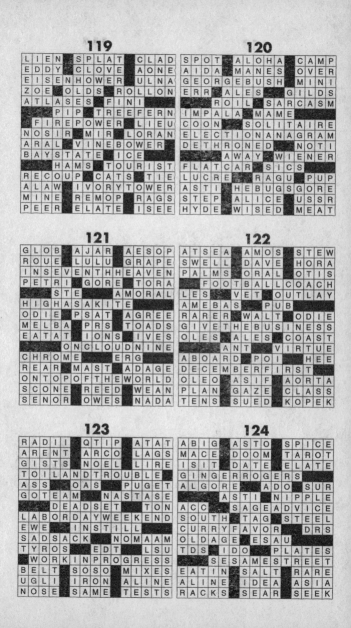

119

```
L I E N   S P L A T   C L A D
E D D Y   C L O V E   A O N E
E I S E N H O W E R   U L N A
Z O E   O L D S   R O L L O N
A T L A S E S   F I N I
      P I P   T R E E F E R N
F I R E P O W E R   L I E U
N O S I R   M I R   L O R A N
A R A L   V I N E B O W E R
B A Y S T A T E   I C E
      H A M S   T O U R I S T
R E C O U P   C A T S   T I E
A L A W   I V O R Y T O W E R
M I N E   R E M O P   R A G S
P E E R   E L A T E   I S E E
```

120

```
S P O T   A L O H A   C A M P
A I D A   M A N E S   O V E R
G E O R G E B U S H   M I N I
E R R   A L E S   G I L D S
      R O I L   S A R C A S M
I M P A L A   M A M E
C O O N   S O L I T A I R E
E L E C T I O N A N A G R A M
D E T H R O N E D   N O T I
      A W A Y   W I E N E R
F L A T C A R   S I C S
L U C R E   R A G U   P U P
A S T I   H E B U G S G O R E
S T E P   A L I C E   U S S R
H Y D E   W I S E D   M E A T
```

121

```
G L O B   A J A R   A E S O P
R O U E   L U L U   G R A P E
I N S E V E N T H H E A V E N
P E T R I   G O R E   T O R A
      S T E   A M O R A L
H I G H A S A K I T E
O D I E   P S A T   A G R E E
M E L B A   P R S   T O A D S
E A T A T   I O N S   I V E S
      O N C L O U D N I N E
C H R O M E   E R G
R E A R   M A S T   A D A G E
O N T O P O F T H E W O R L D
S C O N E   R E E D   W E A N
S E N O R   O W E S   N A D A
```

122

```
A T S E A   A M O S   S T E W
S W E L L   D A V E   H O R A
P A L M S   O R A L   O T I S
      F O O T B A L L C O A C H
L E S   V E T   O U T L A Y
A M E B A S   P U B
R A R E R   W A L T   O D I E
G I V E T H E B U S I N E S S
O L E S   A L E S   C O A S T
      A N T   V I R T U E
A B O A R D   P O I   H E E
D E C E M B E R F I R S T
O L E O   A S I F   A O R T A
P L A N   G A Z E   C L A S S
T E N S   S U E D   K O P E K
```

123

```
R A D I I   Q T I P   A T A T
A R E N T   A R C O   L A G S
G I S T S   N O E L   L I R E
T O I L A N D T R O U B L E
A S S   O A S   P U G E T
G O T E A M   N A S T A S E
      D E A D S E T   T O N
L A B O R D A Y W E E K E N D
E W E   I N S T I L L
S A D S A C K   N O M A A M
T Y R O S   E D T   L S U
      W O R K I N P R O G R E S S
B E L T   S O S O   M I X E S
U G L I   I R O N   A L I N E
N O S E   S A M E   T E S T S
```

124

```
A B I G   A S T O   S P I C E
M A C E   D O O M   T A R O T
I S I T   D A T E   E L A T E
G I N G E R R O G E R S
A L G O R E   A D O   S U R
      A S T I   N I P P L E
A C C   S A G E A D V I C E
S O U T H   T A G   S T E E L
C U R R Y F A V O R   D R S
O L D A G E   E S A U
T D S   I D O   P L A T E S
      S E S A M E S T R E E T
E A T I N   S A L T   R A R E
A L I N E   I D E A   A S I A
R A C K S   S E A R   S E E K
```

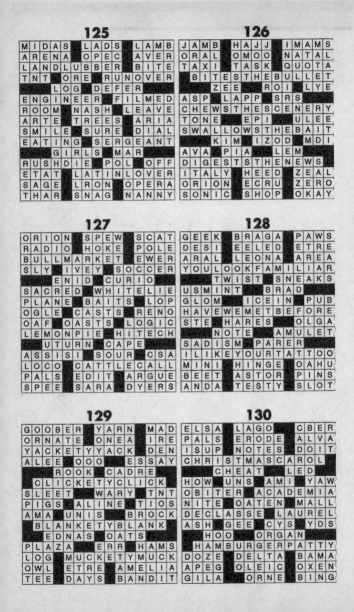

125

```
M I D A S   L A D S   L A M B
A R E N A   O P E C   A V E R
L A N D L U B B E R   B I T E
T N T   O R E   R U N O V E R
      L O G   D E F E R
E N G I N E E R   F I L M E D
R O O M   N A S H   L E A V E
A R T E   T R E E S   A R I A
S M I L E   S U R E   D I A L
E A T I N G   S E R G E A N T
      G I R L S   M A R
R U S H D I E   P O L   O F F
E T A T   L A T I N L O V E R
S A G E   L R O N   O P E R A
T H A R   S N A G   N A N N Y
```

126

```
J A M B   H A J J   I M A M S
O R A L   O M O O   N A T A L
T A X I   T A S K   Q U O T A
B I T E S T H E B U L L E T
      Z E E   R O I   L Y E
A S P   L A P P   S R S
C H E W S T H E S C E N E R Y
T O N E   E P I   U L E E
S W A L L O W S T H E B A I T
      K I M   I Z O D   M D I
A V A   P I A   L E M
D I G E S T S T H E N E W S
I T A L Y   H E E D   Z E A L
O R I O N   E C R U   Z E R O
S O N I C   S H O P   O K A Y
```

127

```
O R I O N   S P E W   S C A T
R A D I O   H O K E   P O L E
B U L L M A R K E T   E W E R
S L Y   I V E Y   S O C C E R
      E N I D   C U R I O
S A C R E D   W H I T E L I E
P L A N E   B A I T S   L O P
O G L E   C A S T S   R E N O
O A F   O A S T S   L O G I C
L E M O N P I E   H I T E C H
      U T U R N   C A P E
A S S I S I   S O U R   C S A
L O C O   C A T T L E C A L L
P A L S   E D I T   A R G U E
S P E E   S A R A   D Y E R S
```

128

```
G E E K   B R A G A   P A W S
D E S I   E E L E D   E T R E
A R A L   L E O N A   A R E A
Y O U L O O K F A M I L I A R
      T W I S T   S N E A K S
U S M I N T   B R A D
G L O M   I C E I N   P U B
H A V E W E M E T B E F O R E
S T E   H A R E S   O L G A
      N O T E   A M U L E T
S A D I S M   P A R E R
I L I K E Y O U R T A T T O O
M I N I   H I N G E   O A H U
B E E T   A S T O R   P I N S
A N D A   T E S T Y   S L O T
```

129

```
G O O B E R   Y A R N   M A D
O R N A T E   O N E A   I R E
Y A C K E T Y Y A C K   D E N
A L E E   O O O   E S S A Y
      R O O K   C A D R E
C L I C K E T Y C L I C K
S L E E T   W A R Y   T N T
P I G S   A L I N E   T I O S
A M A   U N I S   B R O C K
B L A N K E T Y B L A N K
      E D N A S   O A T S
P L A Z A   E R R   H A M S
L O G   M U C K E T Y M U C K
O W L   E T R E   A M E L I A
T E E   D A Y S   B A N D I T
```

130

```
E L S A   L A G O   C B E R
P A L S   E R O D E   A L V A
I S U P   N O T E S   D O I T
C H R I S T M A S C A R O L
      C H E A T   L E D
H O W   U N S   A M I   Y A W
O B I T E R   A C A D E M I A
N I T E   O A T E N   M A L L
D E C L A S S E   L A U R E L
A S H   G E E   C Y S   Y D S
      H O O   O R G A N
H A M B U R G E R P A T T Y
D O Z E   D E L T A   B A M A
A P E G   O L E I C   O X E N
G I L A   O R N E   B I N G
```

The New York Times Crossword Puzzles

The #1 Name in Crosswords

NEW
Sunday Crosswords Volume 30
Crosswords to Exercise Your Brain
Crosswords for Your Breakfast Table
Daily Crosswords Volume 68
More Crosswords for Your Bedside

SPECIAL EDITION
Ultimate Crossword Omnibus
Will Shortz's Favorite Crosswords
Will Shortz's Favorite Sunday
  Crosswords
Will Shortz's Funniest Crosswords

DAILY CROSSWORDS
Daily Omnibus Volume 14
Daily Omnibus Volume 13
Daily Omnibus Volume 12
Daily Crosswords Volume 67
Daily Crosswords Volume 66
Daily Crosswords Volume 65
Daily Crosswords Volume 64
Daily Crosswords Volume 63

EASY CROSSWORDS
Easy Crosswords Volume 5
Easy Crosswords Volume 4
Easy Omnibus Volume 3
Easy Omnibus Volume 2

TOUGH CROSSWORDS
Tough Crosswords Volume 11
Tough Crosswords Volume 10

SUNDAY CROSSWORDS
Sunday Omnibus Volume 7
Sunday Omnibus Volume 6
Sunday Crosswords Volume 29
Sunday Crosswords Volume 28

LARGE-PRINT CROSSWORDS
Large-Print Daily Crosswords
Large-Print Omnibus Volume 5
Large-Print Easy Crosswords

VARIETY PUZZLES
Acrostic Puzzles Volume 9
Sunday Variety Puzzles

PORTABLE SIZE FORMAT
Crosswords to Boost Your
  Brainpower
Easy Crosswords
Crosswords for Your Beach Bag
Super Saturday Crosswords
Sun, Sand and Crosswords
Crosswords for Your Bedside
Crosswords for Your Coffee Break
Crosswords for Your Work Week

FOR YOUNG SOLVERS
Outrageous Crossword Puzzles and
  Word Games for Kids
More Outrageous Crossword
  Puzzles for Kids

 St. Martin's Griffin   Available at your local bookstore or online at nytimes.com/nytstore

NYT 03/04